Christmas 1981

Yes, another Cook book -
Should be a good one -

love -
Mom

HELEN DOLLAGHAN'S BEST MAIN DISHES

HELEN DOLLAGHAN'S

Best

MAIN DISHES

McGRAW-HILL BOOK COMPANY

New York   St. Louis   San Francisco   Mexico   Toronto   Düsseldorf

Book design by Anita Walker Scott

Copyright © 1980 by Helen Dollaghan

2 3 4 5 6 7 8 9   DODO   8 7 6 5 4 3 2 1 0

Library of Congress Cataloging in Publication Data

Dollaghan, Helen.
   Helen Dollaghan's Best main dishes.

   Includes index.
   1. Cookery (Entries) I. Title. II. Title: Best main dishes.
TX740.D6   641.8′2   79-19385
ISBN 0-07-017380-X

Published in association with
SAN FRANCISCO BOOK COMPANY.

For my husband, and in memory of my mother,
Helen Heuer Dollaghan.

Mom taught me how to cook, beginning with
the basics of making gravy.

Cecil, my husband, never complained when the
gravy had a few lumps in it along the way.

CONTENTS

PREFACE

This cookbook has a very simple but heartfelt reason for being: It's my way of saying *thank you* to all of the cooks who contributed the recipes that made it possible—friends, family, and faithful followers of the *Denver Post* food columns who have so generously shared menu ideas with me over the years

I do not, in fact, profess to present new or original recipes in this book, but after testing all of the recipes presented here in my own kitchen many times, they have acquired my personal interpretations. Some of the ingredients or the preparations have been altered to make the recipes easier to understand or to suit the variety of tastes, time schedules, and budgets.

This is not intended to be a basic, "how-to-do-it-all" guide. It *is,* I hope, a book without gimmicks, a carefully selected, well-balanced collection of main-dish recipes representing the kind of cooking that is actually going on in today's best home kitchens. It tries to speak the language of experienced as well as novice cooks.

The book also reflects a cross section of American cookery. Because of the highly mobile population of Denver, a growing metropolis, it is quite rare to find a native who still lives in the city. People from all parts of the nation (and the world) are constantly being transferred in and out. Not to be forgotten are Colorado's visitors who include summer tourists and winter skiers. They are among the many people who have shared their recipes with me.

This book is limited to main dishes but there are a few "extras," such as relishes and breads, offered as menu complements. There is something for everyone with recipes for game, poultry, the most popular cuts of red meat, seafood, as well as for meatless entrées. Some recipes take short cuts or suggest make-ahead techniques, others require more "from scratch" time, and many of them are suitable for entertaining.

The collection goes even a step further by noting any adjustments that are necessary for cooking at both high and low altitudes. Since Denver is a mile above sea level (some 5,280 feet), I have included an explanation at the back of the book of how different altitudes affect cooking.

During the years I have been food editor of the *Denver Post,* I have had innumerable requests from readers to compile a cookbook like this. I appreciated these compliments but seldom gave them more thought than "some day I'll do that." One day, a very special former colleague, Paula Deger Cooper, literally pushed me toward the recipe files saying, "Let's get started on the book." Paula followed up that initial push by offering much help along the way, finally ending up as my chief tester for low-altitude cookery when she later moved to California.

There are many other persons I would like to name in appreciation for their loyalty and support but to do so would make this a very long preface indeed.

Besides, you know who you are.

Denver   H.D.
July 1979

BEEF

Tough as leather, or tender as butter, or any of the stages between, beef has been a popular American meat since the Spaniards brought it to this continent some four hundred years ago. Indians and dust-covered cowboys charred chunks of it over campfires; early-day restaurants in "big" cities pampered their properly-dressed patrons with succulent steaks and roasts, served *au jus* or covered with fancy, seasoned butters or sauces; in homes, stews of beef and garden-fresh vegetables bubbled on top of wood-burning stoves.

Today's meat counter offers a wider variety of beef cuts than ever before. Names of cuts have been standardized too. If you experiment with different cuts, rather than settling only for familiar steaks and roasts, you will add greater variety to your menu while reducing your grocery bill.

Much of the beef available today is quite tender, but even a less-tender cut can be made palatable if it is cooked the right way; for instance, cuts that prove tough if broiled can often be made tender by braising. Meanwhile, be alert to the possibility that a more expensive cut may save you money after all: you may find that the cheaper regular ground beef, for example, yields less meat after the fat has cooked out than the more costly lean or extra-lean beef. Consult reliable and up-to-date basic cookbooks and use information provided by the meat industry to learn about the newest ways to prepare the various cuts.

CORNISH PASTIES

Occupying a very special spot on my kitchen wall is an old, worn-out food chopper, a crescent-shaped piece of tin awkwardly attached to a battered, wooden handle. This *objet d'art* was used by "Nanoo," my late grandmother (or anyone she could recruit in the family), to chop meat and vegetables. Many of the ingredients cut by the old chopper, which was made to fit the curvature of a small, wooden bowl, went into plump meat pies, called pasties (pronounce *past* to rhyme with *fast*). These robust treats, traditionally made with a flaky crust that contained some ground suet, were introduced to America by miners who migrated here from Cornwall, England. Even before the invention of lunch pails, pasties were popular with miners because they could be freshly baked in the morning, wrapped in towels, and carried in pockets or inside shirts to be kept warm for the noontime lunch. Like other recipes with less-than-aristocratic origins, pasties have become a little bit snobbish over the years. Here is an updated version of those wonderful pies made with the old, worn-out food chopper.

¾ pound uncooked beef sirloin steak, trimmed of fat and finely diced

½ pound uncooked pork shoulder, trimmed of fat and finely diced

2 medium, peeled, uncooked potatoes, diced in about ½-inch cubes to make about 2 cups

1 medium onion, chopped

1 cup (about) thinly-sliced, peeled, uncooked rutabagas or turnips *or*

2 cups (about) frozen, unthawed, uncooked mixed vegetables, separated into tiny clusters

Salt and pepper to taste

3 cups unsifted flour

1 teaspoon salt

1 cup solid shortening

6 tablespoons (about) cold water

1 egg beaten with 1 tablespoon water

Mushroom Sauce (optional)

In a large bowl, thoroughly mix together beef, pork, potatoes, onion, the vegetables of your choice, salt, and pepper. Let mixture stand at room temperature while preparing pastry. In a large bowl, mix together flour and 1 teaspoon salt. Blend in shortening with pastry cutter until mixture is crumbly. Gradually sprinkle water over mixture, 1 tablespoonful at a time, tossing lightly with fork after each addition. If pastry appears too dry, add a few drops more water. (Pastry should be slightly more moist than conventional pie pastry, but not as soft as biscuit dough.) Divide pastry into 4 equal portions. Shape each portion into a ball. Roll out each ball between 2 pieces of foil to a 10-inch circle. Working with 1 circle at a time, gently pull foil off top. Using 2 large, ungreased baking sheets for the 4 pastry circles, flip each pastry circle over onto sheet so that remaining foil is on top. Gently pull off foil. Place ¼ of the meat mixture on half of each pastry circle, leaving about 1½ inches of uncovered pastry at the edge. Brush edges of pastry circles with water. Fold uncovered dough over filling, like a big turnover. Bring edge of lower pastry up over edge of top pastry. Pinch edges together and flute them. (If pastry breaks in a few places, just pinch the breaks together or use the smaller ones as "automatic vents".) Prick top of each pasty with fork tines. Just before pasties go into the oven, brush tops and sides of pasties with egg which has been beaten with water. Bake in oven preheated to 375°. After 30 minutes' baking time, switch baking sheets on upper and lower oven racks so that pasties will be done at the same time. Bake another 30 minutes or until pastry is golden brown. (The meat and vegetables should be done in about 1 hour at altitudes above 5,000 feet; in about 50 minutes at altitudes below 5,000 feet.) Serve pasties hot with Mushroom Sauce, if desired (though the sauce is definitely not traditional). Pasties are also fairly tasty cold, carried for lunch. They may be reheated, covered with foil, for about 20 minutes in a moderately hot oven. Makes 4 very large pasties.

Mushroom Sauce

3 tablespoons butter or margarine	½ pound fresh mushrooms, sliced
3 tablespoons flour	and sautéed
Salt and pepper to taste	lightly in about 3 tablespoons
1½ cups milk	butter or margarine

Melt butter or margarine in medium-sized saucepan over moderate heat. Add flour. Stir a few minutes over moderate heat. Add salt and pepper. Gradually add milk, stirring over moderate heat until thickened. Stir in mushrooms. Heat to serving temperature. Makes about 2¾ cups sauce.

CITRUS-SAUCED ROAST

An aromatic marinade, made with grapefruit juice, enhances the meat, then adds snap to a great gravy. Eye-of-round roast benefits from the treatment here, but any beef roast that needs tenderizing can be used.

1 eye-of-round roast (about 3 pounds)	1 medium clove garlic, crushed
½ of a 6-ounce can frozen grapefruit juice, diluted with ¾ cup water (dilute remaining grapefruit juice with 1½ cans water, and drink it)	¼ teaspoon dried leaf basil
	¼ teaspoon dried leaf oregano
	1 medium bay leaf
	¾ teaspoon salt
	¼ teaspoon pepper
½ cup cooking oil	⅓ cup water
½ medium onion, chopped	Grapefruit Gravy Cooked rice or noodles

Place roast in a close-fitting glass bowl. Mix together grapefruit juice, oil, onion, garlic, basil, oregano, bay leaf, salt, and pepper. Pour mixture over roast. Marinate roast, covered, in refrigerator for 12 to 24 hours. Turn roast occasionally during marinating period. Remove meat from marinade and place it, fat side up, on a rack in a shallow roasting pan. Pour water into bottom of pan. Roast, uncovered, in oven preheated to 350° for 30 minutes. Remove bay leaf from marinade and reserve for basting meat and making gravy. Reduce oven temperature to 325°. Roast meat, uncovered, basting occasionally, for about 1 hour longer or until it reaches desired degree of doneness. Allow about 20 minutes to the pound for rare; 22 minutes to the pound for medium; 24 minutes to the pound for well-done. Meat thermometer should register 140°, 160°, and 170°, respectively, for each stage of doneness. (I think it's a shame, however, to roast this cut until well-done, which robs it of juices. If you don't like it rare, please consider the medium cooking stage. At altitudes above 5,000 feet, add 2 or 3 minutes' cooking time to each roasting stage.) Remove roast from pan and keep it warm while preparing gravy. Reserve ¼ cup of the pan drippings for gravy. Serve sliced roast with gravy and cooked rice or noodles. 6 or more servings.

Grapefruit Gravy

¼ cup pan drippings from preceding recipe	1 cup marinade from preceding recipe
½ stick (¼ cup) butter or margarine	1 can (about 13-ounce) beef broth
¼ cup flour	

Place drippings and butter or margarine in medium-sized saucepan over moderate heat. Stir until butter melts. Blend in flour. Continue cooking over moderate heat, stirring, a few minutes. Add marinade and broth. Cook over moderate heat, stirring constantly with a wire whisk, until mixture thickens. Makes about 2 cups gravy.

CATALAN POT ROAST

Because of the different sizes and shapes of pot roasts (with and without the bone), it is very difficult to determine the number of servings each one will yield. Experience with cooking them is the best way to learn this. It is helpful to keep an account of the number of servings in each roast you cook.

¼ teaspoon dried leaf
marjoram
¾ teaspoon salt
¼ teaspoon pepper
1 teaspoon cinnamon
¼ teaspoon ground
cloves
1 tablespoon dry
parsley flakes
1 medium clove
garlic, minced
4 tablespoons olive oil
1 beef rump roast
(4 to 5 pounds)

1 medium, green
pepper, minced
¾ cup chopped onion
2 cans (10½-ounce
each) tomato purée
1 cup dry red wine
½ cup orange juice
1 tablespoon
cornstarch
¼ cup water
1 cup pimiento-stuffed
olives, cut in halves
Boiled potatoes

Combine marjoram, salt, pepper, cinnamon, cloves, parsley, garlic, and 2 tablespoons of the oil. Mix well. Spread mixture over all sides of meat, which has been placed in a bowl. Let meat stand at room temperature 1 hour. Heat remaining oil in Dutch oven over moderate heat. Place roast in Dutch oven and cook over moderate heat until roast is brown on all sides. Remove roast. Add green pepper and onion to drippings; sauté over moderately low heat until onion is transparent. Drain off grease. Add tomato purée, wine, and orange juice. Mix well. Add roast. Bring liquid to boil, reduce heat, and simmer, covered, 3 to 3½ hours or until meat is tender. Remove meat to serving platter; keep warm. Mix together cornstarch and water until smooth, and stir into cooking liquid. Cook over moderate heat, stirring, until thickened. Stir in olives. Serve sauce over sliced meat and potatoes.

ITALIAN-SEASONED POT ROAST

Convenience foods make this roast easy to prepare.

1 beef chuck roast
(about 3 pounds)
Flour
Cooking oil
2½ cups tomato juice

1 package (0.6-
ounce) Italian
salad dressing
mix
Cooked spaghetti,
rice, or noodles

Lightly dust roast on all sides with flour. Heat a small amount of cooking oil over moderate heat in Dutch oven. Add roast. Cook over moderate heat until brown on all sides. Drain off grease. Combine 2 cups of the tomato juice with salad dressing mix. Pour tomato juice mixture around meat. Bake, covered, in oven preheated to 350° for about 2½ to 3½ hours or until done. Remove meat from pan. Bring cooking liquid to boil. Combine remaining ½ cup tomato juice and ¼ cup flour, mixing until smooth. Gradually stir tomato mixture into boiling liquid. Cook, stirring constantly, until thickened. Serve meat and gravy with spaghetti, rice, or noodles. Makes about 6 servings depending on bone and fat content of the roast.

CHICAGO ITALIAN-STYLE BRISKET OF BEEF

Fennel seed, an herb with a flavor mildly reminiscent of licorice, and green chile peppers make an unlikely but flavorsome seasoning combination that perks up a fresh brisket.

1 fresh beef brisket (about 5 pounds) at room temperature	1 can (4-ounce) green chiles, cut in 2-inch strips
Garlic powder	2 teaspoons fennel seeds
Salt and freshly-ground pepper to taste	2 tablespoons brown sugar
1 tablespoon paprika	1 medium onion, sliced and separated into rings

Trim off all but about ¼ inch of fat from brisket. Lay brisket out flat, fat side up. Dust fat side very lightly with garlic powder. Sprinkle with salt, pepper, and 1 teaspoon of the paprika. Arrange chile strips on top and sprinkle with fennel seeds. Reserve a few chile strips for later use. Fold narrow end of brisket to center. Pull short sides of brisket together (they will not quite meet), and tie meat securely to form an oblong shape, about 8 x 5 inches. Place meat, seam sides down, in well-greased pan. Press brown sugar over top of meat. Dust lightly with additional garlic powder, salt, and pepper. Sprinkle remaining paprika on top. Cover top with onion rings and reserved chile strips. Do not add water. Bake, tightly covered, in oven preheated to 275° for 4 to 5 hours or until done. Remove meat from drippings.

Refrigerate meat and drippings in separate containers overnight. Remove and reserve onion rings. Remove string from meat. Spread out meat and cut in thin, diagonal slices across the grain. Arrange slices, slightly overlapping each other, in foil-lined shallow pan. Remove grease from top of refrigerated drippings and discard. Drizzle about ½ cup of the drippings over meat. Arrange reserved onion rings on top. Let meat come to room temperature. Heat, covered, in oven preheated to 375° for about 30 minutes or until hot. 10 or more servings.

POT ROAST DIABLO

This recipe has enjoyed the limelight for more than two decades in the Rocky Mountain Area.

1 beef chuck roast (3 to 5 pounds)	¼ cup chili sauce
	⅔ cup water
¼ cup flour seasoned with salt and pepper	1 tablespoon Worcestershire Sauce
3 tablespoons cooking oil	1 tablespoon vinegar
	1 teaspoon sugar
½ medium onion, chopped	¼ cup water mixed with ¼ cup flour until smooth
⅓ cup water	Cooked noodles
2 tablespoons prepared mustard	

Dredge meat on all sides with seasoned flour. Heat oil over moderate heat in Dutch oven. Add meat. Cook over moderate heat until meat is brown on all sides. Drain off grease. Add onion and ⅓ cup water, stirring it around meat. Bring to boil, reduce heat, and simmer, covered, about 2 hours. If necessary, add water in very small amounts, to keep mixture from becoming dry. Mix together mustard, chili sauce, ⅔ cup water, Worcestershire Sauce, vinegar, and sugar. Pour mixture over meat. Continue to simmer meat, covered, until it is tender. Remove meat from pan. Add enough water, if necessary, to cooking liquid to make 2 cups. Bring liquid to boil. Add flour mixed with water. Cook over moderate heat, stirring with wire whisk, until sauce is smooth and thickened. Slice meat and serve with sauce and noodles. Number of servings depends upon size of roast.

DAY-AHEAD BRISKET WITH BEER

There's no last-minute carving of this meat. It's cooked a day ahead, re-frigerated overnight, then sliced and reheated in its delectable sauce.

Cooking oil
1 fresh beef brisket
(4 to 5 pounds)
1 envelope dry
onion soup mix
1 medium onion,
sliced and separated
into rings

2 medium ribs celery
and some of the
tops chopped
1 cup bottled chili
sauce
½ cup water
1 can (12-ounce)
beer

Heat a small amount of oil in Dutch oven over moderate heat. Add brisket. Cook over moderate heat until brisket is brown on all sides. Drain off grease. Sprinkle dry soup mix over meat. Arrange onion rings and celery on top. Combine chili sauce and water. Pour mixture around meat. Bake, cov-ered, in oven preheated to 350°, allowing about 45 minutes per pound. Baste meat occasionally with its cooking liquid. About 45 minutes before meat is finished, pour beer over top of it. Continue to simmer meat, covered until it is done. Refrigerate brisket, covered, in its cooking liquid overnight. (The refrigeration period helps to tenderize the meat.) The next day, re-move and discard any grease which has formed on top. Slice meat across the grain. Heat slices in the meat's cooking liquid. To serve, pour some of the cooking liquid over slices. Serve remaining cooking liquid in a separate dish. 10 or more servings.

CHINESE TOMATO BEEF

Every stir-fry meal is different, and this one is no exception.

1 pound flank steak,
partially frozen
3 tablespoons soy
sauce or to taste
1½ tablespoons
cornstarch
¼ cup peanut oil
3 medium tomatoes,

unpeeled and
quartered
½ cup chicken broth
½ medium, green
pepper, thinly
sliced
1 tablespoon dry
sherry
Cooked rice

Cut steak across the grain in very thin slices. (It is easier to slice if it is partially frozen.) Combine 2 tablespoons of the soy sauce and 1 tablespoon of the cornstarch. Mix until cornstarch dissolves. Add steak. Stir until steak is coated with soy sauce mixture. Let steak stand at room temperature about 30 minutes so that steak absorbs soy sauce flavor. Heat oil in wok or large skillet over moderate heat. Add steak. Cook over moderately high heat about 30 seconds, stirring constantly. Steak should be slightly rare. Drain steak in colander but reserve drippings that drain from it. Pour off all but about ¼ cup drippings from skillet. Add tomatoes. Cook over moderately high heat, stirring gently, about 1 minute. Add all but 1 tablespoon of the broth. Cook about 30 seconds longer. Add remaining 1 tablespoon soy sauce, green pepper, beef, its drippings, and sherry. Dissolve remaining ½ tablespoon cornstarch in remaining 1 tablespoon broth. Push beef and vegetables to one side of pan. Add cornstarch mixture to cooking liquid. Bring to boil, stirring constantly until thickened. Mix together all ingredients in skillet lightly but thoroughly. Serve over rice. 4 servings.

CORNED BEEF BAKED OMELET ROLL

A cheesy, omelet-like layer is rolled around a corned beef filling, then served with a lemon-flavored sauce for an exciting brunch or supper menu idea. Actually, the baked omelet roll is compatible with all kinds of fillings (try one with canned salmon), so let your imagination take over.

5 tablespoons butter	6 extra-large egg
5 tablespoons flour	whites at room
1 teaspoon salt	temperature
1¼ cups milk	¼ teaspoon cream of
½ cup shredded	tartar
Cheddar cheese	Additional grated
⅓ cup grated Romano	Romano cheese
cheese	Corned Beef Filling
6 extra-large egg	Lemon-Parsley
yolks, beaten	Sauce

Melt butter over moderate heat in a large, heavy saucepan. Add flour and salt. Stir a few minutes over moderate heat. Gradually add milk. Cook over moderate heat, stirring constantly with wire whisk, until mixture is smooth and thickened. Add Cheddar cheese and ⅓ cup Romano cheese. Cook over low heat, stirring, until cheese melts. Remove from heat. Using wire whisk, stir yolks into cheese mixture until thoroughly mixed. Let mixture stand in pan in which it was cooked, at room temperature, while beating egg whites. Beat egg whites until foamy. Add cream of tartar. Beat egg whites until stiff. Fold about ⅓ of the whites into cheese mixture, then carefully but thoroughly fold in remaining whites. Have ready a 10 x 15-inch jelly roll pan which has been greased on bottom and sides, then lined with waxed paper on bottom and sides. Spoon egg mixture into pan, spreading it evenly with rubber spatula to edges of pan. Bake mixture in oven preheated to 350° for 10 to 12 minutes or just until firm to the touch. Do not overcook mixture or allow it to become brown. (At altitudes below 5,000 feet, use the shorter baking period as a guide.) Turn out omelet on a towel which has been sprinkled generously with additional Romano cheese. Carefully remove paper from omelet. Roll omelet from long side together with the towel. (The finished roll will be completely rolled in the towel.) Let stand at room temperature until cool. Unroll omelet. Spread it with Corned Beef Filling, almost to the edges. Roll omelet again, this time without the towel. (Don't worry if a few cracks appear; lightly pat and press them together.) Place roll on a lightly-greased baking sheet. Bake uncovered, in oven preheated to 350° for 15 to 20 minutes or until heated through. Slice and serve with Lemon-Parsley Sauce. 6 to 8 servings.

Corned Beef Filling

1 can (12-ounce) corned beef at room temperature, broken in small pieces with a fork	½ cup finely-chopped celery
	¼ cup well-drained pickle relish
1 tablespoon prepared mustard	½ cup (about) mayonnaise

Thoroughly mix together corned beef, mustard, celery, and pickle relish. Add enough mayonnaise to hold mixture together and to make it fairly moist. Spread mixture on omelet according to preceding directions.

Lemon-Parsley Sauce

2 tablespoons butter	2 tablespoons lemon juice
2 tablespoons flour	
1½ cups chicken broth	3 tablespoons minced parsley
¼ teaspoon salt	
2 egg yolks, beaten	

Melt butter in medium-sized saucepan over moderate heat. Add flour. Stir over moderate heat a few minutes. Gradually add broth and salt. Cook over moderate heat, stirring, until smooth and thickened. Add a small amount of the hot sauce to egg yolks. Add egg yolks to sauce, mixing well with wire whisk. Cook over low heat, stirring constantly, until thickened. Stir in lemon juice and parsley. Serve over slices of Corned Beef Baked Omelet Roll. (This is also an excellent sauce to serve with fish.) Makes about 1¾ cups sauce.

GROUND BEEF CASSEROLE WITH HERB STUFFING

Here's an imaginative way to use some common ingredients.

1½ pounds lean ground beef	⅓ cup butter or margarine
1 egg, beaten	2 cups packaged, herb-seasoned stuffing mix
1 medium onion, chopped	
½ medium, green pepper, chopped	2 medium ribs celery, chopped
½ cup crushed soda crackers	1 can (10¾-ounce) mushroom soup
⅔ cup water	Chopped green pepper to taste

Combine beef, egg, ½ of the onion, green pepper, and crackers. Mix well. Line a 1½-quart round casserole with mixture, pressing it evenly over bottom and up against sides. Combine water and butter or margarine. Heat until butter melts. Add stuffing mix, celery, and remaining onion. Mix lightly but thoroughly. Spoon stuffing in center of casserole. Spoon undiluted soup over stuffing. Sprinkle top with green pepper. Bake, uncovered, in oven preheated to 350° for 1 hour or until stuffing is fluffy. 5 to 6 servings.

INDIAN TACOS

Come on now. Where would a recipe get a name like that? Well, just combine the influences of Mexican and American Indian cookery. The Indian Fry Bread is great for snacks, too.

1½ pounds ground beef	Indian Fry Bread
1 can (6-ounce) tomato paste, mixed with 2 cans water until smooth	Shredded Cheddar cheese
1 can (15-ounce) chili beans	Sliced green onion and some onion tops
1 package (1¼-ounce) taco seasoning mix	Finely-diced, unpeeled tomatoes

Heat a 9- or 10-inch skillet over moderate heat. Crumble beef into skillet. Cook over moderate heat until meat loses red color, breaking up meat in small pieces with edge of a spoon. Drain off grease. In a large bowl, mix together tomato paste-water mixture, beans and their liquid, and dry taco seasoning mix. Using potato masher, mash beans coarsely. Add bean mixture to ground beef. Mix well. Bring to boil, reduce heat, and simmer, covered, about 20 minutes. (Meat mixture can be prepared and frozen before the 20-minute cooking period, but thaw mixture before continuing with directions.) Serve meat mixture over pieces of Indian Fry Bread. Serve small bowls of cheese, onions, and tomatoes on the side to be piled to taste on top of meat mixture. This dish is to be eaten with a fork and knife; not with the hands, taco-style. 6 to 8 servings.

Indian Fry Bread

4 cups unsifted all-purpose flour	1½ teaspoons salt
2 tablespoons (2 tablespoons are correct!) baking powder	2 tablespoons sugar
2 tablespoons cooking oil	1¾ cups warm tap water
	Additional cooking oil

Thoroughly mix together flour, baking powder, 2 tablespoons oil, salt, sugar, and water. Use hands, if necessary, to mix dough. Let dough stand at room temperature 30 minutes. Knead dough until it is smooth and elastic. Roll out dough on well-floured surface to about ¼-inch thickness. Cut dough in rectangles, about 3 x 4 inches. Make a small slit in center of each rectangle with tip of knife (the bread will fry faster and won't get soggy). Heat about ½ inch of additional cooking oil in a large skillet over moderate heat. Oil is hot enough when one of the pieces of dough dropped into it immediately starts to puff up and turn golden brown. Using tongs, drop the pieces of dough into the hot oil. Turn once, and fry until puffy and golden brown. (They will form interesting, irregular shapes.) Drain bread on paper toweling. Leftover bread may be served as a snack with honey. (Recipe is easily cut in half, if desired.)

MEXICAN-STYLE PIZZA

A little bit of Mexican and a little bit of Italian cookery get together in an "All-American" pizza.

1½ pounds lean ground beef
1 can (8-ounce) tomato sauce, diluted with ½ can water
1 package (1¼-ounce) taco seasoning mix
1 package (about 13-ounce) hot roll mix
2 cans (4-ounce each) chopped green chiles, drained

2 green onions and tops, sliced
1 cup shredded, sharp Cheddar cheese
Additional sliced green onions, shredded Cheddar cheese, prepared taco sauce, shredded lettuce, and chopped, fresh tomato (optional)

Heat a 9- or 10-inch skillet over moderate heat. Crumble beef into skillet. Cook over moderate heat until meat loses red color. Break up meat with edge of spoon as it cooks. Drain off grease. Add diluted tomato sauce and dry taco seasoning. Cook over moderate heat, stirring, until taco seasoning dissolves. Prepare hot roll mix according to package directions for making pizza dough (or for hot rolls, if package doesn't specify pizza dough recipe). With greased fingers, pat out dough in greased pizza pan, 12 or 15 inches in diameter. (A larger pan would make a thinner crust. If extra-thin crust is desired, use less dough and bake remainder according to package directions for rolls.) Form a rim of dough around edge of pizza pan. Spread beef mixture over dough. (Do not let dough rise in this recipe.) Sprinkle with green chiles, 2 green onions, and 1 cup cheese. Bake, uncovered, in oven preheated to 425° for about 25 minutes, or until crust is brown and center is done. Cut in wedges to serve. Serve with additional onions, cheese, prepared taco sauce, shredded lettuce, and tomato to be spooned on top, if desired. 6 to 8 servings.

LASAGNA

Still another recipe for Lasagna? Yes, I couldn't resist including it because it has survived the test of time as one of the very best.

1 pound ground beef	1 pound (about)
1 pound bulk Italian	lasagna noodles
sausage	1 tablespoon cooking
3 medium cloves garlic,	oil
minced	1 package (6-ounce)
1 can (8-ounce)	sliced Mozzarella
tomato sauce	cheese
1 can (1-pound)	2 cartons (12-ounce
Italian-style tomatoes	each) small curd
Salt and pepper to	cottage cheese
taste	2 extra-large eggs
1 teaspoon dried leaf	Grated Parmesan
oregano	cheese to taste

Crumble beef and sausage into a large skillet which has been heated over moderate heat. Add garlic; cook over moderate heat until meat loses red color, breaking it up with edge of spoon as it cooks. Drain off grease. Add tomato sauce, tomatoes, which have been cut in small pieces, their liquid, salt, pepper, and oregano. Bring mixture to boil, reduce heat, and simmer, tightly covered, 1 hour. Cook noodles according to package directions, adding cooking oil to the liquid. Drain noodles, then spread them out on foil to keep them from sticking together. Arrange a layer of noodles in a greased, 9 x 13-inch baking dish. Overlap noodles slightly. (The entire pound of noodles won't be used; just enough to make 2 generous layers.) Arrange ½ of the Mozzarella cheese slices on top of noodles, spacing them evenly. Thoroughly mix together cottage cheese and eggs. Spoon ½ of the cottage cheese mixture on top of Mozzarella. Spoon ½ of the meat mixture evenly on top of cottage cheese mixture. Sprinkle with Parmesan cheese. Repeat layers, arranging the noodles again so they just overlap slightly. Bake, uncovered, in oven preheated to 375° for about 30 minutes or until bubbly.

(Mixture may be frozen before cooking, thawed in refrigerator, brought to room temperature, then cooked according to preceding directions.) 8 servings.

ENCHILADA CASSEROLE

What liberties cooks take with the term, Enchilada! Nowadays, it fits a lot of recipes that use tortillas. Here's one of them, a hearty combination which, incidentally, does not freeze well. That's because during thawing, the tortillas tend to absorb the moisture from the other ingredients and become too soft.

10 corn tortillas, 8 inches in diameter	1 can (10½-ounce) mushroom soup
Cooking oil	1 can (1-pound) stewed tomatoes
2 pounds ground beef	½ teaspoon chili powder (optional)
1 medium clove garlic, minced	Salt and pepper to taste
1 medium onion, chopped	1 pound shredded Longhorn cheese
1 can (7-ounce) green chiles, drained and diced	

Cut tortillas in quarters. Heat a small amount of cooking oil in large skillet over moderate heat. Fry tortilla quarters in hot oil for just a few seconds until they are slightly crisp on both sides. Turn them once during frying period. Drain quarters on paper toweling. (Tortilla quarters may be fried 1 or 2 days in advance of using, and refrigerated.) Drain off grease from skillet. Heat cleaned skillet over moderate heat. Crumble beef into skillet. Cook over moderate heat until meat loses red color, breaking up meat with edge of spoon as it cooks. Add garlic and onion during the last 5 minutes of cooking time. Drain off grease. Add chiles, soup, tomatoes, chili powder, salt, and pepper to meat mixture. Mix well. Arrange ½ of tortilla quarters in rows slightly overlapping in greased, shallow, 9 x 13-inch baking dish. Spoon ½ of meat mixture on top of tortillas. Sprinkle ½ of cheese on meat mixture. Repeat layers, ending with cheese. Cover loosely with foil. Bake in oven preheated to 350° for 45 minutes to 1 hour. Decorate edge of baking dish with additional tortilla quarters, if desired. 10 to 12 servings.

TALLERINE GROUND BEEF CASSEROLE

Ripe olives are an unexpected ingredient in this nifty combination.

1½ pounds ground beef
1 medium onion,
    chopped
1 can (10¾-ounce)
    tomato soup
½ cup catsup
1 cup water
1 can (6-ounce)
    pitted ripe olives
1 teaspoon salt
1 can (1-pound)
    whole kernel corn
½ of an 8-ounce
    package noodles
1 cup shredded
    American cheese

Heat a large skillet over moderate heat. Crumble beef into skillet; cook over moderate heat until meat loses red color. Add onion during last 5 minutes of cooking time. Drain off grease. Combine soup, catsup, water, and juice from olives. Add to meat. Cut olives in halves, reserving a few whole olives to garnish top of casserole. Add olive halves, salt, and corn to meat mixture. Break noodles in coarse pieces; add to meat. Bake, covered, in oven preheated to 350° for about 30 minutes or until noodles are done. Stir occasionally during baking. Sprinkle cheese on top. Garnish with whole olives. Uncover and return to oven just until cheese melts. 6 servings.

CARRY-ALONG CASSEROLE

This recipe is so-named because it's great for taking to potluck dinners.

2 pounds ground beef
1 can (6-ounce)
    tomato paste
1 can (15-ounce)
    tomato sauce
1 tablespoon dry
    onion soup mix
    (shake package to
    mix thoroughly
    before measuring)
¾ cup water
1 package (8-ounce)
    noodles, cooked
and drained (less
    noodles may be
    used, if desired)
1 carton (12-ounce)
    small curd cottage
    cheese
1 can (4½-ounce)
    ripe olives, drained
    and sliced
1 cup dairy sour
    cream or plain
    yogurt

Heat a medium-sized skillet over moderate heat. Crumble beef into skillet; cook over moderate heat until meat loses red color. Drain off grease. Add tomato paste, tomato sauce, dry onion soup mix, and water. Mix thoroughly. Bring to boil, reduce heat, and simmer, covered, 20 minutes. Spread ½ of meat mixture in 11 x 7-inch baking dish. Add ½ of the noodles, then ½ of the cottage cheese which has been mixed with ½ of the olives and ½ of the sour cream or yogurt. Repeat layers, ending with cottage cheese mixture. Bake, covered, in oven preheated to 350° for about 30 minutes or until bubbly. 6 to 8 servings.

CHEESE-O-RITOS

Many of Denver's Mexican restaurants serve different versions of this popular dish, listed on menus with different names, of course.

1 can (1-pound) refried beans	6 flour tortillas, 10 inches in diameter
½ teaspoon ground cumin or to taste	¾ pound shredded Colby cheese
¼ teaspoon garlic powder	2 large, fresh tomatoes, peeled and cut in small pieces
1 cup shredded Monterey Jack cheese	Shredded lettuce
1½ pounds ground beef	Dairy sour cream (optional)
3 to 4 cans (6-ounce each) green chile salsa	

Combine beans, cumin, garlic powder, and Monterey Jack cheese in top of double boiler. Cook, covered, over hot water, stirring occasionally, until cheese melts. Keep mixture hot until ready to use. Crumble beef into medium-sized skillet which has been heated over moderate heat; cook, stirring frequently, until meat loses red color. Drain off grease. Add 2 cans of the green chile salsa. Bring to boil, reduce heat to a slow boil, and cook, uncovered, until most of the liquid evaporates. Spread tortillas (no need to heat them) with hot bean mixture. Spread meat over beans, firmly pressing them together. Lightly roll tortillas. Place them, seam sides down, in a single layer in well-greased 9 x 13-inch dish. Pour 1 can of salsa over top and around sides of tortillas. Sprinkle Colby cheese, tomatoes, and onions on top. Bake, uncovered, in oven preheated to 350° for 30 minutes or until bubbly. Serve on plates surrounded with shredded lettuce and additional heated salsa on the side. Sour cream may also be served on the side to be spooned on top of tortillas. 6 servings.

Note: For a spicier flavor, bulk Italian sausage may be substituted for half of the ground beef.

BURGUNDY GROUND BEEF BAKE

The beef doesn't even have to be browned before it's combined with the other ingredients in this moist mixture.

2 pounds extra-lean ground beef	water chestnuts, drained and sliced
1 cup burgundy wine	1 can (1-pound)
4 medium carrots, cut in about 2-inch pieces	tomato wedges, drained (Yes, there are canned
1 cup celery, cut in about 1-inch pieces	tomato wedges. Save the juice for
1 medium onion, sliced and separated into rings	other casseroles, soups, etc.)
½ pound fresh mushrooms, sliced	3 tablespoons quick-cooking tapioca
1½ teaspoons salt	Cooked rice or
1 tablespoon sugar	noodles
1 can (8½-ounce)	

Combine beef and burgundy. Add carrots, celery, onion, mushrooms, salt, sugar, and water chestnuts. Mix well. Add tomato wedges and tapioca. Mix lightly but thoroughly. Place mixture in a 9 x 13-inch pan. Bake, covered, in oven preheated to 300° about 3 hours or until done. (At altitudes below 5,000 feet reduce baking time about 20 minutes.) Uncover during last 30 minutes baking time. Serve over rice or noodles. 8 servings.

CEREAL-TOPPED CASSEROLE

If economy, ease of preparation, and excellent flavor interest you, put this on the menu.

1½ pounds ground beef	whole kernel corn,
½ medium onion, chopped	drained
1½ teaspoons salt	1 package (10-ounce) frozen mixed vegetables, thawed and uncooked
⅛ teaspoon pepper	
½ teaspoon dill weed	
1 envelope (1-ounce) dry onion-mushroom soup mix	1 cup dairy sour cream or plain yogurt
1 cup hot water	2 cups Rice Chex cereal
1 can (8-ounce)	

Heat 9- or 10-inch skillet over moderate heat. Crumble in ground beef. Cook over moderate heat until meat loses red color. Add onion during last 5 minutes of cooking time. Drain off grease. Add salt, pepper, dill weed, and dry soup mix. Mix well. Add water. Mix well. Add corn, mixed vegetables, and sour cream or yogurt. Mix lightly but thoroughly. Spoon into 7 x 13-inch baking dish. (At this point, casserole may be refrigerated, covered, for several hours or wrapped in foil and frozen. It may be stored in freezer up to 3 weeks. Thaw in refrigerator when ready to use.) Let mixture stand until it reaches room temperature. Sprinkle cereal over top. Bake, uncovered, in oven preheated to 350° for 15 minutes. Cover loosely with foil to prevent overbrowning of cereal. Bake about 15 minutes longer or until bubbly. 6 servings.

MOCK MANICOTTI WITH MEAT BALLS

This is made with tiny, tender, rolled pancakes instead of Manicotti tubes. However, the tubes can be substituted for the pancakes, if desired.

Pancakes

6 eggs, beaten	2 cups unsifted flour
2 cups water	¼ teaspoon salt

Combine eggs and water. Mix well. Gradually add flour and salt, beating with wire whisk until smooth. For each pancake drop about 2 tablespoons batter onto moderately hot, greased griddle to make pancakes about 3¼ inches in diameter. Turn pancakes once; cook just long enough for them to become firm. Do not allow them to brown. Remove from griddle and place in single layer on paper toweling. Do not stack pancakes until they are completely cool. Then they may be stacked, covered, and stored at room temperature for several hours. Makes about 38 pancakes.

Ricotta Cheese Filling

1 carton (15-ounce) ricotta cheese	½ teaspoon salt
1 egg, beaten	3 tablespoons minced, fresh parsley
⅓ cup grated Romano cheese	⅛ teaspoon pepper

Mix together all ingredients. Put a scant teaspoonful of ricotta mixture near center of each pancake. Fold over one side of pancake. Close edge with wooden pick.

Meat Balls and Tomato Sauce

2 cans (10½-ounce each) tomato purée	with ½ pound lean ground pork
2 cans (6-ounce each) tomato paste	1 egg, beaten
Water	2 slices bread, trimmed of crusts and torn into small pieces
2½ teaspoons salt	
½ teaspoon Italian herb seasoning or to taste	2 teaspoons minced parsley
1½ pounds lean ground beef *or* 1 pound lean ground beef mixed	¼ teaspoon garlic powder
	⅛ teaspoon pepper
	1 tablespoon grated Romano cheese

Combine tomato purée, tomato paste, 4 cups water, 2 teaspoons of the salt, and Italian herb seasoning in Dutch oven. Bring to boil, reduce heat, and simmer, uncovered, on very low heat for 4 hours. Add ⅔ cup water 3 times at 45-minute intervals during cooking period. Each time water is added, return mixture to boil, reduce heat, and simmer, uncovered. Stir frequently.

Meanwhile, combine ground beef, egg, bread, parsley, garlic powder, remaining ½ teaspoon salt, pepper, and Romano cheese. Mix well. Shape into 18 balls about 1½ inches in diameter. Put meat balls under broiler and broil until brown on all sides, shaking pan frequently to keep them round. Drain balls. Add them to tomato sauce during last 30 minutes of cooking time. Add additional Italian seasoning, if desired, during last ½ hour of cooking time.

TO ASSEMBLE MANICOTTI:

Place about ⅓ of the meat balls and tomato sauce in greased 9 x 13-inch baking dish. Arrange about ½ of the filled pancakes on top. Add about ⅓ more of the meat balls and tomato sauce, then remaining pancakes. Spoon remaining meat balls and tomato sauce on top. (At this point, manicotti may be frozen, but thaw in refrigerator and bring to room temperature before baking.) Bake, covered, in oven preheated to 350° for 30 minutes or until bubbly. Serve with additional Romano cheese, if desired. 8 or more servings.

POTATO PUFF GROUND BEEF CASSEROLE

This is the kind of recipe that mainly requires opening cans and packages, and "throwing together" all of the ingredients.

1 pound ground beef	1 package
½ medium onion, chopped	(1-pound) frozen potato puffs,
½ cup chopped celery	unthawed (These
1 package (10-ounce) frozen peas, unthawed	are precooked mashed potatoes, formed into small
1 can (10¾-ounce) cream of asparagus soup	rounds or other shapes that require only browning
½ cup milk	when served
Salt and pepper to taste	according to package directions.)

Heat a medium-sized skillet over moderate heat. Crumble beef into skillet; cook over moderate heat until meat loses red color. Add onion and celery during the last 5 minutes of cooking time. Drain off grease. Add frozen peas which have been separated into small clusters. Mix together asparagus soup and milk until smooth. Add soup, salt, and pepper to meat mixture. Mix well. Transfer mixture to round, 1½-quart casserole. Arrange frozen potato puffs close together on top to cover entire casserole. Bake, uncovered, in oven preheated to 375° for about 1 hour for altitudes above 5,000 feet; about 45 minutes below 5,000 feet. 4 to 6 servings.

SPEEDY MEAT BALLS AND VEGETABLES

The rice fluffs up during the baking period to indicate the dish is done.

1 pound lean ground beef	¼ teaspoon dry mustard
½ cup packed, shredded American or Cheddar cheese	¼ teaspoon garlic salt
	Pepper to taste
1 teaspoon salt or to taste	2 tablespoons minced onion
1 can (10½-ounce) tomato soup	1 package frozen green beans, thawed but uncooked
1 cup water	
½ cup uncooked rice	1 can (12-ounce) whole kernel corn, drained
¼ teaspoon dried leaf oregano	

Thoroughly mix together beef, cheese, and salt; shape into 10 balls. Combine soup and water in a shallow, 7 x 11-inch baking dish or 10-inch, shallow, casserole; mix until smooth. Stir in rice, oregano, mustard, garlic salt, pepper, and onion. Arrange meat balls close together in center of mixture. Arrange green beans and corn around edge of casserole. Bake, covered, in oven preheated to 350° for about 1½ hours or until rice is fluffy. (At altitudes below 5,000 feet, decrease cooking time about 15 minutes). Turn meat balls occasionally during baking period. 5 to 6 servings.

FRONT RANGE SPAGHETTI PIE

There's nothing new about spaghetti pie. But there's something extra tasty about this version.

6 ounces (about) spaghetti
2 tablespoons butter or margarine
⅓ cup grated Parmesan cheese
2 eggs, well beaten
1 pound ground beef, *or ½ pound* ground beef and ½ pound Italian sausage
1 medium onion, chopped
½ medium, green pepper, chopped
1 can (8-ounce) whole tomatoes
1 can (6-ounce) tomato paste
1 teaspoon sugar
1 teaspoon dried leaf oregano
½ teaspoon garlic salt
1 cup small curd cottage cheese
½ cup shredded Mozzarella cheese

Cook spaghetti according to package directions; drain. (There should be about 3¼ cups cooked spaghetti.) While spaghetti is still hot, thoroughly mix it with butter or margarine, Parmesan cheese, and eggs. Put spaghetti in a buttered 10-inch pie plate with a 2-inch-high rim. With back of spoon spread spaghetti over bottom and up sides of plate to form a "crust." (As it cools it can be spread up the sides if it doesn't stick to sides while still hot.) Heat a 9- or 10-inch skillet over moderate heat. Crumble in beef and sausage if used. Cook over moderate heat until meat loses red color. Break up meat with edge of spoon while it cooks. Add onion and green pepper during last 5 minutes of cooking time. Drain off grease. Cut tomatoes in small pieces. Add tomatoes and their liquid, tomato paste, sugar, oregano, and garlic salt. Cook over moderate heat until hot. Spread cottage cheese over bottom of spaghetti crust. Spoon meat mixture on top of cottage cheese. Bake, uncovered, in oven preheated to 350° for 20 minutes. Sprinkle Mozzarella cheese on top in a small circle in center of pie. Bake about 5 minutes longer or until cheese melts. Let stand about 5 minutes at room temperature before cutting into wedges. 6 servings.

30-MINUTE SPAGHETTI

It's so quick and easy, you might feel a little guilty about how good it tastes. What's more, it isn't even Italian.

2 pounds ground round steak or ground chuck
1 large onion, chopped
1 medium clove garlic, minced
1 medium, green pepper, chopped
1 can (28-ounce) whole tomatoes, cut in pieces
1 can (6-ounce) tomato paste
2 tablespoons Worcestershire Sauce
1 can (3-ounce) sliced mushrooms
2 teaspoons chili powder or to taste
1 package (8-ounce) pasteurized process cheese spread, cut in small pieces
Cooked spaghetti

Heat medium-sized skillet over moderate heat. Crumble meat into skillet. Add onion, garlic, and green pepper. Cook over moderate heat until meat loses red color. Drain off grease. Add tomatoes and their liquid, tomato paste, Worcestershire Sauce, mushrooms and their liquid, and chili powder. Mix well. Bring to boil, reduce heat, and simmer, covered, about 30 minutes. Add cheese. Cook over moderate heat, stirring, until cheese melts. Serve over spaghetti. 8 servings.

FLANK STEAK WITH SAUCE POIVRE VERT

2½ pound flank steak
1 cup dry red wine
2 cloves garlic, mashed
¼ cup cooking oil
Softened butter
Lemon slices
Sprigs of watercress
Sauce Poivre Vert (page 46)

Lightly score steak on both sides. Place in tight-fitting dish. Combine wine, garlic, and oil. Pour over steak and marinate, at room temperature, for 4 hours. In refrigerator, marinate meat about 1 hour longer. Drain meat and blot dry with paper towel. Brush steak with softened butter. Broil about 4 minutes on each side, turning meat once during broiling period. Slice diagonally across the grain. Garnish meat with sliced lemon and watercress and serve with Sauce Poivre Vert. Serves 4 to 6.

EAST 8TH AVENUE CHILI

My sister Kay, (a great cook herself) whipped up this downright good combination one evening during our younger years when we needed something convenient to feed hungry, unexpected visitors. P.S.: This recipe goes easy on chili powder to suit all tastes.

2	pounds ground beef	1 can (28-ounce) whole tomatoes
1	medium onion, chopped	2 cans (1-pound each) dark red kidney beans
1½	teaspoons chili powder or to taste	Ground cumin to taste (optional)
	Salt and pepper to taste	Additional chili powder

Crumble beef into Dutch oven which has been heated over moderate heat. Cook beef until it loses red color, breaking up meat with edge of a large spoon into small pieces as it cooks. Add onion during the last 5 minutes of cooking time. Drain off all but about 1 tablespoon of the grease. Add chili powder, salt, pepper, tomatoes (which have been cut in small pieces), and the tomato liquid. Mix well. Add beans, the bean liquid, and cumin, if desired. Mix lightly but thoroughly (you don't want to break up the beans). Bring mixture to boil, reduce heat and simmer, covered, about 1 hour. Stir mixture occasionally. (When removing the lid from the Dutch oven, you will note that steam has condensed on the bottom of the lid. Wipe off the water spots before returning lid to Dutch oven to prevent the water from dripping back into the chili and thinning it.)

The beauty of this dish is that it can simmer from 1 to 3 hours and still emerge with the same meaty richness and self-thickening cooking liquid.

The chili loses taste, quality, and texture if it is frozen, but it can be stored for up to 3 days in the refrigerator. It will become thicker during the refrigeration period, so add water to obtain desired consistency when reheating. Add bread sticks, crisp, shredded lettuce with your favorite salad dressing, and glasses of ice cold beer for a complete meal. Serve with additional chili powder on the side for those who like a hotter flavor. 8 or more servings.

PAULA'S GREEN PEPPER STEAK

How could this book be complete without a recipe from a colleague and true friend, whose enthusiasm and unceasing help launched the whole project?

1 pound beef round steak, cut about ½-inch thick and trimmed of fat	2 medium, green peppers, cut in about ½-inch strips
1 tablespoon paprika	2 tablespoons cornstarch
2 tablespoons butter or margarine	¼ cup water
2 medium cloves garlic, crushed	¼ cup soy sauce or to taste
1½ cups beef broth	2 large, fresh tomatoes, cut in eighths
1 cup sliced green onions and some of the tops	Cooked rice

With meat pounder or edge of heavy saucer, pound steak to about ¼-inch thickness. Cut steak into strips, about ¼-inch wide. Place meat in a bowl. Add paprika, thoroughly mixing it with steak. Let meat stand at room temperature about 20 minutes. Melt butter or margarine over moderate heat in a 9- or 10-inch skillet. Add steak. Cook over moderate heat until steak is brown on all sides. Add garlic and broth. Bring mixture to boil, reduce heat, and simmer, covered, 30 minutes. Add onion and green pepper. Simmer, covered, about 5 minutes. Mix together cornstarch, water, and soy sauce until smooth. Add cornstarch mixture to meat mixture. Cook over moderate heat, stirring, until mixture is clear and thickened. Add tomatoes. Mix lightly but thoroughly. Serve over rice. 6 servings.

CAMPER'S STANDBY

Pop this in your camper's refrigerator in the morning, and it's ready to tuck into the oven for the evening meal. It's suitable for this kind of treatment at home, too.

2 medium potatoes, peeled and thinly sliced
1 small onion, thinly sliced and separated into rings
Salt and pepper to taste
1 pound lean ground beef

1 can (about 11-ounce) pork and beans
1 can (10¾-ounce) tomato soup
2 lean, uncooked bacon strips, cut in 1-inch pieces
8 strips American cheese (3 x 1 inches each)

Arrange potatoes on bottom of lightly greased, shallow, 10-inch casserole. Scatter onion rings on top. Sprinkle with salt and pepper. Add uncooked ground beef, distributing it evenly with fingertips over onions. Add beans and their liquid. Pour tomato soup over all. (Use spatula to spread each layer evenly.) Scatter bacon pieces on top. Bake, uncovered, in oven preheated to 350° for about 1½ hours or until potatoes are done. (At altitudes below 5,000 feet, reduce cooking time about 15 minutes.) During last 15 minutes of cooking time, place cheese strips on top. 4 servings.

BURGER-OLIVE-TAMALE PIE

Canned tamales are the secret ingredient that makes this special.

1 pound lean ground beef
2 cans (8-ounce each) tomato sauce
2 teaspoons chili powder
½ teaspoon salt

1 can (28-ounce) tamales, drained
6 ounces sliced Cheddar or Monterey Jack cheese
12 to 16 pitted ripe olives

Heat a 9- or 10-inch skillet over moderate heat. Crumble beef into skillet. Cook over moderate heat until beef loses red color. Pour off grease. Add tomato sauce, chili powder and salt. Simmer, covered, about 10 minutes. Remove parchment from tamales. Cut tamales in halves, lengthwise. Cut 2 slices of the cheese into 8 strips, about 1-inch wide; reserve. Dice remaining cheese and stir into meat mixture.

Arrange 8 tamale halves, cut sides down, crosswise, in a 7 x 11-inch, greased, shallow baking dish. Carefully spoon about ½ of the meat mixture between tamales. Arrange remaining 8 tamales, lengthwise, over bottom layer. Carefully spoon remaining meat mixture between rows. Arrange strips of cheese on top of mixture. Bake, uncovered, in oven preheated to 375° for about 25 minutes. Place olives in spaces between tamales and bake about 5 minutes longer. (Assembling this dish is very easy once you get started, though directions may appear complicated.) 4 to 6 servings.

WESTERN VEAL OSCAR

At its best when fresh asparagus is used, this combination of crab, veal, and vegetable is elegant, expensive—and worth it. The limited supply of veal, evident at retail meat counters in Colorado as well as other parts of the nation, is partly responsible for its relatively high cost. But, remember, there is almost no waste in veal and little shrinkage if it is properly cooked, so the cost per serving is not such a bad buy, after all.

1 pound veal cutlets, cut about ½-inch thick	8 small, frozen, precooked crab legs, thawed and removed from shell
Flour	
2 eggs, beaten	2 tablespoons sherry
Fine, dry bread crumbs	8 medium-large, cooked, warm asparagus spears
1 stick (½ cup) butter or margarine	Bearnaise Sauce

Cut veal into 4 serving pieces. Dredge veal generously on both sides in flour, then dip in eggs. Dredge veal generously on both sides in crumbs. Melt ½ of the butter in a large skillet over moderate heat. Add veal. Cook over moderately low heat just until golden brown on both sides. Melt remaining butter in another large skillet over moderate heat. Add crab legs. Sauté crab over moderate heat about 2 minutes. Add sherry. Cook over moderate heat, uncovered, about 5 minutes, turning crab legs frequently. Arrange veal on a platter or individual dinner plates. Top each serving with 2 asparagus spears and 2 crab legs. Spoon Bearnaise Sauce on top. 4 servings.

Bearnaise Sauce

¼	cup dry white wine	1	teaspoon minced parsley
2	tablespoons tarragon vinegar	¾	cup melted butter
1	tablespoon finely-chopped onion	3	extra-large egg yolks, beaten
2	crushed peppercorns		

Put wine, vinegar, onion, peppercorns, and parsley in top of double boiler. Cook mixture over direct moderate heat, uncovered, until it is reduced by half. Place mixture over hot, not boiling, water. Beat together butter, which has been slightly cooled, and beaten egg yolks. Gradually add yolk mixture to wine mixture, stirring constantly with wire whisk. Cook over hot, not boiling water, stirring constantly, until thickened. If mixture starts to separate, beat it very vigorously with wire whisk. Serve immediately. Makes about 1½ cups sauce.

STEAK AND SHRIMP WITH GARLIC BUTTER

When you get the urge to splurge, try this sumptuous offering.

1	stick (½ cup) butter	4	slices (3-ounces each) tenderloin of beef, trimmed of fat
¼	cup minced onion		
⅛	teaspoon pepper		
1	medium clove garlic, minced	8	large shrimp, cooked, peeled, and deveined
¼	cup dry white wine	6	frozen artichoke hearts or halves, cooked
1	tablespoon parsley flakes		
	Cooking oil		Crusty French bread

Melt butter in small skillet over moderate heat. Add onion and sauté over moderately low heat until transparent. Add pepper, garlic, wine, and parsley. Cook over moderate heat, stirring, about 2 minutes. Refrigerate garlic butter for 24 hours. When ready to assemble dish, heat garlic butter until it has melted. Add a small amount of cooking oil to a large skillet. Heat over moderate heat until oil sizzles. Add beef slices (which are called "tournedos" if they are cut from the heart of the tenderloin). Cook beef over high heat 1 minute on each side. Cut each slice of beef into 4 pieces. Arrange 8 pieces in each of 2 individual oven-proof serving dishes. Arrange 4 shrimp and 3 artichokes around the beef in each dish. Pour half the garlic butter in each dish. Bake, uncovered, in oven preheated to 350° for about 12 minutes or until hot. Serve with bread to be broken off in chunks and dunked into the garlic butter. 2 servings.

Note: Recipe may be doubled, tripled, or made in even larger quantities.

BEEROCKS

These little pillows of dough, stuffed with ground beef and sauerkraut, are economical satisfiers that can go hot or cold to the dinner table, into the lunch box or picnic basket, or onto the snack tray. This version of Beerocks is an adaptation of similar Russian and German recipes; here in America, still other versions are known as "Kraut Burgers." One big advantage to this recipe is the time-saving step of refrigerating the foolproof, potato-flour dough overnight.

Dough

2 medium potatoes (about 1 pound), peeled and cut in chunks	⅔ cup cooking oil
	6½ to 7 cups (about) unsifted all-purpose flour
1 package dry yeast	1 egg, beaten with 1 tablespoon water
⅔ cup sugar	Paprika
1½ teaspoons salt	
2 extra-large eggs, well beaten	

Place potatoes in medium-sized saucepan; cover with water. Bring to boil, reduce heat, and simmer, covered, until potatoes are done. Drain potatoes, reserving 1½ cups of the cooking liquid. Mash potatoes to make 1 cup.

(Don't be tempted to use instant mashed potatoes; sorry, but they don't work as well in this recipe.) Keep the mashed potatoes lukewarm in top of double boiler over hot water while preparing remainder of recipe. Reheat, if necessary, 1½ cups of the potato cooking liquid to lukewarm. Pour liquid into large bowl of electric mixer. Sprinkle yeast into potato water; let stand a few minutes, then stir until yeast dissolves. Stir in sugar and salt. Let mixture stand about 5 minutes. Add lukewarm mashed potatoes. Mix on medium-low speed of mixer until well blended. Add eggs and oil. Mix well on medium-low speed of mixer until well blended. Gradually add about ½ of the flour, mixing on medium-low speed of mixer, scraping down sides of bowl frequently with rubber spatula. Work in more flour with your hands until you've made a moderately-stiff dough that is easy to handle. Let dough rest 10 minutes. Turn out dough on lightly-floured surface; knead until it is smooth and elastic. Shape dough into a ball; place in a large, greased bowl. Turn dough to grease top. Cover bowl lightly with plastic wrap. Refrigerate dough about 24 hours. (It will start its rising period in refrigerator.)

Filling

This mixture can be made the day ahead of baking, kept covered and refrigerated, then brought to room temperature before filling Beerocks.

1½ pounds lean ground beef	1 envelope dry onion soup mix
1 can (1-pound) sauerkraut	Cayenne pepper to taste (optional)

Heat a greased, medium-sized skillet over moderate heat. Crumble in ground beef. Cook beef over moderate heat until it loses red color. Break it up in small pieces with edge of a large spoon as it cooks. Drain off all grease. Meanwhile, place sauerkraut in a colander and drain. Then thoroughly rinse sauerkraut with cold water and thoroughly drain again. Place beef in colander with sauerkraut. Mix with fork with large tines. Add dry onion soup mix and cayenne pepper, if desired. Thoroughly mix again with fork with large tines. Let mixture cool to room temperature before mounding it on dough squares. (The reason for using the colander is to allow excess moisture to drain off while mixture is cooling.)

TO ASSEMBLE:

Remove dough from refrigerator. Let dough stand, still lightly covered with plastic wrap for 1 hour at room temperature for altitudes above 5,000 feet;

about 1 hour and 10 minutes for altitudes below 5,000 feet. Punch dough down. Divide it into 3 parts.

Roll out each part of dough between 2 pieces of foil to a rectangle about 12 x 16 inches. Cut each rectangle into 4-inch squares. Place about 1 tablespoon of the filling in center of each square. (The dough squares will accommodate more filling, if desired.) Bring together opposite corners of each square to meet in center. Pinch cut edges together to seal. (With this dough it shouldn't be necessary to moisten edges in order to get them to seal.) Place Beerocks, seam sides down, on greased baking sheets about 1 inch apart. Cover lightly with plastic wrap. Let stand in warm place until puffy; about 15 minutes for altitudes above 5,000 feet; about 20 minutes for altitudes below 5,000 feet. Brush tops and sides with egg which has been beaten with water. Sprinkle tops with paprika. Bake in oven preheated to 375° for 20 to 30 minutes or until golden brown. Makes 3 dozen Beerocks.

Note: When completely cool, Beerocks may be placed in a single layer in a container or wrapped in foil and frozen. To reheat, place Beerocks in foil with a slight opening so steam can escape. Reheat at 300° for about 25 minutes.

FIVE-HOUR STEW

Remember this one? *Denver Post* readers' requests for it over the years indicate they don't want me to forget it.

2 pounds boneless round steak, trimmed of fat and cut in about 1-inch cubes	6 medium carrots, peeled and cut in about 2-inch pieces
2 cans (8-ounce each) tomato sauce	1 cup coarsely-chopped celery
1 cup water	½ medium, green pepper, coarsely chopped
1½ teaspoons salt	
Pepper to taste	1 medium onion, chopped
2 large potatoes, peeled and cut in eighths	1 slice white bread with crusts, torn into small pieces

Mix together steak, tomato sauce, water, salt, and pepper in a Dutch oven. Add potatoes, carrots, celery, green pepper, onion, and bread. Mix well. (Meat need not be browned first for this recipe.) Bake, tightly covered, in oven preheated to 250° for 5 hours, or until meat is tender and vegetables are done. (If the ingredients are at room temperature when mixture goes into the oven, baking time is about the same for all altitudes. The bread and tomato sauce thicken the cooking liquid.) Stir a couple of times during cooking period. 6 or more servings.

QUEEN CITY STEAK AU POIVRE (Pepper Steak)

This copycat version of a classic recipe isn't the least bit hard to swallow.

¼ cup whole peppercorns	3 tablespoons cooking oil
4 boneless, individual steaks, trimmed of fat (boneless New York strip steaks, also called top loin are preferred)	¼ cup plus 1 teaspoon cognac
	½ cup whipping cream, unwhipped
	Salt to taste

Put peppercorns in a plastic bag. Place bag on countertop, and spread peppercorns to eliminate any mounds. Crush peppercorns with the bottom of a heavy saucepan until they become a coarse crumb texture. (Use handle of pan for leverage.) Coat steaks on both sides with crushed peppercorns, firmly pressing them onto steak with fingers. (It might appear to be too much pepper, but the oil fries the pepper and takes much of the hot flavor out of it.) Heat oil in medium-sized, heavy skillet over moderately high heat. The steaks should fit fairly close together in skillet. Fry steaks over moderately high heat to desired degree of doneness, turning once. Drain off grease. Heat ¼ cup of the cognac until steamy. Pour cognac over steaks and ignite. Let cook until flame ceases. Remove steaks to serving platter, and keep warm. Add cream to pan drippings, scraping up and mixing in brown bits that stick to pan. Cook over high heat, stirring constantly, until mixture thickens. Stir in remaining 1 teaspoon cognac. Spoon sauce over steaks. 4 servings.

TURNIP-STEAK SAUTÉ

Those who usually turn up their noses at turnips probably won't even guess the vegetable is in this dish. In fact, most of my "tasters" mistook the turnips for slices of potatoes. The turnips add a distinctively pleasant flavor that can't be copied by "spuds," however.

1 pound round steak, partially frozen
¾ pound turnips
¼ cup cooking oil
4 green onions and some of the tops, thinly sliced
1 small clove garlic, minced
1 cup beef bouillon

½ teaspoon pepper
2 teaspoons soy sauce
1 teaspoon salt or to taste
2 tablespoons cornstarch
¼ cup water
Paprika

Cut meat across the grain in about ¼-inch strips. (It is easier to cut if partially frozen.) Peel turnips; cut in halves, then cut in fairly thin slices. Heat oil over moderate heat in a large skillet. Add meat and cook over moderate heat until brown on all sides. During the last few minutes of cooking time, add onion and garlic. Cook over moderate heat, stirring, until onion is transparent. Drain off excess grease. Add turnips and bouillon. Bring to boil, reduce heat, and simmer, covered, about 15 minutes or until turnips are done. Blend pepper, soy sauce, and salt with cornstarch which has been dissolved in the water. Stir into skillet. Bring to boil, reduce heat, and simmer, stirring, until thickened. Sprinkle with paprika. 4 servings.

ALL-PURPOSE BEEF MARINADE

Any cut of beef that needs tenderizing and/or flavor will benefit from this simple marinade.

¼ cup cooking oil
¼ cup soy sauce
2 tablespoons catsup
1 tablespoon vinegar

¼ teaspoon pepper
2 medium cloves garlic, minced

Combine cooking oil, soy sauce, catsup, vinegar, pepper, and garlic. Mix well. (Even after thorough mixing, some of the oil will separate from other marinade ingredients.) Place meat in close-fitting dish. Pour marinade over meat. Cover and refrigerate small cuts about 8 hours; larger ones and roasts 12 to 24 hours. Beef marinated in this mixture is especially good cooked over charcoal. Makes about ¾ cup marinade. (Recipe is easily doubled for larger cuts of meat.)

CABBAGE-BEEF SKILLET MEAL

Here's a good dish to freeze, then tote on camping trips to be heated over a portable charcoal grill, on a camper's stove—or even over a campfire. Of course, it's good for cooking in the home kitchen, too.

1 pound ground beef	1 cup uncooked
1 can (28-ounce)	elbow macaroni
whole tomatoes	1½ cups coarsely-
1 teaspoon salt or	chopped cabbage
to taste	2 tablespoons minced
1 teaspoon	parsley
Worcestershire	½ cup shredded
Sauce	Cheddar cheese

Heat a large skillet or Dutch oven over moderate heat. Crumble beef into skillet. Cook over moderate heat until meat loses red color, breaking up meat in small pieces with edge of spoon. Drain off grease. Add tomatoes, which have been cut in small pieces, their liquid, salt, and Worcestershire Sauce. Bring mixture to boiling point. Add macaroni. Reduce heat and simmer, covered, about 12 minutes. Add cabbage and parsley, mixing well. Continue cooking about 8 more minutes or until macaroni is done. (At altitudes below 5,000 feet, macaroni will cook a little faster.) Sprinkle cheese on top. Let stand a few minutes until cheese starts to melt, before serving. 4 servings.

Note: To freeze mixture, omit the cheese, and sprinkle it on top during the last stages of the reheating period. The cabbage and parsley may also be added during the reheating period to prevent them from becoming overcooked.

BEEF BELCARO

This is a fancy name for a homespun dish that evolved as a way to use leftover charcoal-broiled steak. Believe it or not, there are those who have it left over! Actually, the recipe is suited to almost any type of leftover beef.

1 pound sirloin steak or steak of your choice

1 cup wide noodles which have been broken in about 2-inch pieces

½ stick (¼ cup) butter

1 can (10½-ounce) vegetable-beef soup

3 tablespoons half-and-half cream

3 tablespoons (about) dairy sour cream

Dash of Worcestershire Sauce

1 tablespoon port wine

Cook steak over charcoal to rare stage. Cut steak in about 1-inch cubes. (2 cups cubed leftover beef roast may be substituted for steak, if desired.) Cook noodles according to package directions; drain thoroughly. Melt butter in large saucepan over moderate heat. Add soup. Cook a few minutes, then add steak. Cook a few more minutes over moderate heat. Add half-and-half cream and enough dairy sour cream for desired consistency. Add noodles, Worcestershire Sauce, and wine. Heat to serving temperature. 4 servings.

BUNDLED BURGER MEAL

When is a hamburger not a hamburger? When it's a juicy meat patty all bundled up in foil with mixed vegetables and French fries.

1 pound lean ground beef

2 packets (1-ounce each) onion gravy mix (shake package to mix ingredients)

1 package (10-ounce)

frozen mixed vegetables

1 package (10-ounce) frozen French fried potatoes

Salt and pepper to taste

Shape meat into 4 patties (meat goes into bundles raw.) Put each burger on square of heavy-duty foil (16 x 16 inches). Sprinkle each burger with ½ packet of dry gravy mix. Thaw vegetables and potatoes just until they can be separated. (They shouldn't be completely thawed because the moisture is necessary during baking.) Put ¼ of the vegetables on top of each burger. Add ¼ of the potatoes, putting a few on top of vegetables and the remainder surrounding burgers. Sprinkle top of mixture with salt and pepper. Bring opposite sides of foil up over food. Make a double fold, leaving air pockets so foil does not touch food. Close ends of foil with double fold. Bundles should be tightly sealed to allow food to steam. Bake in oven preheated to 350° for about 1 hour. 4 servings.

STEAK SICILIANO

Another way to take some of the undesirable chewy quality out of less tender steak.

2½	pound top round steak, cut about 1½-inches thick	1	teaspoon salt
			Pepper to taste
2	cups burgundy wine	1	tablespoon prepared horseradish
1	small clove garlic, minced		
		2	tablespoons dried parsley flakes
1	teaspoon Worcestershire Sauce		
		1	tablespoon prepared mustard
⅛	teaspoon ground oregano	1	tablespoon sugar
		2	tablespoons margarine
1	small onion, minced		Cooked spaghetti

Pierce steak deeply and generously with tines of fork on top surface to allow marinade to penetrate. Place steak in close-fitting, shallow dish. Combine wine, garlic, Worcestershire Sauce, oregano, onion, salt, pepper, horseradish, parsley, mustard, sugar and margarine. Mix well. Cook over moderate heat until margarine melts. Cool mixture to room temperature; pour over steak. Marinate steak, covered, 24 hours in refrigerator, turning steak several times, Drain off marinade but reserve. Broil steak until brown on one side, basting it occasionally with marinade. Turn steak. Pour remaining marinade over it. Broil until it has reached desired stage of doneness. Serve steak with spaghetti, spooning some of the marinade over both. 6 servings.

FRIZZLED DRIED BEEF WITH ZUCCHINI

A humble package of dried beef gets the glamour treatment here.

1 large, unpeeled zucchini squash (about 1 pound)	1 can (8-ounce) water chestnuts, drained and quartered
½ stick (¼ cup) butter or margarine	2 tablespoons sherry
1 package (8-ounce) dried beef	2 teaspoons Worcestershire Sauce
3 tablespoons chopped onion	1 cup (4-ounce) shredded Cheddar cheese
½ pound fresh mushrooms, sliced	6 fresh tomato slices, about ¼-inch thick
1 tablespoon lemon juice	Grated Parmesan cheese
¼ cup flour	Minced parsley
1 teaspoon dry mustard	
2 cups milk	

Cut zucchini in thirds, crosswise. Place zucchini in large saucepan, cover with water, and bring to boil. Reduce heat and simmer, uncovered, about 15 minutes or just until zucchini is crisp-tender. Drain and reserve zucchini. Melt 1 tablespoon of the butter in a 9- or 10-inch skillet over moderate heat. Using kitchen scissors, cut beef into fairly large, bite-size pieces, and drop them into butter. Cook beef, stirring frequently, over moderate heat until it is lightly frizzled. About 5 minutes before beef is done, add onion, mushrooms, and lemon juice, lightly but thoroughly stirring mixture constantly. Place remaining butter in a small, heavy saucepan. Melt butter over moderate heat. Add flour and mustard. Cook a few minutes over moderate heat, stirring. Gradually add milk. Cook over moderate heat, stirring constantly with wire whisk, until mixture is thickened. Add this sauce, water chestnuts, sherry, Worcestershire Sauce, and Cheddar cheese to beef mixture. Mix well. Remove from heat. Stir until cheese starts to melt. Cut each third of the zucchini, lengthwise, into 4 slices. Place 2 of the slices in each of 6, buttered, individual baking dishes (8-ounce size), which have been placed on a baking sheet to facilitate handling. Spoon equal portions of the beef mixture over zucchini. Place a tomato slice on top of each portion. Sprinkle with Parmesan cheese. Place dishes under broiler, about 10 inches from source of heat. Broil until cheese is lightly browned. Garnish with parsley. 6 servings.

TOMATO-SIMMERED SHORT RIBS WITH CREAMY GRAVY

Too often slighted, beef short ribs can be skillfully braised to perfection for some mighty good eating.

3 to 4 pounds beef short ribs, cut into serving pieces	½ teaspoon dried leaf marjoram
1 medium clove garlic, minced	Salt to taste
1 large onion, chopped	4 medium carrots, cut in thick slices
1 can (1-pound) stewed tomatoes	1 large green pepper, cut in thick strips
1 medium bay leaf	¼ cup flour
½ teaspoon dried leaf rosemary	½ cup water
½ teaspoon dried leaf thyme	1 cup plain yogurt or dairy sour cream
	Cooked noodles

Brown ribs on all sides in greased Dutch oven over moderately low heat. During last few minutes of browning time, add garlic and onion. Drain off excess grease. Add tomatoes, bay leaf, rosemary, thyme, marjoram, and salt. Bring to boil, reduce heat, and simmer, covered about 1 hour. Turn ribs occasionally during cooking period. Add carrots and green pepper. Cook another ½ hour until meat is tender and carrots are done. (At altitudes above 5,000 feet, total cooking time may have to be extended to 2 hours.) Remove ribs and vegetables from cooking liquid. Remove and discard bay leaf. Refrigerate ribs and vegetables in a container overnight. Refrigerate cooking liquid in another container overnight. Just before serving, remove and discard fat which has risen to top of refrigerated cooking liquid. Add enough water to cooking liquid, if necessary, to make 2 cups. Place cooking liquid in Dutch oven; cook over moderate heat until hot. Mix together flour and water until smooth. Stir flour mixture into hot cooking liquid. Cook over moderate heat, stirring, until slightly thickened. Add short ribs and vegetables. Cook over moderate heat, stirring occasionally, until meat is heated through. Stir in yogurt or sour cream. Heat just to serving temperature, stirring frequently. Do not allow mixture to boil. Serve ribs, vegetables, and gravy with noodles. 4 or more servings.

ZESTY MEAT LOAF

Bored with the same old meat loaf? Try this carrot-studded treat.

2 pounds lean ground beef	¼ cup chopped onion
1 cup shredded, sharp Cheddar cheese	1 medium carrot, shredded
½ cup dry bread crumbs	2 eggs, beaten
	½ cup bottled Thousand Island salad dressing

Combine all ingredients. Mix thoroughly. Form mixture into a loaf shape and place in a greased, shallow pan. Bake, uncovered, in oven preheated to 350° for about 1 hour or until done. (Cooking time will vary, depending on the thickness of loaf.) 6 to 8 servings.

FISH AND SEAFOOD

Who wouldn't enjoy a succulent salmon steak or white-meated lobster tail, simply broiled or cooked in any number of ways to quick perfection?

But let's face facts.

Some of the tastiest ways to serve fish or seafood—by adding only light, delicate sauces that allow the fish or seafood to retain its identity—are beyond the budgets of many Americans, especially where inland markets must charge high prices for the fresh or frozen fish that is flown to them. In this section, you'll find a wealth of ideas for *extending* some of the more expensive seafoods by combining them with inexpensive ingredients that, in many cases, will increase the nutritional value of the dish.

Along with such good combinations, we can also appreciate beautiful, rich, homemade sauces made with puréed, fresh vegetables to keep the caloric content light without foregoing flavor.

Let's face facts again. Many busy cooks who don't own food processors or blenders to perform the puréeing task rely on that handy can of soup, seasoning mix, or other convenience food that is tucked in the cupboard, ready at a moment's notice for inclusion in a recipe. So you'll also find here some delicious ways to take advantage of these shortcuts.

When you *can* splurge on full, main-course servings of our nutritious, finny, and hard-shelled friends that are spanking fresh or fresh-frozen from the "briny deep," remember an important rule: avoid overcooking to prevent dry, tasteless results. To help frozen fish retain its moisture, allow it to thaw slowly in the refrigerator before cooking.

SALMON-RICE PIE

A cream sauce sprinkled with stuffed olive slices enriches wedges of this pie.

1 can (1-pound) salmon, drained and flaked	2 tablespoons lemon juice
2 cups cooked rice	1½ teaspoons salt or to taste
2 tablespoons fresh, minced parsley	¼ teaspoon pepper or to taste
1 tablespoon minced onion	3 eggs, well beaten
½ cup chopped celery	Olive Sauce
	Lemon wedges
	Pimiento-stuffed olives, sliced

Combine salmon and rice, mixing lightly but thoroughly. Add parsley, onion, celery, lemon juice, salt, pepper, and eggs. Mix lightly but thoroughly. Spoon mixture into well-greased 9-inch pie plate. Bake, uncovered, in oven preheated to 350° for 35 to 45 minutes or until firm. (Altitudes below 5,000 feet will require the shorter baking period.) Let stand about 10 minutes before cutting in wedges to serve. Serve with Olive Sauce. Garnish with lemon wedges and olive slices. 6 servings.

Olive Sauce

2 tablespoons butter or margarine	1 cup milk
2 tablespoons flour	½ cup sliced, pimiento-stuffed olives
¼ teaspoon dry mustard	Salt to taste

Melt butter or margarine in small saucepan over moderate heat. Add flour and mustard. Cook a few minutes over moderate heat, stirring. Gradually add milk. Cook over moderate heat, stirring constantly with wire whisk, until smooth and thickened. Remove from heat. Add olives and salt. Mix well. Makes about 1½ cups sauce.

SAUCE POIVRE VERT

This green peppercorn sauce adds tantalizing flavor when used as a topping for broiled salmon steaks, beef, or poultry.

3 tablespoons plus 2 teaspoons butter	specialty sections of stores)
3 tablespoons chopped shallots or green onions	1½ teaspoons prepared Dijon-style mustard
¼ cup cognac	½ teaspoon beef flavor base (available at spice counters and in specialty sections of stores)
3 teaspoons green peppercorns, drained and mashed with back of spoon (green peppercorns are available in	1 cup whipping cream, unwhipped

Melt 3 tablespoons of the butter in medium-sized skillet over moderate heat. Add shallots or green onions. Sauté a few minutes over moderate heat, stirring. Add cognac. Bring to boil, reduce heat to medium and cook, uncovered, until mixture is reduced to half the original amount. Add peppercorns, mustard, beef flavor base, and cream. Cook over moderate heat, stirring, until thickened. Add remaining 2 teaspoons butter. Stir until melted. Serve over broiled salmon steaks, flank steak or other beef, chicken or duck. Makes about 1¼ cups.

Note: Green peppercorns add exciting new flavor to potato chip dips, stuffings, salad dressings, and fish or meat casseroles. Mash them with back of spoon when using them so they become more evenly distributed in the food.

HALIBUT OR SALMON WITH PUFFED TOPPING

Fish can be an unpredictable lot when it comes to estimating cooking times for them. Their size and flesh warmth (do they go straight from the refrigerator to the stove?) as well as that ever-present factor of oven temperature variance, all influence their cooking times. However, there is one definite rule: don't overcook these nutritious catches. They all require tender treatment.

2 pounds halibut, cut in serving pieces, *or* 2 pounds salmon steaks or fillets (thawed, if frozen)	¼ cup grated Parmesan cheese
	¼ teaspoon Worcestershire Sauce
Melted butter, margarine, or cooking oil	1 extra-large egg white at room temperature
Salt and pepper to taste	2 tablespoons chopped green onion
⅓ cup mayonnaise	

Brush halibut or salmon generously with melted butter, margarine or oil. Sprinkle with salt and pepper. Place fish, not touching each other, in foil-lined pan. Broil about 4 inches from source of heat, about 4 minutes on each side, turning once. Combine mayonnaise, Parmesan cheese, and Worcestershire Sauce. Beat egg white until stiff. Fold egg white into mayonnaise mixture. Sprinkle fish with onions. Spoon cheese mixture on top. Place under broiler a few minutes until topping is puffed and golden, and fish flesh is opaque when tested with fork. 4 servings.

JUICY SALMON PATTIES

You can make 4 juicy, thick patties from a small can of salmon.

1 can (about 7-ounce) salmon, drained and flaked
1 extra-large egg, beaten
½ teaspoon bottled steak sauce
Uncooked, "concentrated

nutrition" cereal flakes or uncooked oatmeal
Cooking oil
Tartar sauce (optional)
Dill sauce (optional)

Combine salmon, egg, and steak sauce. Mix thoroughly. Add enough cereal flakes or oatmeal to hold mixture together but do not make it too stiff. Divide mixture into 4 equal portions. Shape each portion into a patty about 3 inches in diameter. Heat a small amount of cooking oil over moderate heat in a medium-sized skillet. Add patties. Cook over moderate heat a few minutes just until golden brown on each side. Turn only once during cooking period. Serve with your favorite tartar sauce or the following dill sauce, if desired. 4 servings.

Dill Sauce

2 tablespoons butter or margarine
2 tablespoons flour
1 cup evaporated milk
⅓ cup water

1 egg yolk, beaten
Salt and pepper to taste
1 teaspoon dill weed or to taste

Melt butter or margarine in small skillet over moderate heat. Add flour. Cook a few minutes over moderate heat, stirring. Gradually add evaporated milk and water. Cook over moderately low heat, stirring, until thickened. Stir a small amount of the hot sauce into egg yolk. Stir yolk mixture in remaining hot sauce, using wire whisk. Cook over moderately low heat, stirring, until thickened. Remove from heat. Add salt, pepper, and dill. Makes about 2½ cups sauce.

TUNA-COTTAGE CHEESE COMBO

Cottage cheese increases the nutritional value of this dish.

1 cup cottage cheese	¼ cup slivered
2 cups cooked rice	almonds
2 cans (about	1 can (8-ounce)
7 ounces each)	tomato sauce
tuna, drained	⅛ teaspoon pepper
and flaked	½ teaspoon garlic
¼ cup sliced ripe	salt
olives	¼ cup grated
	Parmesan cheese

Combine cottage cheese, rice, tuna, olives, almonds, tomato sauce, pepper and garlic salt. Mix lightly but thoroughly. Spoon mixture into greased, round 1½-quart casserole. Sprinkle top with Parmesan cheese. Bake, covered, in oven preheated to 325° for 35 to 45 minutes or until mixture is bubbly. (At altitudes below 5,000 feet, it will cook faster.) 4 to 6 servings.

HEARTY TUNA LOAF

This will bake by the time you've tossed together a crisp green salad to go with it.

4 tablespoons butter	crumbled into
or margarine	pea-size pieces
2 tablespoons bottled	(this keeps cheese
garlic spread	from melting
concentrate	too fast)
1 loaf (1 pound)	1 can (4-ounce)
soft French-style	mushroom stems
bread	and pieces, drained
1 can (about	3 tablespoons
9 ounces) tuna,	mayonnaise
drained and flaked	2 tablespoons sweet
1½ cups sharp	pickle relish
Longhorn cheese,	10 thin slices tomato

Heat together butter or margarine and garlic spread until melted and well blended, stirring occasionally. (Or use your own thick, garlic-butter recipe.) Cut bread in half, lengthwise. Scoop out a trench about 2-inches wide down center of each half. Brush garlic mixture over cut portions of bread. Combine scooped out bread, which has been torn in small pieces, with tuna, 1 cup of the cheese, mushrooms, mayonnaise, and pickle relish. Mix well. Divide tuna mixture in half. Fill each trench with ½ of tuna mixture. Sprinkle about 2 tablespoons of remaining cheese over top of tuna mixture. Arrange 5 tomato slices on top of cheese. Sprinkle tomatoes with remaining cheese. Place loaves on a foil-lined baking sheet. Bake in oven preheated to 400° for about 10 to 15 minutes or until hot. Place under broiler for a few minutes to lightly brown tops, if desired. Cut in fairly large slices to serve. 6 servings.

TUNA CRUNCH PIE

A crust crunchy with oats, cheese, and walnuts contrasts beautifully with the creamy, dill-flavored filling.

1¼ cups shredded Swiss or Cheddar cheese	tuna, drained and flaked
1 cup unsifted all-purpose flour	2 extra-large eggs, beaten until light and fluffy
1 cup quick-cooking oats, uncooked	½ cup dairy sour cream or plain yogurt
1 teaspoon salt	¼ cup mayonnaise
1 teaspoon paprika	2 tablespoons chopped pimiento
1 stick (½ cup) butter or margarine, softened	2 tablespoons grated onion
½ cup finely-chopped walnuts	¼ teaspoon dried dill weed
2 cans (about 7 ounces each)	2 drops red pepper sauce or to taste

Combine ¾ cup of cheese, flour, oats, salt, and paprika; mix well. Cut in butter with pastry cutter or 2 knives until mixture resembles coarse crumbs.

Stir in walnuts. (Mixture will be stiff.) Reserve 1 cup of the mixture for pie topping. Firmly press remaining mixture onto bottom and up sides of a well-greased, 10-inch pie plate with sides that are 2-inches deep. Spread tuna over bottom of crust. Beat together eggs, sour cream or yogurt, and mayonnaise until well mixed; blend in remaining ½ cup of the cheese, pimiento, onion, dill, and red pepper sauce. Pour mixture over tuna. Sprinkle with reserved crumb mixture. Bake, uncovered, in oven preheated to 400° for about 35 minutes or until golden brown. Cool about 10 minutes before cutting into wedges to serve. 6 to 8 servings.

STUFFED TROUT A LA ROCKIES

In the Rocky Mountain West, many tourists and resident fishermen have the opportunity to savor the inimitable flavor of trout, spanking fresh from high mountain streams. But smoking or freezing the fish is a necessity, also, for it must not be wasted. Frozen trout tends to become dry during cooking and can always stand a "lift" in the way of a sauce, stuffing, or garnish that adds moisture. Here is one of the most popular stuffings to appear in the *Denver Post* food columns during the past twenty years. It also makes a great stuffing for red snapper or other fish of your choice.

1 tablespoon butter or margarine	Juice of ½ medium lemon
1 small green onion, minced	¼ cup half-and-half cream
3 small ribs celery, minced	Salt and pepper to taste
¾ cup finely-chopped, cooked shrimp	Cracker crumbs
1 tablespoon dried parsley flakes	1 large trout, cleaned
1 egg, beaten	Lean bacon strips

Melt butter or margarine over moderate heat in a small skillet. Add onion and celery; sauté over moderately low heat until onion is transparent. Remove from heat. Add shrimp, parsley, egg, lemon juice, cream, salt, and pepper. Add just enough cracker crumbs to hold mixture together. Loosely stuff trout with mixture, allowing it to bulge a bit. (Trout is not skewered closed in this recipe. Feel free to bone trout, if you keep its shape without removing the head and tail. However, bones left in the fish are not at all that unpleasant in this case.) Place trout on its side on a greased rack in a shallow pan. Cover trout with strips of bacon. Bake, uncovered, in oven preheated to 350° until trout flesh is opaque when tested with fork. Allow about 20 minutes per pound, stuffed weight. Place any leftover stuffing in foil or covered baking dish, and bake it right along with the trout. If bacon gets too crisp during last part of baking period cover trout loosely with foil. Number of servings depends on size of trout.

PAN-FRIED TROUT WITH SAUCES

Want to start a culinary controversy? Then ask your friends what they think is the best way to make potato salad, chili—or fry trout. That glistening king of lake and stream is at its best, I think, lightly coated with flour, flipped into sizzling bacon grease for a few minutes, then brought to the table with head intact. There is a certain beauty in having the trout look whole and natural. Besides, the connoisseur will eat the small muscle in the jaw bone below the eye of the trout. This very delicate portion, about the size of a thumbtack head, lifts out easily with a touch of the fork. A light but buttery sauce always enhances the fish.

Pan-Fried Trout

For each trout, fry 1 slice of bacon. Remove bacon from skillet; drain on paper toweling. Reserve drippings. Sprinkle cleaned trout inside and out with lemon juice, salt, and pepper. Lightly dredge trout on all sides with flour. Heat about ¼ inch of the reserved bacon drippings in a skillet large enough to accommodate trout without bending it. Add trout; fry over moderate heat just until golden brown on each side. Turn only once during frying period. Cooking time depends on size of trout. Trout is done when tested with fork to reveal opaque flesh. Garnish trout with bacon. Serve trout with one of the following sauces if desired.

Mushroom Sauce

½ stick (¼ cup) butter or margarine	1 tablespoon lemon juice
½ pound fresh mushrooms sliced	Salt to taste

Melt butter or margarine over moderate heat in medium-sized skillet. Add mushrooms. Sauté mushrooms over moderately low heat just a few minutes until golden colored. Stir frequently. Add lemon juice and salt. Toss to mix.

Dill Butter

1 stick (½ cup) butter	3 tablespoons lemon
2 teaspoons dried	juice or to taste
dill weed or to taste	

Melt butter in small saucepan. Add dill and lemon juice. Heat to serving temperature.

Amandine Sauce

½ stick (¼ cup)	Lemon juice to taste
butter or margarine	Minced fresh parsley
½ cup blanched,	to taste
slivered almonds	

Melt butter or margarine in small saucepan, over moderate heat. Add almonds. Cook over moderate heat, stirring constantly, just until almonds are golden colored. Add lemon juice and parsley.

TUNA MAYONNAISE PUFF

How about some simple sophistication?

¼ cup flour	1 can (9-ounce)
¼ teaspoon salt	tuna (or salmon),
Pepper to taste	drained and flaked
½ cup mayonnaise	4 egg whites at
¼ cup milk	room temperature

Stir flour, salt, and pepper into mayonnaise. Mix until smooth. Add milk. Mix until smooth. Fold in tuna. Beat egg whites until stiff. Gently fold whites into tuna mixture until thoroughly blended. Pour mixture into greased, 1½-quart soufflé dish. At altitudes above 5,000 feet, bake in oven preheated to 350° for about 50 minutes or until top is firm. At altitudes below 5,000 feet, reduce baking time about 10 minutes. Serve immediately. 4 servings.

SHOESTRING TUNA SALAD SUPREME

Here's a guess-what's-in-it combination. Crisp shoestring potatoes are likely to puzzle taste buds, but will please them too.

1 can (about 7 ounces) tuna, drained and flaked
1 medium, red apple, unpeeled and diced
½ medium onion, chopped
1 large carrot, shredded
¾ to 1 cup mayonnaise (diluted, if desired, with a small amount of milk and stirred until smooth)
1 can (4-ounce) shoestring potatoes
Salad greens
Olives, hard-cooked egg quarters, tomato slices, and/or fresh grapes for garnish

Combine tuna, apple, onion, and carrot. Mix lightly but thoroughly. Add enough mayonnaise to moisten mixture to desired consistency. Just before serving, lightly fold in shoestring potatoes. Serve on salad greens and garnish with olives, egg quarters, tomato slices, and/or grapes. 4 servings.

ORANGE SAUCE FOR BROILED LOBSTER TAILS

Let this serve as a refreshing substitute for the usual "drawn butter."

1 can (6-ounce) frozen orange juice, thawed and undiluted
¼ cup lemon juice
½ teaspoon dry mustard
¼ teaspoon dried leaf rosemary
½ teaspoon celery salt
½ teaspoon onion powder
½ teaspoon salt
¼ teaspoon aromatic bitters
1 stick (½ cup) butter, cut in chunks

In a medium-sized saucepan, combine undiluted orange juice, lemon juice, mustard, rosemary, celery salt, onion powder, salt and bitters. Mix well with wire whisk. Bring mixture to boiling point stirring constantly. Cook at rolling boil, uncovered, about 1 minute. Remove from heat. Add butter. Mix with wire whisk until butter melts. Use mixture as a basting liquid while lobster tails are boiling, then as a sauce for dipping the lobster meat. Makes enough sauce for 6 medium, broiled lobster tails.

TROUT IN WHITE WINE

The cooking liquid for this luscious concoction is later converted into a delicate sauce that is served over rice.

4	cleaned trout, about 14-inches long (smaller trout may be used)		Juice from 1 medium lemon
½	stick (¼ cup) plus 2 tablespoons butter or margarine	1½	cups dry white wine
		½	cup water
		4	tablespoons flour
1	medium onion, finely chopped	½	cup milk
			Salt and pepper to taste
			Cooked rice
			Slivered almonds

Using a very sharp knife, bone trout by first cutting off head. Then insert knife next to backbone at tail and make a deep slit the entire length of trout up to head. Repeat process on other side of backbone. Cut off tail and backbone in front of it. With a fork, hook onto backbone and pull it out or gently push flesh away from bones with blade of knife. Fold fillets together in original position. (If smaller trout are used, they need not be boned, and can be cooked whole.) Place fish in single layer in lightly-greased, close-fitting, shallow pan. Melt 2 tablespoons of the butter or margarine over moderate heat in small skillet. Add onion; sauté over moderately low heat until onion is transparent. Remove from heat. Add lemon juice, wine, and water. Mix well. Pour mixture over fish. Bake, covered, in oven preheated to 350° for about 20 minutes or until fish flesh is opaque when tested with fork. Melt remaining ½ stick butter in small skillet. Add flour. Cook a few minutes over moderate heat, stirring. Gradually add all of cooking liquid from trout, and milk. Cook over moderate heat, stirring, until thickened. Add salt and pepper. Place trout on a bed of rice, spoon sauce over trout and sprinkle with almonds. 4 servings.

SAUCY SOLE

One of Denver's culinary prize-winning restaurateurs prefers his sole this way. If you must, use thawed frozen sole, but fresh sole is better for this kind of cooking treatment because the flesh is firmer.

4 tablespoons cornstarch	2 egg whites at room temperature
1½ cups rich chicken broth	½ teaspoon salt
1 teaspoon soy sauce	Vegetable oil for deep-fat frying
2 teaspoons sugar	3 tablespoons finely-slivered water chestnuts
1 tablespoon vinegar	
1 pound fresh sole fillets, cut in about 2-inch pieces	Cooked rice
2 tablespoons water	Paprika

Mix 2 tablespoons of the cornstarch with about 3 tablespoons of the chicken broth until smooth. Add cornstarch mixture, soy sauce, sugar, and vinegar to remaining broth which has been put in a large saucepan. Bring to boiling point, reduce heat and simmer, stirring occasionally, until sauce thickens. Remove sauce from heat. Cover sauce and allow it to come to room temperature while completing remainder of recipe. Thoroughly dry sole pieces with paper towelling. In a medium bowl, mix water with remaining 2 tablespoons cornstarch until smooth. Add egg whites and salt; mix thoroughly, using wire whisk. Using fingers dip sole pieces, a few at a time, into cornstarch mixture to coat all sides. (Cornstarch mixture helps hold fish together and seals in moisture.) Stir cornstach mixture periodically after dipping sole in it. In deep, heavy pan, heat cooking oil to about 375° or until a small cube of bread browns in it in about 1 minute. Add sole pieces, a few at a time. Cook sole 1 minute or less. Do not fry pieces long enough to become brown. Drain sole on paper toweling. Add sole and water chestnuts to sauce. Mix lightly but thoroughly; heat just to serving temperature. Serve sole and sauce over rice and garnish with paprika. 4 servings.

ROMAINE-STEAMED FILLETS

White-meated fish fillets stay moist while they steam under a bed of Romaine lettuce.

¼ teaspoon turmeric	1 medium onion, sliced
½ teaspoon salt	and separated into
¼ teaspoon pepper	rings
½ teaspoon dry	1 pint cherry
mustard	tomatoes, halved
¼ teaspoon dried leaf	½ medium bunch
basil	Romaine lettuce,
1 pound thick perch	trimmed of coarse
fillets or other	ends
fillets of your choice	2 tablespoons
(thawed, if frozen)	Worcestershire Sauce
⅓ cup olive oil	Cooked rice
½ medium, green pepper,	
diced	

Combine turmeric, salt, pepper, mustard, and basil. Rub one side of each fillet with mixture. Heat oil over moderately low heat in a heavy skillet or Dutch oven, large enough so fillets can be arranged in a single layer. Place fillets in oil with seasoned sides up. Sprinkle green pepper over fillets. Scatter onion rings on top. Arrange tomato halves on fish in centers of the onion rings. Cover entire dish with a layer of Romaine leaves. Sprinkle Worcestershire Sauce over Romaine leaves and tightly cover pan. Increase heat to moderate or just until mixture gets quite steamy. Reduce heat to moderately low. (Temperature should maintain steam but not be hot enough to fry fish.) Steam mixture about 20 minutes or until fish flesh is opaque when tested with fork. Moisture will collect from the tomatoes and Romaine as it wilts. Serve fish, vegetables and pan drippings over rice. 4 servings.

COMPANY FISH ROLL-UPS

This elegant entrée—fish fillets rolled around a saucy, chopped spinach mixture and topped with a lemony cheese sauce—is economical for three reasons: it is a vegetable and main dish rolled into one, none of the fish is wasted, and there is very little shrinkage during the baking period.

2 tablespoons butter
or margarine
2 tablespoons flour
½ teaspoon salt
¼ teaspoon paprika
1¼ cups half-and-half
cream
1 cup shredded
Cheddar cheeese
Grated rind and
juice of ½
medium lemon

1 package (10-ounce)
frozen chopped
spinach, thawed,
uncooked, and
thoroughly drained
in colander
2 tablespoons finely-
sliced green onion
6 sole, haddock, or
flounder fillets
(about 1½ pounds)
Cooked rice

Melt butter or margarine in medium-sized skillet over moderate heat. Add flour, salt, and paprika. Stir a few minutes over moderate heat. Gradually add cream. Cook over moderate heat, stirring until thickened. Add ½ cup of the cheese, lemon rind, and lemon juice. Remove from heat; stir until cheese melts. Squeeze as much moisture as possible out of thoroughly-drained spinach, using back of large spoon to press it against sides of colander or squeeze spinach between hands. Add onion to ⅓ cup of the cheese sauce and add to spinach. Mix well. Place equal amounts of spinach mixture on wide end of fillets. Roll up fillets and place, seam sides down, in close-fitting, shallow baking dish. (Their sides should touch to hold them together.) Spoon remaining cheese sauce over top of fillets. Bake, uncovered, in oven preheated to 350° for 25 to 35 minutes or just until centers of fillet rolls look opaque when a knife is inserted in them. Sprinkle with remaining ½ cup cheese during about the last 6 minutes baking time. Serve with rice. 6 servings.

LEMON-BROILED HALIBUT

Quick and satisfying, yet very special.

2 large halibut steaks,
about ½-inch thick
6 tablespoons butter
or margarine, melted
½ teaspoon salt
½ teaspoon pepper

1 teaspoon
Worcestershire Sauce
2 tablespoons lemon
juice
Paprika

Place halibut steaks, without sides touching, in foil-lined broiler pan. Mix together butter or margarine, salt, pepper, Worcestershire Sauce and lemon juice. Drizzle mixture over halibut and sprinkle with paprika. Broil fish about 4 inches from source of heat for 3 to 5 minutes on each side or until halibut flesh is opaque when tested with fork. Baste halibut once or twice with pan drippings. (Broiling time can only be estimated because of variance in size and shape of fish.) 4 servings.

FISH FILLETS A LA FLORIDA

The sauce is tangy and refreshing with juice and sections of fresh grapefruit.

2 tablespoons margarine or cooking oil	1 cup unsweetened grapefruit juice
¼ cup chopped onion	¼ cup chopped, fresh parsley
1 pound flounder, haddock, or sole fillets	1 tablespoon flour
¼ pound fresh mushrooms, sliced	1 chicken bouillon cube
Salt and pepper to taste	Fresh grapefruit sections

Place 1 tablespoon of the margarine or oil in a large skillet over moderate heat. Add onion. Sauté over moderately low heat, stirring frequently, until onion is transparent. Place fillets on top of onion in a single layer. Sprinkle fillets with mushrooms, salt, and pepper. Add grapefruit juice. Bring to a slow bubbling, not boiling, point to keep fish moist but still tender and firm while cooking. Reduce heat and simmer, covered, about 5 minutes. Add parsley. Simmer, covered, about 4 minutes longer or until fish is opaque when tested with fork. Remove fish to heated serving platter; keep warm. Reserve 1⅓ cups of the cooking liquid. In a small pan, melt remaining 1 tablespoon margarine or oil over moderate heat. Add flour. Cook over moderate heat a few minutes, stirring. Gradually add reserved 1⅓ cups cooking liquid and bouillon cube. Cook over moderate heat, stirring frequently until mixture thickens and bouillon cube dissolves. (Bouillon cube should provide the additional amount of salt to suit most tastes.) Pour sauce over fish. Garnish with grapefruit sections. 4 servings.

ECONOMY FISH FILLET CAKES

This recipe is totally deceiving. Obviously simple to put together, it cooks in a hurry, and the big surprise comes when you bite into the crunchy little cakes and discover their delightful flavor.

¾ pound uncooked fish fillets, coarsely chopped (about 2 cups; turbot, cod, perch, etc. may be used)

1 can (8-ounce) whole kernel corn, drained, *or* 1 cup leftover, cooked, drained, whole kernel corn

1 can (8-ounce) cut, green beans, drained and coarsely chopped

or 1 cup leftover, cooked, drained beans, coarsely chopped

½ cup finely-shredded, uncooked carrots

4 medium, green onions and some of the tops, chopped

2 extra-large eggs, beaten

¾ cup unsifted flour

Salt and pepper to taste

Cooking oil

Combine fish, corn, beans, carrots, onions, and eggs. Mix well. Add flour, salt, and pepper. Mix well. Heat a large skillet with about ¼ inch of cooking oil in it over moderate heat. Drop fish mixture by heaping tablespoonsful into skillet. Cook cakes over moderate heat until brown on each side. Turn only once during cooking period. Drain cakes on paper toweling. Add more oil as needed. Keep fried cakes warm in low oven. Makes about 14 cakes, each 3-inch size, or 4 to 6 servings.

THREE-STEP COQUILLE SAINT-JACQUES

Here's a short but impressive version of Coquille Saint-Jacques, the French description of scallops served in their shells. If you don't have large scallop shells or individual baking dishes, the mixture can go straight from the skillet into a large serving dish. Small servings of the scallops make an elegant first course.

1 pound scallops (thawed, if frozen)	Juice of 1 medium lemon
Flour seasoned with salt and pepper to taste	1½ cups whipping cream, unwhipped
3 tablespoons butter	Salt and pepper to taste
3 tablespoons cooking oil	Fine, dry bread crumbs (optional)
½ pound fresh mushrooms, sliced	Finely-shredded Gruyere cheese to taste

Lightly dredge scallops in seasoned flour. In a large skillet, heat butter and oil over moderate heat until butter melts. Add scallops. Cook over moderate heat just until scallops are golden brown on all sides. Remove scallops from skillet. Add mushrooms, lemon juice, and cream to the pan drippings; season with salt and pepper. Cook sauce over moderate heat, stirring frequently, until slightly thickened. If a thicker sauce is desired, blend in enough bread crumbs to get desired consistency. Add scallops. Heat to serving temperature. Do not let mixture reach boiling point during any of the cooking stages. Spoon mixture into 4 to 6 large scallop shells or individual baking dishes or into a large, oven-proof, serving dish. Sprinkle cheese on top. Place under broiler about 7 inches from source of heat for just a few minutes until cheese melts. 4 to 6 servings.

OYSTERS TETRAZZINI

A superlative way to stretch a pint of oysters, this version of Italian Tetrazzini combines seasoned stuffing mix with this traditional use of pasta.

¼ pound fine noodles, cooked and drained	1 teaspoon salt or to taste
1 stick (½ cup) butter or margarine	⅛ teaspoon pepper
1 cup dry, herb-seasoned stuffing mix	2 teaspoons Worcestershire Sauce
¼ cup grated Parmesan cheese	1 pint oysters
¼ cup flour	3 cups milk
	¼ cup sherry

Rinse noodles with water; drain thoroughly. (More noodles may be used, if desired.) Place noodles in greased, shallow, 10-inch or 11 x 7-inch baking dish. Melt butter or margarine in medium-sized saucepan. Thoroughly mix 4 tablespoons of the melted butter with stuffing mix and cheese. Leave remaining butter in pan. Add flour, salt, pepper, and Worcestershire Sauce to remaining butter. Cook over moderate heat, stirring a few minutes. Drain oysters and add enough water to oyster liquid, if necessary, to make ½ cup. Gradually add oyster liquid and milk to flour mixture. Cook over moderate heat, stirring until thickened. Add sherry. Mix well. Arrange oysters on noodles. Spoon sauce over top. Sprinkle with stuffing mixture. Bake, uncovered, in oven preheated to 400° for about 30 to 45 minutes or until brown and crusty on top. (At altitudes below 5,000 feet, check mixture after it has cooked about 30 minutes.) 6 servings.

SEAFOOD-VEGETABLE DELIGHT

Not overpowered by starchy binders, this casserole uses fine, dry bread crumbs to tie it all together. Omit the crab, and you have a beautiful, fresh vegetable combination.

½ stick (¼ cup) butter or margarine	uncooked, fresh or frozen crab meat, cut in small pieces (thaw if frozen)
1 small onion, chopped	
3 small zucchini squash, unpeeled and sliced	1⅓ cups diced Swiss cheese
½ medium clove garlic, crushed or minced	1 cup canned, fine, dry Italian-style bread crumbs
3 large, fresh tomatoes, cut in small pieces	1 teaspoon salt
	1 teaspoon pepper or to taste
½ pound (about)	1 teaspoon dried leaf basil

Melt butter or margarine in medium-sized skillet over moderate heat. Add onion, zucchini, and garlic. Sauté a few minutes over moderate heat until onion is transparent, stirring frequently. Combine zucchini mixture with tomatoes, crab, 1 cup of cheese, ¾ cup of the bread crumbs, salt, pepper, and basil. Mix lightly but thoroughly. Turn mixture into 2-quart round casserole. Sprinkle top with remaining cheese and bread crumbs. Dot with additional butter or margarine. Bake, uncovered, in oven preheated to 375° for 30 minutes or until bubbly. 4 to 5 servings.

CRAB AND CHICKEN ELEGANT

Amazing—how a small amount of luxury-priced crab can retain its identity when it's combined with less-costly chicken.

3 whole chicken breasts	½ cup dry white wine
Salt and pepper to taste	2 egg yolks, beaten
1 medium rib celery and leaves, cut in coarse chunks	1 cup partially-cooked peas (preferably fresh)
1 medium bay leaf	1 can (about 7-ounce) crab meat *or* 6 ounces fresh, cooked crab meat *or* 6 ounces frozen crab meat, thawed
1 small carrot, cut in chunks	
3 tablespoons butter or margarine	
1 cup sliced, fresh mushrooms	½ cup whipping cream, whipped until stiff
¼ cup chopped onion	¼ cup grated Parmesan cheese
3 tablespoons flour	Paprika
1½ cups chicken broth	

Place chicken breasts in a large pan. Add salt, pepper, celery, bay leaf, carrots, and enough water to barely cover chicken. Bring to boil, reduce heat and simmer, covered, until breasts are done. (Skim off residue that floats on top of water during first part of cooking period.) Remove chicken from broth. Strain and reserve broth, discarding vegetables and bay leaf. (Part of this broth may be used later but I think canned chicken broth adds more flavor to this particular dish.) Remove skin and bones from chicken. Cut chicken in thin slices or bite-size pieces. Spread chicken evenly over bottom of lightly-greased shallow baking dish, 7 x 11-inches. Melt butter or margarine in a medium-sized skillet over moderate heat. Add mushrooms and onions; sauté over moderately low heat until onion is transparent, stirring frequently. Add flour, salt, pepper, and cook a few minutes over moderate heat, stirring lightly. Gradually add broth (either canned or reserved from breasts) and wine. Cook over moderate heat, stirring, until thickened. Stir a small amount of hot mixture into egg yolks. Add yolks to hot sauce. Cook over moderately low heat, stirring constantly, about 2 minutes. Remove from heat. Add peas and crab. Mix gently but thoroughly. Gently fold in whipped cream. Pour sauce over chicken. Sprinkle with cheese and paprika. Bake, uncovered, in oven preheated to 325° for about 20 minutes or until heated through. 6 servings.

THREE-IN-ONE SEAFOOD CASSEROLE

Here's a superb blend of scallops, shrimp, and crab meat.

1 cup dry white wine	4 tablespoons flour
1 small onion, thinly sliced	1 cup half-and-half cream
1 tablespoon minced parsley	⅓ cup grated Cheddar cheese
1 teaspoon salt	½ pound small, cooked, peeled, deveined shrimp
1 pound uncooked scallops (thaw, if frozen)	½ pound cooked, shelled crab, flaked (lobster meat may be substituted)
½ stick (¼ cup) butter or margarine	
2 teaspoons lemon juice	
1 can (3-ounce) sliced mushrooms	

Combine wine, onion, parsley, salt, and scallops in large saucepan. Bring to gentle bubbling (not boiling) point. Reduce heat and simmer, covered, just until scallops are done. Remove scallops from liquid; cut them in halves. To the liquid add 2 tablespoons of the butter or margarine, lemon juice, and broth drained from mushrooms. Heat until butter melts. Add enough water to this liquid to make 2 cups. In another large saucepan, melt remaining butter or margarine. Add flour. Stir a few minutes over moderate heat. Gradually add wine mixture and cream. Cook, stirring, over moderate heat until thickened. Add cheese, stirring until cheese melts. Add scallops, mushrooms, shrimp, and crab. Heat to serving temperature. 6 to 8 servings.

NEPTUNE INTERNATIONAL

Only a few other menu accompaniments are required for this rich entrée—perhaps a fruit salad and a green vegetable.

1 can (10¾-ounce) cream of shrimp soup	½ pound fresh mushrooms, sliced
1½ cups milk	½ cup chopped green pepper
½ pound peeled, cooked, deveined shrimp	3 tablespoons chopped onion
1 can (4-ounce) water chestnuts, drained and sliced	1½ teaspoons salt
	½ teaspoon pepper
1 can (about 7 ounces) crab meat	1 package (8-ounce) noodles, cooked and drained
	½ cup grated Cheddar cheese

Combine soup and milk. Mix well. Add shrimp, water chestnuts, crab, mushrooms, green pepper, onion, salt, and pepper. Mix lightly but thoroughly. Arrange about ⅓ of the noodles on bottom of greased, shallow 9 x 13-inch casserole. Spoon about ½ of the shrimp mixture on top of noodles. Repeat layers. Sprinkle with cheese. Bake, uncovered, in oven preheated to 350° just until bubbly. 8 servings.

SCALLOPED OYSTERS

Add some elegance to a roast turkey or chicken dinner with this simple but scrumptious casserole.

½ pound soda crackers, coarsely crushed	butter or margarine, softened
1 pint medium oysters	Salt and pepper to taste
1 stick (½ cup)	1 cup milk

Place ½ of the crackers, then ½ of the oysters and their liquor in greased, round, 2-quart casserole. Dot with ½ of the butter. Season with salt and pepper. Repeat layers. Carefully pour milk over top. Bake, covered, in oven preheated to 350° for 35 to 45 minutes. (At altitudes below 5,000 feet, use the shorter baking period as a guide.) 6 servings.

SEAFOOD NERO

As food prices rise, and our budgets flounder, this recipe should increase in popularity. Since 1969 it has been making Denver's party circuit rounds, appearing at dinners as well as luncheons.

2 tablespoons butter or margarine	1 teaspoon salt or to taste
2 tablespoons minced onion	2 cans (8-ounce each) tomato sauce
1 medium clove garlic, minced	¼ cup prepared mustard
1 pound uncooked, shelled, deveined, medium-sized shrimp	½ teaspoon red pepper sauce
1 pound uncooked fillet of flounder, cut in coarse pieces *or* 1 pound uncooked scallops (any frozen fish should first be thawed)	½ cup dairy sour cream
	½ cup cornflake crumbs tossed with 1 tablespoon butter or margarine
	Lemon wedges
	Buttered noodles or rice
1 can (8-ounce) minced clams	

Melt butter or margarine in large skillet over moderately low heat. Add onion, garlic, and shrimp. Cook over moderately low heat just until shrimp start to turn pink and are almost done. Add flounder during the last 5 minutes cooking time (if scallops are used, add them at the beginning along with shrimp). Stir mixture frequently during cooking period, adding a little more butter if necessary. Spoon mixture into a shallow, 9 x 13-inch casserole. Drain clams and reserve liquid. Sprinkle clams on mixture in casserole. Mix together ⅓ cup of the clam liquor with salt, tomato sauce, mustard, and red pepper sauce; bring to boiling point, stirring occasionally. Remove from heat. Blend in sour cream. Add sauce to ingredients in casserole. Mix lightly but thoroughly. Sprinkle cornflake crumbs on top. Bake, uncovered, in oven preheated to 400° for about 15 minutes or just until bubbly. Garnish with lemon wedges. Serve with buttered noodles or rice. 8 servings.

EILEEN'S MILD CURRY INDIENNE

From one of the "Mile High City's" most talented interior decorators comes this delight. The curry flavor is there but it's not strong enough to offend anyone.

½ stick (¼ cup) butter or margarine
1 cup finely-diced, peeled eggplant (choose small to medium eggplant; it contains less water than large eggplant)
1 medium onion, chopped
1 large, peeled, tart apple, finely diced
1 cup chopped celery
1 tablespoon curry powder
6 tablespoons flour
2 cups chicken broth
1 tablespoon lemon juice
1 cup milk
¾ teaspoon salt
White pepper to taste
2 cups diced, cooked chicken
2 cups medium, cooked, shelled, deveined shrimp *or* 2 cans (4½-ounce each) shrimp
6 whole hard-cooked eggs, quartered (optional)
Hot, cooked rice
Chopped peanuts
Chutney
White raisins which have been soaked until plump in dry white wine, then drained
Chopped green onion and tops
Crisp fried bacon, crumbled
Bananas, peeled and cut diagonally in about 1-inch slices

Melt butter or margarine in large skillet or Dutch oven. Add eggplant, onion, apple, and celery. Sauté over moderate heat until onion is transparent. Add curry powder and flour. Cook a few minutes over moderate heat, stirring. Gradually add chicken broth, lemon juice, and milk. Cook over moderate heat, stirring until thickened. Add salt, pepper, chicken, shrimp, and eggs. Heat to serving temperature. Serve curry with rice and condiments, each in a small separate bowl: peanuts, chutney, raisins, green onion, crumbled bacon and banana pieces. (This is the traditional way to serve curry. However, condiments are optional, and this is a delicious dish even without them.) 6 servings.

TOMATO CRAB BISQUE

Don't be the least bit embarrassed about serving this luscious combination just because it takes advantage of convenience foods. Add a salad and hot rolls to complete the entrée.

1 can (10¾-ounce) green pea soup
2 cans (10¾-ounce each) tomato soup
2 cups half-and-half cream
1 teaspoon Worcestershire Sauce
3 tablespoons sherry
1 can (6½-ounce) crab meat, drained and flaked
Parsley

Combine undiluted soups, cream, Worcestershire Sauce, and sherry. Mix with rotary beater or electric mixer until smooth. Blend in crab, lightly but thoroughly. Heat to serving temperature. Garnish with parsley. 6 servings as a main dish; about 10 servings as a before-dinner soup.

SHRIMP ENTRÉE SOUP

For a yummy meal, serve this soup with hot corn meal muffins and a fruit salad.

6 slices lean bacon
½ cup chopped onion
1 medium clove garlic, minced
1 can (28-ounce) whole tomatoes
1 medium, green pepper, chopped
¼ teaspoon red pepper sauce
½ teaspoon black pepper
1 medium bay leaf
1 large carrot, thinly sliced
2 medium ribs celery, sliced
2 medium potatoes, peeled and cubed
2 teaspoons salt or to taste
2 cans (4½-ounce each) shrimp or 1 package, (10-ounce) frozen, uncooked, shelled shrimp, thawed or 10 ounces fresh, uncooked shrimp, shelled and deveined

Fry bacon until crisp in Dutch oven. Drain and crumble bacon. Sauté onion and garlic over moderately low heat in 2 tablespoons of the bacon drippings until onion is transparent. Add tomatoes, which have been cut in small pieces, and their liquid. Add green pepper, red pepper sauce, black pepper, bay leaf, carrots, celery, potatoes, and salt. Bring to boiling point, reduce heat and simmer, covered, until potatoes are done. Add shrimp. (If canned shrimp are used, drain and rinse with cold water before adding to soup.) Continue to cook until canned shrimp are heated through, or, if frozen or fresh shrimp are used, cook just until done. Remove bay leaf. Garnish each serving with crumbled bacon. 4 servings.

CRAB BRUNCH BAKE

When you run out of ideas for brunch, try this casserole. It goes together pronto.

2 tablespoons butter or margarine	7 ounces) crab meat, drained and cut in small pieces
⅓ cup chopped celery	(lobster meat may be substituted)
1 cup sliced, fresh mushrooms	2½ cups cooked rice
3 tablespoons flour	½ cup (or more to
½ teaspoon salt	taste) toasted,
⅛ teaspoon pepper	slivered almonds
1½ cups milk	¼ cup buttered
1 cup shredded Cheddar cheese	bread crumbs
1 can (about	Dried parsley flakes

Melt butter or margarine over moderate heat in large saucepan. Add celery and mushrooms. Cook over moderate heat, stirring, about 2 minutes. Sprinkle flour, salt, and pepper over mushroom mixture; mix gently but thoroughly. Gradually add milk. Cook over moderate heat, stirring constantly, until thickened. Remove from heat. Add cheese. Mix lightly but thoroughly. Combine crab, rice, and almonds. Add crab mixture to mushroom mixture. Mix lightly but thoroughly. Spoon mixture into lightly-greased, shallow 7 x 11-inch baking dish. Sprinkle top with buttered crumbs. Bake, uncovered, in oven preheated to 350° just until bubbly. Garnish with parsley. 4 servings.

CRAB OR SHRIMP-BROCCOLI CASSEROLE

Speed up the preparation by making the crust the day before serving, refrigerate, then bring to room temperature before adding the filling.

Herb-Bread Crust

4 slices soft bread with crusts, torn into small pieces
¼ cup chopped green onion
2 tablespoons fresh, minced parsley

½ teaspoon dried leaf basil
½ teaspoon salt
¼ teaspoon pepper
½ stick (¼ cup) butter or margarine, melted

Combine bread, onion, parsley, basil, salt, and pepper. Add butter or margarine. Mix to thoroughly coat bread with butter. Press mixture on bottom of greased, 8-inch square pan. Bake in oven preheated to 350° for about 20 minutes or until golden brown.

Filling

½ stick (¼ cup) butter or margarine
¼ cup flour
½ teaspoon celery salt
Salt and pepper to taste
1½ cups milk
1 package (10-ounce) frozen chopped broccoli, uncooked, thawed, and drained
1 can (about 7-ounce) crab,

drained and flaked
or 2 cans (about 4-ounce each) large shrimp, drained
¼ cup chopped green onion
2 tablespoons chopped pimiento
¼ cup dry bread crumbs tossed with 1 tablespoon melted butter

Melt butter or margarine. Add flour, celery salt, salt, and pepper. Cook a few minutes over moderate heat, stirring. Gradually add milk. Cook over moderate heat, stirring, until thickened. Add broccoli, crab or shrimp, onion, and pimiento. Spoon mixture into baked Herb-Bread Crust. Sprinkle top with bread crumbs. Bake, uncovered, in oven preheated to 400° for about 15 minutes or until bubbly. 4 servings.

SHRIMP-CRAB PUFF

Good recipe ideas never die; they don't even fade away.

12 slices white sandwich bread
4 eggs, beaten
3 cups milk
Salt and pepper to taste
1 can (4½-ounce) small shrimp, drained
1 can (7½-ounce) crab, drained and flaked
1 cup chopped celery
1 can (10¾-ounce) mushroom soup
1½ cups grated Cheddar cheese

Trim crusts from bread. Cut each slice in half. Arrange 12 halves of bread in single layer on bottom of greased, shallow 9 x 13-inch baking dish. Thoroughly beat together eggs, milk, salt, and pepper. Pour over bread in dish. Combine shrimp, crab, and celery. Spoon crab mixture evenly on bread. Top with remaining halves of bread. Refrigerate, covered, 24 hours. Spoon undiluted mushroom soup on top of bread. Bake, uncovered, in oven preheated to 350° for about 1½ hours or until puffy and golden brown. (Baking time is longer than usual because the dish is cold when it goes into the oven. However, at altitudes below 5,000 feet, baking time can be reduced about 5 minutes.) Sprinkle cheese on top during last 15 minutes of baking time. Let stand a few minutes, then make cuts between bread halves. 12 servings.

FAST FISH BAKE

Here's a last-minute way to dress up fish fillets.

1½ to 2 pounds fish fillets of your choice (thaw, if frozen)
2 tablespoons butter or margarine
¼ cup chopped green pepper
1 cup soft, fresh
whole-wheat bread crumbs
½ cup shredded Cheddar cheese
¼ cup mayonnaise
2 tablespoons prepared mustard
Salt and pepper to taste

Place fillets in single layer in greased, shallow, close-fitting baking dish. Melt butter or margarine over moderate heat in medium-sized skillet. Add green pepper. Cook over moderate heat, stirring about 2 minutes. Remove skillet from heat. Add bread crumbs, cheese, mayonnaise, and mustard to green pepper. Mix lightly but thoroughly. Add salt and pepper. Mix again. Spread mixture on top of fish. Bake, uncovered, in oven preheated to 350° for 20 to 30 minutes or until fish flesh is opaque when tested with fork. 4 to 6 servings.

YOU-DECIDE SEAFOOD QUICHES

Confession: I couldn't decide which of the following, highly-pleasing quiche recipes is the best—so you be the judge. But I am certain that the colorful tomato aspic ring will complement either quiche when served for luncheon along with hot rolls. For the quiche shells, try the recipe for Extra-Rich Pastry Shells on page 158.

Shrimp Quiche

Pastry for 2 pie shells, 9 inches each
1 cup shredded Swiss cheese
1 tablespoon flour
2 cans (4½-ounce each) small shrimp, drained
3 extra-large eggs, slightly beaten

1 can (13-ounce) evaporated milk
⅓ cup water
2 tablespoons minced green onion
1 tablespoon dried parsley flakes
⅛ teaspoon nutmeg
¼ teaspoon salt
⅛ teaspoon pepper

Roll out pastry and place in pie plates; flute edges. Prick bottom and sides of pie shells with fork tines in several places. (This helps shells bake evenly. If you're a perfectionist, cover the pastry with waxed paper, and weight it down with dry beans to keep pastry even while baking. However, I think this is a waste of time when you're using extra moist fillings, as in these quiches. A slight wave here and there in the pastry shouldn't offend anyone.)

Bake pie shells in oven preheated to 350° for about 7 minutes or just until firm but not brown. (Pie shells are partially baked to prevent them from becoming soggy when filling is added.) Combine cheese and flour. Mix well. Sprinkle ½ of the cheese mixture over bottom of each pie shell. Arrange equal amounts of shrimp on top of cheese. Combine eggs, evaporated milk, water, onion, parsley, nutmeg, salt, and pepper. Mix well. Carefully pour ½ of the mixture over shrimp in each pie shell. Bake, uncovered, in oven preheated to 375° for 30 to 40 minutes or until knife inserted in center comes out clean. Cool on rack about 10 minutes before serving. Cut in wedges to serve. Makes 8 to 12 servings as a main dish; more servings when cut in thin wedges, and served as hors d'oeuvres.

Seafood Quiche With Madeira

Pastry for 1 pie shell, 9-inch size, to fit pie plate with sides 2 inches deep
3 tablespoons butter or margarine
2 tablespoons minced green onion and some of the tops
1 cup (about) cooked seafood, cut in small bite-size pieces (crab meat, lobster, chopped shrimp, tuna, salmon; a combination of these or fish of your choice may be used)
2 tablespoons dry madeira, dry vermouth, or dry white wine
3 extra-large eggs, lightly beaten
1 cup whipping cream, unwhipped
1 tablespoon tomato paste
½ teaspoon salt
⅛ teaspoon pepper
¼ cup shredded Swiss cheese

Roll out pastry and place in pie plate; flute edges. Prick bottom and sides of pie shell with fork tines in several places. Bake pie shell in oven preheated to 350° for about 7 minutes or just until firm but not brown. Melt butter or margarine over moderate heat in medium-sized skillet. Add onion. Sauté over moderately low heat until onion is transparent. Remove from heat. Add seafood and wine. Mix well. Combine eggs, cream, tomato paste, salt, and pepper. Using wire whisk, mix until mixture is smooth. Add egg mixture to seafood mixture. Mix lightly but thoroughly. Pour mixture into pastry shell. Sprinkle with cheese. Bake, uncovered, in oven preheated to 375° for 30 to 40 minutes or until knife inserted in center comes out clean. Cool on rack about 10 minutes before serving. Cut in wedges to serve. 4 to 6 servings.

Crimson Aspic Ring

2 cans (1-pound each) stewed tomatoes
2 packages (3-ounce each) strawberry or raspberry gelatin
4 teaspoons prepared horseradish
1 tablespoon minced onion
3 teaspoons salt or to taste

2 tablespoons chopped green pepper
2 tablespoons chopped celery
2 or 3 drops red pepper sauce
Salad greens
Cottage cheese
Mayonnaise

Heat tomatoes in medium-sized saucepan to boiling point. Remove from heat. Add gelatin. Stir until gelatin dissolves. Add horseradish, onion, salt, green pepper, celery, and red pepper sauce. Mix well. Spoon mixture into 1½- or 2-quart ring mold. Refrigerate until firm. Invert aspic onto salad greens. Fill center with cottage cheese. Serve with mayonnaise on the side. 6 to 8 servings.

BEER BATTER FOR FISH OR VEGETABLES WITH RED SAUCE

Cover chunks of fish or vegetables with this batter, plunge them into hot oil, and watch them turn into fluffy, golden-brown nuggets. An added attraction is the nippy sauce to be used as a dip.

1 cup unsifted all-purpose flour
1 egg, beaten
1 teaspoon salt
½ teaspoon pepper
1 tablespoon sugar
1 tablespoon cooking oil
1 heaping teaspoon baking powder

Cold beer
Uncooked fillet of sole, cut in 2-inch pieces (see other fish and vegetable suggestions below)
Cooking oil for frying
Red Sauce

Combine flour, egg, salt, pepper, sugar, oil, and baking powder. Gradually add enough beer, starting with about ½ cup, to make mixture the consistency of thick pancake batter. **Mix** until smooth. Using tongs or fork, **dip** pieces of sole in batter, allowing excess to drain off. Fry sole in 2 or 3 inches of moderately hot cooking oil just until brown and puffy on both sides. Turn once during cooking period. Makes enough batter for about 2 pounds fish.

Note: This batter also is excellent for frying uncooked, shelled, deveined shrimp, onion rings or uncooked zucchini squash, cut in about ¼-inch slices.

Red Sauce

1 cup catsup	1 tablespoon
Juice from ½ lemon	Worcestershire Sauce
2 tablespoons prepared	4 or 5 drops (or to taste)
horseradish	red pepper sauce

Combine all ingredients. **Mix well. Serve** cold as a dip for fish or zucchini fried in beer batter.

COD FISH STEAKS WITH PICKLE SAUCE

The crunchy dill pickles as well as their liquid add "oomph" to a sauce which enhances the flavor of white-fleshed cod.

½ cup dill pickle liquid, drained from dill pickles	1 cup dill pickles which have been cut in about ¼-inch slices
1½ cups chicken broth or bouillon	4 cod fish steaks, about 1-inch thick and weighing about 2 pounds (cod fish fillets may be substituted; they will take less time to cook)
4 teaspoons cornstarch	
¼ teaspoon dried leaf thyme	
¼ teaspoon dry mustard	
1 teaspoon dried leaf basil	
Pepper to taste	½ pound sliced fresh mushrooms
3 medium carrots, cut in strips	1 large, fresh tomato cut in wedges
1 large onion, sliced	

Combine pickle liquid and broth or bouillon with cornstarch in large pan. Stir until cornstarch dissolves. Add thyme, mustard, basil, and pepper.

Bring to boil, stirring constantly. **Reduce heat** and simmer, stirring, until thickened. Add carrots. Simmer covered, until carrots are almost done. Add onion and pickles. Place fish in a single layer in 11 x 7-inch shallow baking dish. Pour sauce over fish and bake, covered, at 375° for 15 minutes. Add mushrooms and tomato. Baste fish and vegetables with sauce. Bake, covered, about 10 minutes longer or until fish flesh is opaque when tested with a fork. Transfer fish and vegetables to serving dish. Serve sauce on the side to be spooned over fish. 4 servings.

GENERAL SLAY'S RED SNAPPER

The recipe for this stuffed, baked beauty, which basks in a buttery tomato mixture, is a favorite of General Alton D. Slay, commander of Air Force Systems Command, Andrews Air Force Base, Washington D.C. General Slay, who can still find time to cook, was commander of Denver's Lowry Air Force Base in the early '70s. This recipe received very favorable comments after it was printed in the *Denver Post* food columns.

5 slices very dry white
  bread with crusts,
  torn into small pieces
1 cup milk
⅓ stick butter or
  margarine
½ cup chopped onion
⅓ cup minced parsley
1 can (6-ounce)
  crab meat, drained
  and flaked
Cayenne pepper to
  taste
Salt to taste

Paprika to taste
2 whole red snappers
  (1½ to 2 pounds
  each)
Thin slices of butter
Lemon slices
2 cans (1-pound
  each) whole
  tomatoes, well
  drained (Save liquid
  for flavoring
  casseroles, soups,
  etc.)

Combine bread and milk. Let stand until bread absorbs milk. Melt butter or margarine in large skillet over moderate heat. Add onion. Sauté over moderately low heat until onion is transparent. Add bread mixture, parsley, crab, cayenne pepper, and salt. Sprinkle inside of snappers with salt and paprika. Pack stuffing lightly in cavities of snappers. Place leftover stuffing in a mound in center of well-greased, shallow 9 x 13-inch pan. Place a snapper, on its side, on each side of stuffing. Place about 4 thin slices of butter on top of each snapper. Place lemon slices on top of butter. Carefully spoon whole tomatoes into space at ends of pan. Season tomatoes with salt and pepper. Bake uncovered, in oven preheated to 375° for about 45 minutes or until fish flesh is opaque when tested with fork. (Baking time depends on size of fish. Start testing it after about 30 minutes.) Baste fish occasionally with pan juices during baking. Serve extra stuffing and tomatoes in separate dishes. 4 to 6 servings.

LAMB

The sophisticated taste of today's consumers has led many of them to use lamb in order to vary the menu and enjoy a change from beef, pork, and poultry. An excellent source of protein as well as B-vitamins and minerals, lamb is just about as versatile as any other meat. Since it comes from young sheep, you can usually count on it to be tender also.

Baked, broiled, barbecued, or braised, this fine-textured meat takes to all kinds of cooking techniques, and is compatible with innumerable seasonings and other ingredients for flavor changes.

Some of the recipes in this section are from the best kitchens of Colorado's sheep ranches, which are located mainly on the state's Western Slope, unfolding from the top of the Continental Divide. Unlike some other domestic animals, sheep aren't finicky about climate and can withstand the cold mountain air at altitudes up to 12,000 feet as well as the warmth of grazing lands near the desert.

LAMB SHANKS A LA VERMOUTH

Sweet is the meat that clings to the bones of lamb shanks. Don't neglect them. I first became acquainted with this recipe twenty years ago.

4 lamb shanks (¾ to 1 pound each)	1 can (10¾-ounce) beef consommé
½ medium lemon	1 cup water
½ teaspoon garlic powder	½ cup dry vermouth
1 cup (about) flour seasoned with salt and pepper	4 medium carrots, cut in about 2-inch chunks
½ cup cooking oil	4 medium ribs celery, cut in about 2-inch chunks
1 medium onion, chopped	

Place shanks in a shallow dish. Rub shanks on all sides with cut side of lemon, gently squeezing some of the juice on the meat as you go. Sprinkle shanks with garlic powder; let stand about 10 minutes at room temperature. Put flour in paper bag. Add shanks, one at a time, and shake until coated with flour. Reserve any flour left in bag. Heat oil in a large skillet over moderate heat. Add shanks. Cook over moderate heat until meat is brown on all sides. Remove shanks and all but 4 tablespoons drippings from the skillet.

Heat the 4 tablespoons drippings over moderate heat. Add onion. Sauté over moderately low heat, stirring frequently, until onion is transparent. Add 4 tablespoons of the reserved flour to onions. Cook a few minutes over moderate heat, stirring. Gradually add consommé, water, and vermouth. Cook over moderate heat, stirring, until mixture is slightly thickened. Put shanks in a single layer in a shallow, 9 x 13-inch baking dish. Pour vermouth mixture over shanks. (At this point, the dish may be refrigerated, covered, up to 24 hours. This saves last-minute preparation, and also adds more flavor to the meat.) Bring mixture to room temperature. Bake, covered with foil, in oven preheated to 325° for 1½ hours. Turn shanks. Tuck carrots and celery between shanks. Bake, covered, about 30 minutes longer or until carrots are done. (At altitudes below 5,000 feet, reduce total baking time about 15 minutes.) 4 servings.

JOHNNY VAN'S LEG-OF-LAMB

This recipe for juicy slices of broiled lamb, first marinated the easy way in teriyaki sauce, is a favorite of John Vanderhoof, former governor of Colorado. Vanderhoof bones his own leg of lamb, but for those less proficient in the art of deboning, let a friendly butcher do it.

3 pounds (about) boned leg of lamb Garlic salt	1 bottle (5-ounce) teriyaki sauce

If necessary, have butcher bone or "butterfly" a leg of lamb. (It won't resemble the artistic shape of a butterfly at all, but simply means removing the bone and shank while keeping the meat in one piece.) Trim off as much fat as possible from meat. Lay lamb open, book style. Using sharp knife, score lamb on both sides, making a crisscross pattern with slashes about ¼-inch apart. Sprinkle lamb generously on both sides with garlic salt. Rub salt in well with fingertips. Place lamb in shallow, close-fitting glass dish, keeping it open in butterflied shape. Pour teriyaki sauce over lamb. Marinate at room temperature at least 1 hour, turning meat occasionally. For a stronger teriyaki flavor, marinate lamb several hours or overnight in refrigerator, turning meat occasionally. Cook lamb, keeping it open in butterflied shape, over hot charcoal for about 10 minutes or less on each side or until meat has reached desired degree of doneness. Lamb may also be cooked, keeping it open in butterflied shape, under oven broiler. In this case, place meat 8 to 10 inches from source of heat. (Because 1 side of the boned leg will be thicker than the other side, you will have varying degrees of doneness to suit tastes for well done, medium and slightly rare. Cut in thin slices to serve. (Any cold, leftover lamb is a delicacy for sandwiches.) 8 servings.

MOUSSAKA

A classic Greek dish, this version of Moussaka is moist with Monterey Jack cheese instead of the traditional Parmesan cheese. There are three basic steps to the recipe: the sauce, which can be prepared in advance, refrigerated, then heated before assembling the recipe, the meat mixture, which can be made in advance, even frozen, thawed, and brought to room temperature; and the eggplant, which should be fried just before assembling. Leftovers reheat nicely.

3 medium eggplants, peeled and cut crosswise in ½-inch slices (The use of medium-sized eggplants, which contain less moisture than large ones, eliminates the need for the conventional method of salting, draining, and drying the slices with paper toweling before they are fried.)
Flour
Olive oil
1½ pounds uncooked ground lamb
1 large onion, chopped
1 medium clove garlic, minced
1 can (8-ounce) tomato sauce
Salt and pepper to taste
¼ teaspoon cinnamon
½ teaspoon dried leaf oregano
1 tablespoon dried parsley flakes
White Sauce
2 cups (about 8 ounces) shredded Monterey Jack cheese
1 cup dry, fairly-coarse bread crumbs

Dredge both sides of eggplant slices with flour. Heat, over moderate heat, about 1½ inches of olive oil in each of 2 large skillets. (Using 2 skillets speeds up frying time.) Add eggplant slices to oil. Cook over moderate heat, turning once, just until eggplant is lightly brown on each side. Drain eggplant on paper toweling. Heat about 2 tablespoons olive oil in a fairly large skillet over moderate heat and crumble in lamb. Cook over moderate heat, breaking up lamb with edge of spoon, until it is brown. Add onion and garlic during last few minutes cooking time. Drain off grease. Add tomato sauce. Mix well. Bring to boil, reduce heat and simmer, covered, about 10 minutes. Add salt, pepper, cinnamon, oregano, and parsley. Mix well. Arrange about ⅓ of the eggplant slices in a single layer on bottom of greased, 9 x 13-inch baking dish. Spoon ½ of the meat mixture on top. Spoon about ⅓ of the White Sauce evenly over meat. Sprinkle sauce with 1 cup of the cheese and ⅓ cup of the crumbs. Repeat layers, ending with crumbs. (There will be 3 layers of eggplant, White Sauce, and crumbs; 2 layers of meat and cheese.) Bake, uncovered, in oven preheated to 350° for 30 to 40 minutes or until top is lightly brown. Let stand a few minutes before cutting into squares to serve. 8 to 10 servings.

Note: Ground beef chuck can be substituted for lamb, if desired.

White Sauce

6 tablespoons butter or margarine	3 eggs, well beaten
6 tablespoons flour	Salt and pepper to taste
3 cups milk	

Melt butter or margarine over moderate heat in medium-sized saucepan. Add flour. Cook a few minutes over moderate heat, stirring constantly. Gradually add milk. Cook over moderate heat, stirring until thickened. Stir a small amount of hot mixture into eggs. Gradually add eggs to remaining hot mixture, stirring with wire whisk until smooth. Cook a few minutes over moderately low heat, stirring constantly, until thickened. Add salt and pepper. Makes 3½ cups sauce.

PRUNE SAUCE SUZETTE FOR LAMB

Tired of the usual mint jelly with lamb? Then try this tempting variation. Plump the prunes by putting them in a vegetable steamer and steam until they are soft.

½ cup lemon juice	prunes, pitted and
1 cup currant jelly	halved
2 tablespoons slivered	2 medium oranges,
orange rind	peeled and sectioned
1 tablespoon slivered	½ stick (¼ cup)
lemon rind	butter
2 cups plumped	2 tablespoons brandy

Heat lemon juice and jelly, stirring until smooth. Add orange and lemon rinds and prunes. Bring to boil, reduce heat and simmer, covered, about 5 minutes. Add orange sections and butter. Heat over moderate heat, stirring frequently until butter melts. Add brandy. Mix well. (Brandy may be heated in a small pan, poured over sauce, and flambéed, if desired.) Serve sauce with sliced, roast lamb or lamb chops. Makes about 3½ cups.

LAMB SHANKS ITALIANO

Properly braised, lamb shanks can be tenderized to perfection. Here the cooking liquid forms a thick sauce that's spooned over the shanks and vegetables at serving time.

4 lamb shanks (¾ to	1 envelope (about
1 pound each)	1 ounce) dry
1 cup dry red wine	onion soup mix
1 can (6-ounce)	3 medium zucchini
tomato paste	squash, unpeeled and
1 cup water	sliced diagonally in
1 medium clove	about 2-inch pieces
garlic, minced	1 package (8-ounce)
¼ teaspoon dried leaf	frozen artichoke
oregano	hearts, thawed, *or*
¼ teaspoon dried leaf	1 can (14-ounce)
rosemary	artichoke hearts,
¼ teaspoon dried leaf	drained
basil	

Brown shanks on all sides under broiler. Transfer shanks to Dutch oven. Combine wine, tomato paste, water, garlic, oregano, rosemary, basil, and dry soup mix. Mix well. Pour mixture over shanks. Bake, covered, in oven preheated to 325° for about 2 hours or until shanks are tender. Add zucchini about 20 minutes before cooking time is completed. Add artichoke hearts about 15 minutes before cooking time is completed. (At altitudes below 5,000 feet, reduce total cooking time about 15 minutes.) 4 servings.

PIQUANT LAMB WITH SQUASH

Here's a harmonious blend of fresh vegetables and meat. The combination will surprise you.

1½ pounds Italian sausage, cut in about 1½-inch lengths

2 pounds uncooked lamb, cut in 1-inch cubes

½ medium onion, chopped

1 medium clove garlic, minced

2 tablespoons flour

2 cups beef broth

1 cup dry red wine

1 can (28-ounce) whole tomatoes

1 teaspoon paprika

½ teaspoon dried leaf thyme

2 medium bay leaves

½ teaspoon dried leaf rosemary

1 teaspoon salt

½ teaspoon pepper or to taste

1 tablespoon dried leaf basil

1 teaspoon ground ginger

1 butternut squash (about 2 pounds), peeled, seeded and cut in 1-inch cubes

2 medium zucchini squash, unpeeled and cut in ½-inch slices

½ pound fresh mushrooms, sliced

Grated Romano cheese to taste

½ cup mint jelly

1 cup dairy sour cream

Heat a Dutch oven over moderate heat. Rub one of the cut sides of a piece of sausage over bottom and part way up sides of pan to grease it. Add all of sausage. Cook sausage over moderate heat until brown on all sides. Remove sausage from pan. Drain off all but about 2 tablespoons of the grease. Heat this grease over moderate heat. Add lamb. Cook over moderate heat, stirring frequently, until lamb is brown on all sides. Sprinkle onion, garlic, and flour over meat. Cook a few minutes over moderate heat, stirring. Add sausage, broth, wine, and tomatoes, which have been cut in small pieces, and tomato liquid. Add paprika, thyme, bay leaves, rosemary, salt, pepper, basil, and ginger. Mix well. Bring to boil, reduce heat and simmer, covered, about 1½ hours. Add butternut squash. Simmer, covered, 25 minutes. Add zucchini squash. Simmer, covered, about 20 minutes. Add mushrooms. Simmer, covered, about 5 minutes longer. (At altitudes below 5,000 feet, slightly reduced time suggested for each cooking period.) Remove bay leaves. Sprinkle with cheese. Have ready dairy sour cream mixture. To make, melt mint jelly, cool slightly and mix with the sour cream, which should be at room temperature. Serve lamb mixture with sour cream mixture on the side to be spooned over each serving. 6 to 8 servings.

PASTA STUFFED WITH LAMB AND WHEAT GERM

A superb way to present pasta with a different twist, that's also nutritious.

8	manicotti shells	¼	cup grated Parmesan cheese
2	tablespoons butter or margarine	1	teaspoon dried leaf oregano
½	cup chopped onion	½	teaspoon dried leaf basil
⅛	teaspoon garlic powder	½	teaspoon salt
2	cans (15-ounce each) tomato sauce	¼	teaspoon pepper
1	pound uncooked ground lamb	1	package (6-ounce) sliced Monterey Jack cheese
⅔	cup toasted wheat germ		Minced parsley

Cook manicotti shells in boiling, salted water according to package directions. Drain off boiling water. Add warm, tap water to manicotti shells, and let them stand in water until ready to fill. (It keeps them from sticking together.) Melt butter or margarine over moderate heat. Add onion. Sauté over moderate heat until onion is transparent. Add garlic powder and tomato sauce. Crumble lamb into another skillet. Cook over moderate heat until meat loses red color. Drain off grease. Add wheat germ, Parmesan cheese, oregano, basil, salt, pepper, and ¾ cup of the tomato sauce mixture. Mix well. Carefully place manicotti shells on paper toweling to drain. Gently stuff shells with meat mixture, packing it in tightly. Pour remaining tomato sauce mixture into 7 x 11-inch, shallow baking dish. Place manicotti in 1 layer over tomato sauce. Place cheese slices on top of manicotti, covering shells completely. Bake, covered, in oven preheated to 425° for about 25 minutes or until heated through. Sprinkle top with parsley. 4 servings.

Note: Ground beef tastes as good as lamb in this recipe.

TARTLY SWEET GLAZED LAMB

Roasted at a low temperature with the fell (a paper-like covering left on the meat to help retain its shape), leg of lamb will ooze with juices when it's carved into thin slices. They will be extra tender if the meat is roasted only to the deliciously rare or medium stage. At altitudes below 5,000 feet, a 300° oven temperature is recommended; above 5,000 feet, it's best to increase the temperature to 325°.

1	leg of lamb (about 5 pounds)	½	cup currant or other tart, red jelly
1	teaspoon salt	1	tablespoon lemon juice
1	teaspoon dry mustard		
½	teaspoon ground ginger	1	medium lemon, thinly sliced
¼	teaspoon pepper		

Place lamb on rack, fat side up, in shallow roasting pan. Mix together salt, mustard, ginger, and pepper. With fingertips, rub this mixture over top of meat. Insert meat thermometer in thickest part of meat. (Don't let thermometer touch a bone.) Roast, uncovered, without any liquid in pan, in oven preheated to 300° or 325°. Allow 20 to 25 minutes per pound for rare (140° on meat thermometer), 25 to 30 minutes per pound for medium (160° on meat thermometer), and 30 to 35 minutes for well done (170° on meat thermometer). It isn't necessary to baste meat with drippings during roasting period. Mix jelly with lemon juice, using a fork or wire whisk to break up jelly. About ½ hour before roasting period is completed, arrange lemon slices on top of lamb. (If necessary, secure slices to meat with wooden picks). Spoon jelly mixture between lemon slices. When roasting is complete, remove lamb from oven, and let "rest" about 15 minutes before carving. About 10 servings.

ROUNDUP ROLL

If this bears a sneaky resemblance to Beef Wellington, it's because of the lamb-onion mixture that snuggles in a roll of quick bread dough. The rosy-colored, easy-to-handle dough can also be used to encase whole, fat olives, or meat, fish and poultry hors d'oeuvre mixtures, or for making deep-dish pie, for meat pie toppings—or any idea of your imagination.

Lamb Filling

1½	pounds ground lamb	¼	teaspoon pepper
¾	cup chopped celery	1	can (15-ounce)
½	cup chopped onion		tomato sauce
½	teaspoon salt		

Heat a greased, 9 or 10-inch skillet over moderate heat. Crumble in lamb. Cook over moderate heat, breaking up lamb in small bits with edge of spoon, until lamb is slightly brown. Add celery and onion about 5 minutes before cooking time is completed. Place mixture in colander; let stand until all grease is drained off. Return mixture to skillet. Add salt, pepper, and 1½ cups of the tomato sauce. (Reserve remaining tomato sauce for dough.) Mix well. Bring mixture to boil, reduce heat to moderate, and cook, uncovered, until mixture thickens and most of the liquid has evaporated. Refrigerate mixture until cold. (It shouldn't be spread over dough while warm.)

Dough

3 cups all-purpose flour (at altitudes below 5,000 feet, sift flour before spooning it into measuring cup; at altitudes above 5,000 feet, spoon flour into cup without sifting it— the dough needs the additional flour obtained, without sifting, at higher altitudes)

4 teaspoons baking powder (that's right: 4 teaspoons!)

1 teaspoon salt

¼ teaspoon ground marjoram

⅛ teaspoon ground sage

6 tablespoons shortening

Tomato sauce reserved from previous recipe plus enough cold water to make 1 cup

1 egg beaten with 1 tablespoon water

Sift together flour, baking powder, salt, marjoram, and sage. Cut in shortening until mixture resembles coarse meal. Gradually stir in tomato sauce-water mixture, then use hands to mix dry ingredients with liquid. Dough will be stiff. Knead dough on unfloured surface until smooth and elastic. Work in any flour left in mixing bowl while kneading dough. Roll out dough between 2 pieces of foil into a rectangle about 11 x 16 inches. Use hands and fingers to pat and stretch dough evenly. Remove both pieces of foil from dough. (At this point, dough may be left covered with foil, and allowed to stand at room temperature up to 1½ hours, if you want to eliminate last minute preparation.)

TO ASSEMBLE:

Spread cooled meat mixture evenly over dough, leaving about a 1-inch border on all sides. (It may appear that there is too much meat mixture, but dough is stiff enough to hold it.) Roll dough, starting from long side, jelly roll fashion. With water-moistened fingers, press center and end seams together to seal tightly. If dough tears, just pinch it together with fingers. Place the roll on a lightly-greased baking sheet, seam side down. Generously brush top and sides of roll with egg-water mixture. Bake, uncovered, in oven preheated to 375° for about 35 minutes or until very well browned. Do not undercook or dough in the center will not be baked. (The roll bakes in about the same time for all altitudes.) Don't worry if some drippings escape from roll during baking. Loosen bottom of roll from baking sheet with large spatula. Let roll stand on baking sheet about 15 minutes before cutting into thick slices to serve. Serve with Cheese Sauce on the side, to be spooned over slices. 8 servings.

Note: Ground beef is easily substituted for the lamb, if desired.

Cheese Sauce

2 tablespoons butter or margarine	1¾ cups milk
2 tablespoons flour	1 cup shredded, sharp Cheddar cheese
Salt and pepper to taste	

Melt butter or margarine in medium-sized saucepan over moderate heat. Add flour. Cook over moderate heat, stirring, a few minutes. Gradually add milk. Cook over moderate heat, stirring with wire whisk, until thickened. Add cheese. Cook over moderately low heat, stirring with wire whisk, until cheese melts and mixture is smooth. Makes about 2½ cups.

FRESH VEGETABLE-LAMB STEW

A hearty kind of meal that uses vegetables from your garden—if you're lucky enough to have one.

Cooking oil	¼ teaspoon (or to taste) dried leaf thyme
1½ pounds lamb shoulder, cut in 1-inch cubes	1 medium bay leaf
1½ teaspoons sugar	3 medium potatoes, peeled and cut in quarters
1 teaspoon salt	
¼ teaspoon pepper	4 medium carrots, sliced
2 tablespoons flour	
1 cup chicken broth	6 small onions
1 cup dry white wine	½ pound fresh green beans, snapped in halves
2 medium, fresh tomatoes, cut in small pieces	
1 medium clove garlic, minced	1 pound fresh green peas, shelled just before serving

Heat a small amount of oil in Dutch oven over moderate heat. Add lamb. Cook over moderate heat, stirring frequently, until lamb is brown on all sides. Drain off grease. Sprinkle meat with sugar, salt, pepper, and flour. Cook over low heat a few minutes, stirring. Add chicken broth, wine, tomatoes, garlic, thyme, and bay leaf. Mix well. Bring to boil, reduce heat and simmer, covered, about 1 hour. Add potatoes, carrots, and onions. Bring to boil, reduce heat and simmer, covered about 5 minutes. Add beans, cover, and continue cooking about 12 minutes. Add peas and cook about 8 minutes or until all vegetables are tender. 4 to 6 servings.

WESTERN SLOPE LAMB RIBLETS

Shoppers who limit their choices to lamb roasts and chops are missing the mighty good eating found in other cuts, such as that in the skinny bones of lamb riblets.

3½ pounds lamb riblets	1 tablespoon Worcestershire Sauce
1 medium onion, chopped	1 teaspoon marjoram
1 large fresh tomato, cut in small pieces	1 teaspoon salt
¼ cup diced green pepper	¼ teaspoon dried leaf basil
¼ cup diced celery	¼ teaspoon dried leaf thyme
1 can (15-ounce) tomato sauce	1 medium bay leaf, crushed
½ cup water	½ teaspoon red pepper sauce, or to taste
1 medium clove garlic, minced	
1 tablespoon brown sugar	

Place riblets on rack in shallow roasting pan. Bake, covered with foil, in oven preheated to 325° for 1 hour and 15 minutes. Combine all the remaining ingredients. Mix well. Pour off drippings from riblets. Remove rack from pan. Replace riblets in pan and pour sauce over meat. Bake, covered, at 325° for about 45 minutes longer or until riblets are done. 4 servings.

LAMB CHOPS WITH APRICOT SAUCE

Meaty lamb arm or blade shoulder chops can be broiled in the same way as delicate loin cousins, but they are extra pleasing when braised in this simple sauce. When used alone, the sauce adds importance to broiled lamb chops of your choice when it is spooned over them.

2 tablespoons cooking oil	¾ cup plus 3 tablespoons apricot nectar
4 arm or blade lamb chops, about ½-inch thick, trimmed of fat	1 tablespoon lemon juice
Salt and pepper to taste	1 tablespoon raisins (or more to taste)
	1 tablespoon cornstarch

Heat oil in large skillet or Dutch oven over moderate heat. Add chops. Cook over moderate heat until chops are brown on both sides, turning them once. Drain off grease. Sprinkle chops with salt and pepper. Combine ¾ cup of the apricot nectar, lemon juice, and raisins. Pour mixture over and around chops. Bring to boil, reduce heat and simmer, tightly covered, about 35 minutes or until chops are tender. Remove chops to heated platter. Mix cornstarch until smooth with remaining 3 tablespoons apricot nectar. Heat cooking liquid in pan over moderate heat and add cornstarch mixture. Cook over moderate heat, stirring until thickened. Pour sauce over chops. 4 servings.

To make the sauce to use as a topping for broiled lamb chops: Place ¾ cup apricot nectar, 1 tablespoon lemon juice and 1 tablespoon raisins in small pan; heat until hot, over moderate heat. Mix until smooth 2 teaspoons cornstarch and 2 teaspoons cold water or apricot nectar. (The preceding recipe calls for 1 tablespoon cornstarch because more cooking liquid develops when the chops are braised in the sauce.) Stir cornstarch mixture into hot mixture. Cook over moderate heat, stirring, until thickened. (At altitudes above 5,000 feet, always cook cornstarch mixtures over direct heat; they won't thicken if cooked in top of double boiler over hot water.) Makes about 1 cup.

CABBAGE-WRAPPED LAMB IN GARLICKY TOMATO SAUCE

This recipe was printed in the *Denver Post* some twenty years ago. Believe it or not, we still get requests for it.

¾ pound uncooked ground lamb	1 cup cooked rice
¾ pound uncooked bulk pork sausage	2 extra-large eggs, slightly beaten
1 teaspoon salt or to taste	1 head (about 1¾ pounds) cabbage
¼ teaspoon pepper	Garlicky Tomato Sauce
½ cup chopped onion	

Mix together lamb, sausage, salt, pepper, onion, and rice. Add eggs. Mix well. (Mixture will be moist.) Divide mixture into 12 equal portions. Place them on a sheet of foil, and form each portion into oblong-shaped bundles. Let bundles stand on foil, uncovered, at room temperature, while preparing cabbage. (This permits mixture to dry out a bit and also lose its chill before being wrapped in cabbage leaves.) Remove coarse, outer leaves from cabbage. Place cabbage head in a large kettle of boiling water. There should be enough water to almost cover cabbage. Cook at rolling boil about 4 minutes or just until outer cabbage leaves start to wilt. Place cabbage in colander. Let drain and cool until it can be handled. (Don't allow cabbage to become cold, however, or leaves won't be pliable.) Remove 12 of the largest, whole, outer leaves. Reserve remaining cabbage for later use. Cut out, in a V-shape, the thick base of the vein from each whole cabbage leaf. Discard cut-out portions. Place a meat bundle in the center of each cabbage leaf. Bring up ends and sides of leaf around meat to completely enclose it, overlapping sides of leaf. Secure at seam with wooden pick. (One pick for each bundle should be enough.) Place bundles, seam sides down, in single layer in ungreased, shallow, close-fitting pan. Bundles should touch each other. Remove core from reserved cabbage and quarter. Holding each quarter over bundles, cut cabbage in coarse pieces, letting them fall on bundles, then spread evenly over top. Pour hot Garlicky Tomato Sauce over top. (Don't worry if pan is quite full, and mixture mounds slightly. Cabbage will shrink during cooking so there shouldn't be any run-over drippings.) Cover pan with a large piece of foil and press edges of foil against pan. Bake, covered, in oven preheated to 350° for 1 hour. Uncover, fluff up tomato sauce on top with a fork, and bake 30 minutes longer or until cooking liquid is reduced to desired consistency. (If flour was omitted in Garlicky Tomato Sauce, the cooking liquid will be thin. A thin sauce, incidentally, makes a wonderful dunking mixture for chunks of crusty bread.) When serving, warn diners about the wooden picks! Makes 6 servings of 2 bundles each with some of the extra cabbage in Garlicky Tomato Sauce spooned over them.

Note: This dish is also tasty made with extra lean, ground beef.

Garlicky Tomato Sauce

3 tablespoons cooking oil	3 tablespoons flour (optional)
1 medium onion, chopped	1 teaspoon salt
	¼ teaspoon pepper
4 or 5 medium cloves garlic, minced or mashed	2 tablespoons dried leaf parsley
	1 can (28-ounce) whole tomatoes

Heat oil in medium-sized pan over moderate heat. Add onion and garlic. (If you have a food processor, use the steel blade to chop onion and garlic.) Sauté onion mixture over moderate heat, stirring frequently, until onion is transparent. Add flour (for a thicker sauce), salt, pepper, and parsley. Cook over moderate heat a few minutes, stirring. Place tomatoes and their liquid in a small bowl. Cut tomatoes in small pieces with a sharp knife. (It isn't even necessary to handle the tomatoes; just run a small, sharp knife through each tomato to cut it into several pieces.) Beat tomatoes with egg beater until they are broken into even smaller pieces. Add tomatoes to onion mixture. Mix well. Bring to boil, reduce heat and simmer, covered, 15 minutes. (This sauce can be made a day ahead, refrigerated and reheated until hot before using in recipe.)

CASSOLETTE OF LAMB AND VEGETABLES

Not to be confused with cassoulet, a French stew of beans and pork, the similar-sounding cassolette means individual, oven-proof dishes of varying sizes and shapes. In France, cassolettes are used for hors d'oeuvres, entrées, and desserts. In America, they are more likely to be used for individual casseroles.

2 pounds lamb (from the leg), trimmed of fat and cut in about 1-inch cubes
Flour seasoned to taste with salt, pepper, celery seed, and garlic salt.
12 peeled white onions, about the size of walnuts (thaw if frozen)
3 large carrots, cut in fairly thick slices

3 large ribs celery, cut in fairly thick slices
1 large potato or more to taste, peeled and cut in about ½-inch cubes
Bay leaves
Whole cloves
Dry red wine or equal portions of dry red wine, and beef bouillon mixed together
French bread (optional)

Thickly coat lamb in seasoned flour. (It will help to thicken the cooking liquid.) Distribute ½ of the lamb cubes in 6 greased, individual casseroles of at least 3-cup size with deep sides. (Isn't it nice not to have to brown the meat?) Place equal amounts of onions, carrots, celery, and potatoes in each casserole. Add remaining lamb cubes. Place a small piece of bay leaf and 1 whole clove on top of meat. (The clove may be stuck in an onion so that it is easy to find for removal later.) Add enough of the wine or wine mixture to almost cover meat and vegetables. Bake, tightly covered, in oven preheated to 350° for about 1½ hours or until lamb and vegetables are done. Remove bay leaves and cloves. (If a large casserole is used, instead of individual ones, increase cooking time by 15 minutes or longer.) If desired, serve with chunks of French bread to be dipped in the wine cooking liquid. 6 servings.

LAMB ON A SPIT

When this marinated meat comes off the spit, it will lure even lamb-doubters to the dining table.

1 medium, green pepper, finely-diced	⅛ teaspoon red pepper sauce
2 medium, fresh tomatoes, peeled and cut in small pieces	1 cup port wine
	1 cup water
	½ cup olive oil
1 medium onion, finely chopped	1 teaspoon salt or to taste
2 tablespoons dried parsley flakes	1 teaspoon pepper or to taste
3 medium cloves garlic, minced	1 leg of lamb or lamb shoulder roast
¼ teaspoon dried leaf marjoram	(about 6 pounds), boned, rolled and
⅛ teaspoon dry mustard	tied for spit-cooking

In a glass dish that makes a close-fitting container for meat, combine green pepper, tomatoes, onion, parsley, garlic, marjoram, mustard, and red pepper sauce. Mix well. Add wine, water, and olive oil. Mix well. Add salt and pepper. Add lamb. Refrigerate, covered, about 12 hours, turning lamb occasionally. Drain lamb but reserve marinade. Place lamb on spit. Cook on rotisserie of outdoor grill or on oven rotisserie. Cooking time will vary depending on the method used so rely on your handy meat thermometer.

When inserted in meat, it should register about 140° for rare, 160° for medium, and 170° for well done. Brush lamb frequently with marinade during cooking. (If desired, serve leftover marinade as a relish-sauce with slices of lamb or save it to marinate other meat. Allow about ⅓ pound of boned meat for each serving.

SWEET AND SOUR LAMB

This enticing way to serve roast lamb, the second time around, comes from one of Colorado's sheep ranch kitchens.

2 tablespoons olive oil	2 tablespoons
6 cups (about)	cornstarch
coarsely-cut pieces	¼ cup vinegar
of roast lamb	2 tablespoons soy sauce
1 medium onion,	1 can (1-pound,
thinly sliced and	4-ounce) pineapple
separated into rings	chunks
2 cups water	Salt to taste
2 chicken or beef	1 medium, green
bouillon cubes	pepper, cut into strips
⅓ cup packed brown	Buttered noodles or
sugar	rice

(This recipe is at its best when the leftover lamb comes from a leg or shoulder roast that has first been rubbed with olive oil, then sprinkled generously with lemon juice, salt, pepper, dried leaf oregano, and garlic powder. The dry seasonings should be rubbed into the roast with fingertips. To reduce shrinkage and retain moisture, pamper lamb roasts with a low oven temperature, of about 325°.)

Heat olive oil in medium-sized skillet over moderate heat. Add lamb and cook over moderate heat just until lamb is warm. Add onion during last few minutes cooking time. Add water, bouillon cubes, and brown sugar. Bring to boil, reduce heat and simmer, covered, 15 minutes. Combine cornstarch, vinegar, soy sauce, and juice drained from pineapple. Stir until cornstarch dissolves. Gradually add mixture to lamb. Cook over moderate heat, stirring until thickened, adding more cornstarch if a thicker consistency is desired. Add pineapple chunks, salt to taste, and green pepper. Cook over moderate heat just until pepper is tender but still crisp. Serve over buttered noodles or rice. 6 to 8 servings.

MYSTERY LAMB KABOBS

A distinctive marinade using buttermilk along with seasonings adds a tangy flavor to chunks of lamb. Actually, this marinade isn't all that mysterious. The acidity of the buttermilk helps tenderize the meat, making the marinade "a natural" for other cuts also, such as cubed beef round steak.

1 cup buttermilk	Fresh corn-on-the-cob, cut in 1-inch slices
1½ tablespoons Worcestershire Sauce	Whole, small boiling onions
1 teaspoon lemon pepper	Fresh red and green peppers, cut in 2-inch pieces
2 teaspoons salt	Unpeeled, uncooked zucchini squash, cut in 2-inch slices
1 medium clove garlic, crushed	Large, fresh mushroom caps
2 tablespoons cooking oil	Melted butter
1½ to 2 pounds uncooked lamb cubes for kabobs, cut in about 1½-inch pieces	Uncooked bean sprouts or cooked rice

In a shallow, glass dish, mix together buttermilk, Worcestershire Sauce, lemon pepper, salt, garlic, and oil. Add lamb in a single layer. Stir lamb to coat all sides with marinade. Pierce each cube of meat with fork tines to allow penetration of the marinade. Refrigerate lamb, covered, about 6 hours. (If marinade is used for beef round steak cubes, refrigerate the beef up to 24 hours.) Cook corn in boiling water to cover, a few minutes or just until barely soft. Place onions and peppers in a strainer over a pan of boiling water (or put them in a vegetable steamer) and steam just until they are barely soft. (They will retain their color and flavor if not cooked in water.) Remove meat from marinade. On skewers, alternate meat with corn (push skewers through cob part of corn), onions, peppers, zucchini, and mushroom caps. Broil on the outdoor grill or in the oven broiler, about 9 inches from source of heat, until meat reaches desired degree of doneness. Brush vegetables frequently with butter during broiling period. Serve kabobs on a bed of bean sprouts or buttered rice. 6 or more servings, depending on the amount of vegetables used.

MEATLESS ENTRÉES

It isn't necessary to be a vegetarian to know that some meatless (or fishless) dishes can be as nutritionally well-balanced and satisfying as those containing meat, poultry, or seafood. Indeed, demand is growing for meatless recipes which use ingredients such as cheese, eggs, and vegetables to create nourishing, enjoyable, and economical main dishes.

The recipes in this section are designed to serve as inspiration for those interested in improvising their own meatless entrées when—if for no other reason—you want to take the ho-hum out of meal preparation. You'll find many of these dishes quite economical, especially if you use fresh vegetables from your own garden.

As an added attraction, I have included recipes for salads, corn bread, and other quick breads (all tested for any altitude) that will complement any main dish of your choice.

BROWN RICE-CHEESE STUFFED GREEN PEPPERS

Green peppers filled with this moist, nutritious mixture are particularly impressive when served on dinner plates with slim wedges of peeled cantaloupe or other melon of your choice and garnished with fresh, vitamin A-filled parsley sprigs.

6 large green peppers (about 2 pounds)	diced, unpeeled tomatoes
3 cups cooked brown rice (not instant)	1⅛ teaspoons salt or to taste
2 cups (about 8-ounce) shredded Swiss or Cheddar cheese	1 teaspoon paprika
	4 teaspoons Worcestershire Sauce
2 large, fresh, finely-	3 extra-large eggs, lightly beaten
	¾ cup water

Cut a thin slice off top of each pepper. (Save cut-off portions for use in salads, casseroles, etc.) Remove seeds and membrane from peppers. Parcook peppers in boiling water to cover about 10 minutes for altitudes above 5,000 feet, about 8 minutes for altitudes below 5,000 feet. Combine rice (rice should be warm or at room temperature), cheese, ¾ cup of the tomatoes, 1 teaspoon of the salt, paprika, 3 teaspoons of the Worcestershire Sauce, and eggs. Mix well. Spoon mixture into peppers. (Don't be afraid to pack it slightly.) Place peppers in close-fitting pan, 8 x 8 inches or 9 x 9 inches. Combine water, remaining tomatoes, remaining ⅛ teaspoon salt, and remaining 1 teaspoon Worcestershire Sauce. Pour mixture over and around peppers. Bake, uncovered, in oven preheated to 375° for about 45 minutes or until peppers are soft when pierced with fork and rice mixture is heated through. 6 servings.

EGGPLANT-ZUCCHINI CASSEROLE
WITH GREEN CHILE-CORN SPOON BREAD

This meatless casserole is very satisfying, especially when served with the Mexican-inspired bread.

2 cans (8-ounce each) tomato sauce
¼ cup water
2 teaspoons Worcestershire Sauce
1 teaspoon salt
½ teaspoon dried leaf oregano
2 medium cloves garlic, minced
1 medium eggplant, peeled and cut in ¼-inch slices
2 medium zucchini squash, unpeeled and cut in ½-inch slices

1 cup uncooked spaghetti which has been broken into about 1-inch pieces
3 medium ribs celery, coarsely chopped
1 medium, green pepper, coarsely chopped
8 ounces (about) Mozzarella cheese slices, cut in 18 pieces, each about 2-inches wide and 3½-inches long
Green Chile-Corn Spoon Bread

Combine tomato sauce, water, Worcestershire Sauce, salt, oregano, and garlic. Mix well. Arrange ½ of eggplant slices in single layer in greased, shallow, 9 x 13-inch baking dish. Arrange ½ of squash slices, ½ of spaghetti, ½ of celery, and ½ of green pepper evenly on top of eggplant. Evenly space 9 of the cheese slices on top. Spoon on ½ of the tomato mixture. Repeat layers. Bake, covered, in oven preheated to 350° for about 1 hour and 15 minutes or until casserole is bubbly. (At altitudes below 5,000 feet, a slightly shorter baking time will be required.) Serve with Green Chile-Corn Spoon Bread, if desired. 8 servings.

Green Chile-Corn Spoon Bread

This can bake right along with the preceding casserole since it requires the same oven temperature.

1 cup yellow corn meal	1 can (1-pound) cream-style corn
1½ teaspoons baking powder at altitudes above 5,000 feet; 1¾ teaspoons baking powder at altitudes below 5,000 feet	¼ cup cooking oil or bacon drippings at room temperature but not solidified
	1 cup milk
	1 can (4-ounce) diced green chiles
	Paprika

Stir together corn meal and baking powder in large bowl. Add corn and oil or bacon drippings. Mix well. Add milk, chiles, and their juice. Mix well. Spoon mixture into ungreased, round, 1-quart casserole. Bake, uncovered, in oven preheated to 350° for about 45 minutes or until golden brown but not dry. (At altitudes below 5,000 feet, slightly less baking time will be required.) Sprinkle with paprika. Mixture should be spooned out of casserole for serving. Serve as a bread and/or vegetable with main dish of your choice. 6 servings.

Note: Leftovers may be reheated by sprinkling a small amount of water on top, then baking the bread in 375° oven, covered, about 10 minutes or until warm.

SOUR CREAM PANCAKES

These hefty pancakes come to us from one of Wyoming's noted cooks, the wife of a rancher. For a quick supper dish, serve with your favorite topping and creamy, scrambled eggs to which chopped green pepper, onion, and pimiento have been added. Garnish the pancake platter with fresh fruit.

½ teaspoon baking soda	1 teaspoon salt
1 cup dairy sour cream	2 tablespoons sugar
1 cup buttermilk	2 cups unsifted flour
1 teaspoon baking powder	4 extra-large eggs
	½ teaspoon vanilla

Stir baking soda into a small amount of the sour cream; set aside. In a large bowl, mix together remaining sour cream and buttermilk. Add baking powder, salt, sugar, and flour. Mix well. Add eggs, one at a time, mixing well after each addition. Add sour cream with soda and vanilla. Mix well. For extra-thin pancakes, add a small amount of water to batter. Drop spoonfuls of batter onto moderately hot grill which has about ⅛ inch of melted shortening on it. Cook pancakes over moderate heat until bubbles form on uncooked side. Turn pancakes. Cook until golden brown. Pancakes can be made in any size. This recipe makes about 36 pancakes about 2½ inches in diameter.

SKI-COUNTRY FONDUE WITH SPINACH SALAD

Since the fondue craze hit the country a number of years ago, this easy-to-prepare dish has remained a favorite for many hostesses. This fondue is especially compatible with a nutritious spinach salad.

¾ cup beer	1 tablespoon flour
½ teaspoon minced garlic flakes	Red pepper sauce to taste
1 cup (about 4 ounces) shredded, sharp Cheddar cheese	1 tablespoon Kirsch or to taste
2 cups (about 8 ounces) shredded Swiss cheese	Cubes of bagels, pumpernickel, rye, or onion bread

Place beer in a pottery fondue dish or other flameproof dish. Heat beer over moderately low heat just until it is bubbly. Add garlic. Thoroughly toss together Cheddar and Swiss cheese. Add flour to cheese. Thoroughly toss together again. Very gradually add cheese to beer, stirring constantly. Cook, stirring constantly, over moderately low heat just until cheese has melted and mixture is smooth. Do not allow mixture to boil. Just before serving, stir in red pepper sauce and Kirsch. Place the fondue dish over an alcohol burner with a slow flame. Keep hot but not simmering. Spear cubed bagels, pumpernickel, rye, or onion bread with fondue fork and swirl in fondue mixture. (The more you swirl, the less chance the fondue will separate.) If fondue becomes too thick over warmer while it is being eaten, thin to desired consistency with more beer. Serve with the following spinach salad, if desired. 4 servings.

Spinach Salad with Tangy, Cooked Dressing

1 egg	¼ pound bacon, fried, drained and crumbled (optional)
¾ cup sugar	
½ cup vinegar	
1 teaspoon salt	Use any or all of the following ingredients to taste: sliced, fresh mushrooms; coarsely-chopped, hard-cooked eggs; shelled sunflower seeds; sliced water chestnuts; fresh bean sprouts; fresh alfalfa sprouts
1 medium onion, chopped	
⅛ teaspoon dry mustard or to taste	
⅛ teaspoon Worcestershire Sauce or to taste	
2 pounds uncooked, fresh spinach, torn in large, bite-size pieces	

Crack egg into a medium-sized saucepan and beat lightly. Add sugar, vinegar, and salt. Mix well. Cook over moderate heat, stirring frequently, just until mixture reaches boiling point and is thickened. (It won't become real thick.) Add onion, mustard, and Worcestershire Sauce. Transfer mixture to a bowl; cool slightly, then refrigerate until chilled. Makes about ¾ cup dressing. Just before serving, toss together spinach, bacon, mushrooms, eggs, sunflower seeds, etc. Add desired amount of dressing. Toss together again, lightly but thoroughly. 4 servings.

CONFETTI CORN CAKE WITH CORN BREAD

Any way you slice it, here's a fresh approach to combining carbohydrates, vegetable protein, and dairy products. Serve this dish with a fresh fruit salad. Baked by itself, the corn bread recipe I've included (which is cake-like rather than crumbly) makes a luscious addition to any meal.

2 packages (about 10-ounce each) frozen mixed vegetables, cooked until barely tender and drained (or substitute fresh,	cooked vegetables of your choice)
	Salt and pepper to taste
	Non-Crumbly Corn Bread
	Zippy Cheese Sauce

Arrange vegetables in greased, 9-inch pie plate. Add salt and pepper to vegetables. Prepare Non-Crumbly Corn Bread and carefully spoon batter on top of vegetables. Bake, uncovered, in oven preheated to 350° for about 25 minutes or until corn bread is golden brown and wooden pick inserted in center comes out clean. (At altitudes below 5,000 feet, slightly less baking time may be required.) Cut in wedges. Serve with Zippy Cheese Sauce. 6 servings.

Non-Crumbly Corn Bread

3 tablespoons butter or margarine, softened	off with knife or spatula
2 tablespoons sugar	3 teaspoons baking powder
2 extra-large egg yolks	½ teaspoon salt
1 cup yellow corn meal	1 cup milk
1 cup unsifted all-purpose flour, spooned into cup to measure, then leveled	2 extra-large egg whites at room temperature

Cream together butter or margarine and sugar in large bowl of mixer. Add egg yolks, mixing at low speed until blended. Mix together corn meal, flour, baking powder, and salt in another bowl. Alternately add dry ingredients with milk to egg yolk mixture, beating at medium speed and scraping frequently down sides of bowl with rubber spatula. Mix just until ingredients are blended. Beat egg whites until stiff. Thoroughly fold whites into corn meal mixture. Spoon batter onto vegetables, according to preceding directions, or use the following procedure for baking the corn bread by itself:

Spoon batter into greased, 8 x 8-inch pan. Bake in oven preheated to 425° for about 20 minutes or until wooden pick inserted in center comes out clean. (Baking time is about the same for all altitudes, but the wooden pick test is really the best guide.) Cool corn bread in pan about 10 minutes. Loosen sides with spatula. Cut in squares to serve.

Note: A higher oven temperature is required when corn bread is baked alone than when batter is used in preceding recipe.

Zippy Cheese Sauce

2 tablespoons butter or margarine	1½ cups milk
2 tablespoons flour	1½ cups shredded, sharp Cheddar cheese
½ teaspoon salt	
½ teaspoon dry mustard	½ teaspoon Worcestershire Sauce

Melt butter or margarine in a medium-sized skillet over moderate heat. Add flour, salt, and mustard. Cook over moderate heat, stirring, a few minutes. Gradually add milk. Cook over moderate heat, stirring, until mixture is thickened. Remove from heat. Stir in cheese and Worcestershire Sauce. Mix until cheese melts. Makes about 2 cups sauce.

CAULIFLOWER-TOMATO-CHEESE BAKE
WITH ONION BREAD SQUARES

A creamy cheese sauce brings tomatoes and fresh or frozen cauliflower together. Add the onion-flavored bread for a special meal.

Cooking oil	1½ cups shredded
1 medium onion,	Cheddar cheese
thinly sliced and	1 medium head
separated into rings	cauliflower *or* 2
2 medium, fresh	packages (about
tomatoes, sliced	10 ounces each)
2 tablespoons butter	frozen cauliflower
or margarine	Salt and pepper
2 tablespoons flour	to taste
1¼ cups milk	Onion Bread
	Squares

Heat a small amount of cooking oil in a large skillet over moderate heat. Add onion; sauté over moderate heat, stirring, for about 2 minutes. Place tomato slices on top of onion. Cook, covered, over moderately low heat just until tomatoes are soft. Melt butter or margarine over moderate heat in a medium-sized saucepan. Add flour. Stir a few minutes more over moderate heat, then gradually add milk. Cook over moderate heat, stirring, until thickened. Remove from heat. Add 1 cup of the cheese. Stir until cheese melts. Cut off and discard coarse stalks of cauliflower. Separate cauliflower into flowerettes and cook in boiling water to cover, just until they are crisp-tender. Drain. (If frozen cauliflower is used, cook according to package directions just until crisp-tender.) Spread cauliflower over bottom of greased, shallow, 10-inch baking dish. Spoon onion-tomato mixture evenly over cauliflower. Pour cheese sauce evenly over top. Sprinkle with remaining ½ cup cheese. (At this point, casserole may be frozen. When ready to use, thaw and bake, uncovered, at 350° just until bubbly.) Place casserole under broiler about 7 inches from source of heat just until cheese melts and mixture is slightly brown. Serve with Onion Bread Squares. 6 servings.

Onion Bread Squares

2 tablespoons butter or margarine	2 extra-large eggs
3 cups diced onions	¾ cup milk
½ cup diced green pepper	¾ cup dairy sour cream
2 cups packaged biscuit mix	½ teaspoon salt
	¼ teaspoon pepper

Melt butter or margarine in medium-sized skillet over moderate heat. Add onions and green pepper. Sauté over moderate heat, stirring frequently, until onion is transparent. Combine biscuit mix, 1 of the eggs, and milk. Mix well. Spoon dough into a greased, 8 x 8-inch pan. Spread onion mixture over dough. Beat remaining egg with sour cream, salt, and pepper. Spoon this mixture evenly over onion mixture. Bake, uncovered, in oven preheated to 400° for about 25 minutes or until wooden pick inserted in center comes out clean. Cut bread in squares, and serve warm.

Note: At altitudes below 5,000 feet, it is not necessary to use extra-large eggs; medium to large eggs may be used. Baking time can also be reduced about 5 minutes.

THE ARCHBISHOP'S MEATLESS MEAL

This casserole, created by the Most Reverend James V. Casey, Roman Catholic Archbishop of Denver, dates back to the days when Catholics were not allowed to eat meat on Fridays. Archbishop Casey concocted it to pinch-hit for fish or macaroni and cheese, and it goes nicely with just about any soup of your choice.

1 package (6-ounce) long-grain and wild rice	2 medium, fresh tomatoes, peeled and cut in small pieces
1 cup sliced ripe olives	Salt and pepper to taste
1 cup (about 4 ounces) shredded Cheddar cheese	¼ teaspoon onion salt (optional)
2 cans (3-ounce each) whole mushroom caps, drained	¾ cup boiling water

Prepare rice according to package directions, but use only 2 cups water. Add olives, cheese, mushrooms, tomatoes, salt, pepper, and onion salt if desired. Put mixture in greased, round, 2-quart casserole. Pour boiling water over top. Bake, covered, in oven preheated to 350° for about 45 minutes for altitudes above 5,000 feet, about 35 minutes for altitudes below 5,000 feet. Uncover and bake about 15 minutes longer for all altitudes. 6 servings.

SIMPLIFIED CHILES RELLENOS JOSÉ

In the traditional Mexican manner, green chile peppers (usually stuffed with cheese) are individually covered with an egg batter and fried in hot oil. There is no need to take that time-consuming step in this version of the dish, a favorite of Denverites.

1 can (1-pound, 10-ounce) whole, green, mild chiles or 18 whole, canned chiles	5 extra-large eggs
	¼ cup unsifted flour
	1¼ cups milk
	½ teaspoon salt
	Pepper to taste
1 pound Monterey Jack cheese, cut in strips about 1-inch wide, 3-inches long, ¼-inch thick	Red pepper sauce to taste
	½ pound shredded Cheddar cheese
	Paprika

Carefully rinse seeds from chiles with cold water. Spread chiles in single layer on paper toweling. Carefully pat them with another piece of paper toweling until they are dry. Carefully slip a strip of Monterey Jack cheese into each chile. Using a rotary beater or electric mixer, thoroughly beat eggs. Gradually add flour, beating until smooth. Add milk, salt, pepper, and red pepper sauce. Beat thoroughly. Arrange ½ of the stuffed chiles in a well-greased, shallow, 7 x 11-inch baking dish. Sprinkle with ½ of the Cheddar cheese and a generous amount of paprika. Repeat layers, ending with paprika. Carefully pour egg mixture over top. Bake, uncovered, in oven preheated to 350° for about 45 minutes or until knife inserted in custard-like mixture between chiles comes out clean. (At altitudes below 5,000 feet, test for doneness after 30 minutes of baking time.) Serve with a fruit salad or tossed green salad and hot rolls. 6 servings.

MUSHROOM-POTATO SOUP

Fresh mushrooms and half-and-half cream are 2 expensive ingredients that go into a relatively inexpensive soup. That's because the mixture is extended with potatoes and carrots to yield a generous number of servings and is hearty enough to serve as a main dish.

5 tablespoons butter or margarine	2 teaspoons salt or to taste
2 leeks, chopped (about 2 cups); green onions and some of the tops may be substituted	Ground pepper to taste
	1 medium bay leaf
	2 pounds potatoes, peeled and diced
2 large carrots, thinly sliced	1 pound fresh mushrooms, sliced
6 cups rich chicken broth	1 cup half-and-half cream
2 teaspoons dill weed	¼ cup flour

Melt 3 tablespoons of the butter or margarine in a large kettle. Add leeks and carrots. Sauté over moderate heat a few minutes, stirring frequently. Add broth, dill, salt, pepper, bay leaf, and potatoes. Bring to boil, reduce heat, and simmer, covered, until potatoes are done. Melt remaining butter or margarine in a large skillet. Add mushrooms. Sauté over moderate heat, stirring frequently, until mushrooms are golden colored. Remove bay leaf from potato mixture. Gradually stir half-and-half cream into flour; mix until smooth. Add mushrooms and cream mixture to potato mixture. Cook over moderate heat, stirring constantly, until soup has thickened. Garnish with more dill weed, if desired. 6 or more servings as a main dish soup.

TOMATOES AU GRATIN
WITH OLIVE SKILLET BREAD

Garden-fresh tomatoes can be enjoyed as a main dish when they are given this deluxe treatment. Serve the casserole, if you wish, with wedges of hot, olive-studded bread.

1¾ cups dry Italian-style bread crumbs

4 large, fresh tomatoes, unpeeled, and cut in about ¼-inch slices

2 teaspoons sugar

1 teaspoon salt

1 teaspoon paprika

⅓ teaspoon dry mustard

2 cups (about 8 ounces) shredded Cheddar cheese

1 cup cooked elbow macaroni (optional)

½ stick (¼ cup) butter or margarine, melted

Generously grease bottom and sides of a shallow, 10-inch casserole. Sprinkle about ⅓ of the crumbs over bottom of casserole. Place about ⅓ of the tomatoes in a single layer on crumbs. Combine sugar, salt, paprika, and mustard. Mix well. Sprinkle about ⅓ of the sugar mixture on tomatoes. Sprinkle about ⅓ of the cheese on top. If macaroni is used, sprinkle all of it on cheese. Repeat layers of crumbs, tomatoes, sugar mixture, and cheese drizzling melted butter or margarine over the top bread crumb layer before adding the last layer of tomatoes. Bake, covered, in oven preheated to 375° for about 30 minutes. Uncover and bake about 10 minutes longer. Serve with Olive Skillet Bread, if desired. 4 to 6 servings.

Olive Skillet Bread

1 can (3½-ounce) pitted ripe olives, drained and cut in wedges

4 cups buttermilk baking mix

½ teaspoon garlic powder

¼ cup instant mashed potato flakes

3 tablespoons minced onion

1 cup shredded Monterey Jack cheese

½ cup dairy sour cream

¾ cup milk

2 tablespoons melted butter

1 egg, lightly beaten

1 egg, beaten with 1 tablespoon water

Combine olives, baking mix, garlic powder, dry potato flakes, onion, and cheese. Mix well. Combine sour cream, milk, butter, and plain, beaten egg. Mix well. Add liquid ingredients all at once to dry ingredients. Stir just until dry ingredients are moistened. Turn dough into well-greased, 9-inch cast iron or other heavy skillet. Spread dough fairly even in skillet. Brush top with egg which has been beaten with water. Bake on bottom rack of oven that has been preheated to 375° for about 45 minutes or until wooden pick inserted in center comes out clean. (At altitudes below 5,000 feet, slightly less baking time will be required.) Serve warm, cut in wedges. Makes 1 round loaf, 9-inch size.

MAIN DISH BLACK BEAN SOUP

This version of a Guatemalan specialty uses tiny, dry, blackish beans which have a high nutrient value and are grown in several sections of this country. These beans are not as popular here as other types of dry beans, probably because their color is not too appetizing, but the flavor is highly acceptable.

3 pounds dry black beans (available in specialty food stores)	1 tablespoon dried parsley flakes
1 large onion, quartered	1 teaspoon black pepper
1 large green pepper, quartered	1 teaspoon dried leaf oregano
4 quarts water	1 teaspoon dried leaf thyme
1 medium onion, finely chopped	2 teaspoons vinegar
1 medium, green pepper, finely chopped	2 teaspoons sugar
1 can (6-ounce) tomato paste	Green pepper strips, hard-cooked egg slices and/or lemon slices
1 tablespoon Worcestershire Sauce	Cooked rice or warmed flour tortillas (optional)
1 tablespoon garlic salt	

Thoroughly wash and drain beans. (There is no need to soak them overnight.) Combine beans, quartered onion, quartered green pepper, and water in 6-quart kettle. Bring to boil, reduce heat, and simmer, covered, about 3 hours or until beans are nearly tender. Add chopped onion, chopped green pepper, tomato paste, Worcestershire Sauce, garlic salt, parsley, black pepper, oregano, thyme, vinegar, and sugar. Mix well. Bring to boil, reduce heat, and simmer, covered, about 45 minutes or until beans are done. Stir occasionally. Taste during cooking period, and add more of any one of the listed seasonings if necessary. Also, add more water if thinner consistency is desired. Serve as a soup in bowls or on rice or tortillas. Garnish with green pepper strips, egg, and/or lemon slices. (Soup freezes nicely.) Makes about 6 quarts.

SPINACH CHEESE PIE

This dish makes no apologies for taking full advantage of convenience foods. Those who like just a little bit of meat can add the bacon.

1 package (8-ounce) refrigerator crescent rolls
1 cup (about 4 ounces) shredded Cheddar cheese
3 eggs, slightly beaten
1 cup evaporated milk
2 teaspoons Worcestershire Sauce
½ teaspoon salt
½ teaspoon onion salt or to taste
Pepper to taste

1 package (about 10-ounce) creamed spinach, frozen in pouch; cooked according to package directions
1 can (about 2½-ounce) mushrooms, drained
8 slices bacon, crisply fried, drained, and crumbled (optional)
Grated Parmesan cheese to taste

Unroll crescent rolls. Press dough evenly, sealing seams, to form a crust in a 10-inch pie plate. Sprinkle Cheddar cheese evenly over top of dough. Combine eggs, evaporated milk, Worcestershire Sauce, salt, onion salt, and pepper. Mix well. Add cooked spinach, mushrooms, and ½ of the bacon, if desired. Spoon mixture onto cheese in pie plate. Sprinkle top with Parmesan cheese. Bake, uncovered, in oven preheated to 350° for 35 minutes. Sprinkle remaining bacon on top, if desired. Bake, uncovered, about 25 minutes longer or until knife inserted in center comes out clean. (At altitudes below 5,000 feet, start testing pie for doneness after about 15 minutes during the final stage of baking.) 6 to 8 servings.

PORK

A cross section of Americana is represented in this selection of pork recipes, which includes Oriental- and Mexican-influenced entrées as well as Continental and traditional American family-style dishes. Recipes for ham are accompanied by suggestions for glazes, basting liquids, and ways to use the rosy meat when it is reduced to humble leftovers. An all-purpose white sauce mix (which can be kept handy in the refrigerator) is also included in this section, but you'll find it useful for saucing all meats, poultry, fish, or vegetables.

Very different from the cuts that came from its corpulent ancestors, today's pork is much leaner and has fewer calories and a higher protein content. Though it is still important to cook pork until it is well done, it should not be overcooked either. The latest pork industry research recommends an internal temperature (on the meat thermometer) of 170° to 180°; older recipes required 185°. Those longer cooking periods in addition to yesteryear's less-desirable quality of pork probably help to account for the popular belief that the meat tends to be tough and dry—but that is simply not true of the juicy pork cuts available at the modern meat counter.

KATSUDON

Katsudon (pork in a bowl) is a classic Japanese main dish so versatile that you can serve it with just about any type of salad or vegetable without worrying that their flavors will clash.

1 pound boneless, uncooked pork shoulder, loin, etc., cut in about 1-inch pieces (pork should be weighed after bones are removed)	1 medium onion, cut in half, crosswise with the grain, then cut in thin slices
Flour	2 cups water
2 eggs, beaten	¼ cup soy sauce
Very fine cracker crumbs	2 teaspoons sugar or to taste
Cooking oil	Salt and pepper to taste
	Egg topping (optional)
	Cooked rice

Place pork, a few pieces at a time, in a paper bag which holds a generous amount of flour. Shake pork until it is generously coated on all sides with flour. Dip pork in eggs. Then place pork in a paper bag with a generous amount of cracker crumbs. Shake bag until pork is generously coated with crumbs. Heat about ½ inch of cooking oil in a 9- or 10-inch skillet over moderate heat. Fry pork pieces in oil over moderately high heat until they are brown and crisp on all sides. Add more oil, if necessary, as pieces are cooked. Drain pork on paper toweling. Drain off grease from skillet and add onion, water, soy sauce, sugar, salt, and pepper. Mix well. Bring mixture to boiling point. Add pork. Cook pork, uncovered, over moderate heat about 30 minutes or until sauce is reduced and thickened to desired consistency. (The crumb-flour coating on the pork will help thicken the sauce.) If desired, pour 2 beaten eggs over top of pork mixture. Cook over moderate heat, covered, until egg topping is firm. Serve pork mixture over rice. 6 servings.

SMOTHERED BURRITOS WITH GREEN CHILE

Mexican dishes are "hot," in terms of appeal, in the Rocky Mountain region. Here is one of the "best of the best" ways to present Mexican food.

Green Chile

2 pounds uncooked pork, trimmed of excess fat and cubed	2 cans (28-ounce each) whole tomatoes, mashed with potato masher in their liquid
1 medium onion, chopped	2 cans (4-ounce each) diced, mild green chiles (1 can hot green chiles may be substituted for a spicier flavor)
2 medium cloves garlic, minced	
2 tablespoons chili powder	
Salt and pepper to taste	

Heat a heavy kettle over moderate heat. Add pork. Cook over moderate heat, stirring, until grease starts to collect. Continue cooking, stirring occasionally, until pork is brown on all sides. Add onion and garlic during last 5 minutes of cooking time. Drain off grease. Combine chili powder, salt, pepper, tomatoes, and chiles. Add tomato mixture to pork. Bring to boil, reduce heat, and simmer, tightly covered, 3 hours. Serve as a sauce for Smothered Burritos. (Green Chile also freezes nicely.) Makes about 2 quarts.

Smothered Burritos

6 flour tortillas, 8-inch size	Diced onions to taste
1 can (28-ounce) refried beans	Chopped, fresh tomatoes to taste
1 cup (or more to taste) Green Chile from preceding recipe	Shredded lettuce
	Shredded Longhorn cheese to taste

Spread tortillas with beans. Roll tortillas, jelly-roll fashion. Place tortillas, seam sides down, in single layer in greased pan. Pour Green Chile over top and around sides. Sprinkle with onions, tomatoes, lettuce, and generous portions of cheese. Bake, uncovered, in oven preheated to 350° for about 20 minutes or until burritos are thoroughly heated. Serve extra Green Chile on the side to be spooned over burritos. 6 servings.

PORK CREOLE WITH SAUERKRAUT RELISH

Combining pork with sauerkraut is a time-honored idea that takes a new direction here. The sauerkraut is in the form of a delicious cold relish.

Cooking oil	1 can (4-ounce) sliced mushrooms, drained
1 pound uncooked pork, trimmed of fat and cut in 1-inch cubes	½ medium green pepper, chopped
1 medium onion, chopped	Worcestershire Sauce to taste
1 medium clove garlic, minced	Cayenne pepper to taste
1 can (1-pound) whole tomatoes	Salt and pepper to taste
1 large rib celery with leaves, chopped	Cooked rice

Heat a small amount of cooking oil in large skillet over moderate heat. Add pork. Cook over moderate heat until pork is brown on all sides. Add onion and garlic during last few minutes of cooking time. Drain off grease. Add tomatoes, which have been cut in pieces, the tomato liquid, celery, mushrooms, green pepper, Worcestershire Sauce, cayenne, salt, and pepper. Bake, covered, in oven preheated to 350° for about 1 hour. Serve with rice. 4 servings.

Sauerkraut Relish

1 cup sugar	water, and thoroughly drained again
½ cup vinegar	
1 can (1-pound) sauerkraut, drained, rinsed with cold	1 cup chopped onion
	1 cup chopped celery
	1 cup chopped pimiento

Heat together sugar and vinegar, stirring until sugar dissolves. Do not allow mixture to come to boil. Combine vinegar mixture with sauerkraut, onion, celery, and pimiento. Mix well. Refrigerate, covered, at least 24 hours. Serve as a relish and/or salad.

STIR-FRY PORK WITH ALMONDS

A delicious Oriental-influenced dish, certain to please.

2 tablespoons cornstarch	1 can (8-ounce) water chestnuts, drained and sliced
2 tablespoons soy sauce	1 package (6-ounce) frozen snow peas, thawed and uncooked or 1 package (9-ounce) frozen, cut green beans, thawed and uncooked
⅛ teaspoon garlic powder	
1 pound lean, boneless, uncooked pork, cut in small strips	
4 tablespoons cooking oil	
¾ cup whole, blanched almonds	1 cup chicken broth
1 large onion, sliced ½-inch thick, then cut slices in half	½ teaspoon celery seed
	Hot cooked rice

Combine cornstarch, soy sauce, and garlic powder. Stir until cornstarch dissolves. Combine pork with cornstarch mixture; mix thoroughly to coat pork on all sides. Let stand at room temperature for 20 minutes. Stir occasionally. Heat 1 tablespoon of the oil in large skillet or wok. Add almonds. Cook over moderately high heat, stirring constantly, about 2 minutes or until almonds are golden brown. Remove almonds from skillet. Add remaining 3 tablespoons of oil to skillet. Add pork and juices from cornstarch mixture, and onion. Fry over moderately high heat, stirring constantly, just until pork is done. Add almonds, water chestnuts, snow peas or beans, chicken broth, and celery seed. Cook over moderately high heat, stirring constantly, until pan juices are thickened and vegetables are crisp-tender. Serve over rice. 4 to 6 servings.

SLOW COOKER CHILE VERDE

This zesty pork-tomato mixture is something nice to come home to.

Cooking oil
1½ pounds boneless, uncooked pork shoulder cut in 1½-inch cubes (beef chuck may be substituted)
1 can (28-ounce) whole tomatoes
½ cup beef consommé
2 tablespoons lemon juice
1 medium clove garlic, crushed
¼ teaspoon sugar
1 teaspoon ground cumin
¼ teaspoon cloves
1 can (7-ounce) whole green chiles, cut in thin strips
⅓ cup chopped parsley
Salt to taste
Tortillas or cooked rice

Heat a small amount of cooking oil in large skillet over moderate heat. Add meat, and cook over moderate heat until it is brown on all sides. Drain off off grease. Add tomatoes which have been cut in fairly large pieces, the tomato liquid, consommé, lemon juice, garlic, sugar, cumin, cloves, chiles, parsley, and salt. Bring to boiling point. Place mixture in 3½-quart electric, slow-cooking pot. Cook on low heat 6 to 8 hours according to manufacturer's directions. Chile Verde may also be cooked on top of the stove. In this case, simmer it, covered, about 2½ hours. Serve in bowls as a soup-stew or over tortillas or rice. 6 servings.

SPICY GLAZE FOR ROAST PORK

This simple glaze may be used with any type of pork roast. Remember, pork should always be cooked to the well-done stage in case there are trichinae in the meat. Internal temperatures for pork roasts, registered by a meat thermometer, should range from 170° to 180°. When the flesh of the meat is pricked, the juices that run out of it should be clear. A 325° oven temperature is recommended for most pork roasts, but cooking times vary because of the differences in the shape and size of cuts. Consult a basic, dependable cookbook for more detailed information on roasting pork.

1 cup brown sugar	1 tablespoon (or more
¼ cup pineapple juice	to taste) prepared
2 tablespoons vinegar	Dijon-style mustard

Combine brown sugar, pineapple juice, vinegar, and mustard. Mix well. Spoon ½ of the mixture over pork roast of your choice during the last 45 minutes of cooking time. Spoon remaining mixture over roast during the last 20 minutes of cooking time.

PORK CHOP STUFFING CASSEROLE

Smoked pork chops, which do not have to be browned, may be substituted for fresh chops.

2 tablespoons cooking oil	1 can (10¾-ounce) undiluted cream of celery soup
6 pork chops, cut about ¾-inch thick	½ cup water
2 medium onions, chopped	2 medium tart, unpeeled apples, coarsely chopped
Salt to taste	
1 package (8-ounce) herb-seasoned stuffing mix	3 cups unpeeled zucchini squash

Heat oil in large skillet over moderate heat. Add chops, and cook over moderate heat until they are lightly brown on both sides. Remove chops from skillet. Add onions to drippings. Sauté onions over moderately low heat until they are transparent. Drain off all but about 2 tablespoons drippings. Add salt and stuffing mix to onions. Mix well. Mix together soup and water until smooth. Add soup, apples, and zucchini to stuffing mixture. Mix lightly but thoroughly. Spoon mixture evenly over bottom of a greased, 9 x 13-inch baking dish. Place chops in a single layer on top of stuffing. Bake, tightly covered with foil, in oven preheated to 325° for about 40 minutes. Remove foil. Bake, uncovered, about 15 minutes longer or until chops are done. (At altitudes below 5,000 feet, decrease total cooking time about 10 minutes.) 6 servings.

THREE WAY CHINESE PORK NUGGETS

These can be served as hors d'oeuvres or in two different main dishes.

2 eggs, beaten	1 pound uncooked
1½ teaspoons salt	pork tenderloin, cut
⅓ cup plus 2 table-	in small pieces
spoons water	about ¾-inch thick
1 cup unsifted flour	Oil for deep-fat
	frying

Combine eggs, salt, and water. Gradually add flour. Mix with wire whisk until smooth. Using a fork, dip pork pieces in egg batter to thoroughly coat each piece. Have ready a fairly large, deep-fat fryer or deep, heavy pan about ½ full of oil which has been heated to about 375° or is hot enough to brown a bread cube in about 1 minute. Fry a few nuggets at a time in the oil just until batter is golden brown and pork is done. Drain nuggets on paper toweling and use in one of the following recipes. (Nuggets may be frozen at this point. If frozen, thaw them in refrigerator before using.)

Hors d'oeuvres

Pork Nuggets can be served warm or at room temperature. Spear nuggets with wooden picks and dip them into hot mustard, your favorite sweet-sour sauce, or the following plum sauce.

1 cup plum jam	1 teaspoon lemon juice
1 teaspoon dry mustard	1 teaspoon grated
¾ teaspoon ginger	lemon rind
½ teaspoon salt	2 dashes red pepper
1 teaspoon onion juice	sauce or to taste

Melt jam over low heat in small pan. Add mustard, ginger, salt, onion juice, lemon juice, lemon rind, and red pepper sauce. Simmer until hot.

Sweet-Sour Pork Nugget Main Dish

1 can (14-ounce) pineapple chunks
6 tablespoons cider vinegar
½ cup brown sugar
1 tablespoon soy sauce
1 medium, green pepper, cut in 1-inch squares
1 tablespoon cornstarch mixed until smooth with 1 tablespoon water
Pork Nuggets from preceding recipe
8 to 10 cherry tomatoes
Cooked rice

Drain pineapple, and reserve liquid. Add enough water to pineapple liquid to make 1 cup. Combine pineapple liquid, vinegar, brown sugar, and soy sauce in medium saucepan. Mix well. Bring mixture to boiling point. Add green pepper and pineapple chunks. Cook, uncovered, at slow boil about 2 minutes. Add cornstarch mixture. Cook over moderate heat, stirring, until thickened. Add as many Pork Nuggets as desired, and cherry tomatoes. Heat just to serving temperature. Serve with rice. 4 to 6 servings.

Pork Nuggets and Pea Pod Main Dish

1 tablespoon soy sauce
½ cup water
1 medium clove garlic, minced
¼ cup slivered almonds
2 tablespoons sherry
¼ teaspoon (or to taste) 5-spice (an optional seasoning containing 5 different spices from the Far East; available in food specialty stores)
1 silver-dollar sized piece of fresh ginger root, slivered (fresh ginger root cuts easier if it is partially frozen)
2 cups (about) fresh snow pea pods
Pork Nuggets from preceding recipe
1 tablespoon cornstarch, mixed until smooth in ½ cup water
Cooked rice

Combine soy sauce, water, garlic, almonds, sherry, and 5-spice. Bring to boil, reduce heat, and simmer mixture, covered, about 5 minutes. Add ginger root and pea pods; bring to boil. Cook, uncovered, at rolling boil about 1 minute. Add as many Pork Nuggets as desired, and cornstarch mixture. Mix lightly but thoroughly. Cook over moderate heat, stirring, until mixture thickens and pea pods are crisp-tender. Serve with rice. 4 to 6 servings.

BAVARIAN PORK CHOP BAKE

This combination, requiring only six ingredients, goes especially well with a tossed green salad.

Cooking oil
6 to 8 pork chops, about ¾-inch thick
Salt and pepper to taste
1 can (29-ounce) sauerkraut, drained
2 medium, tart apples, unpeeled and coarsely chopped
1 medium onion, chopped
1 tablespoon brown sugar
1 teaspoon caraway seeds

Heat a small amount of oil over moderate heat in large skillet. Add pork chops. Cook over moderate heat until chops are brown on both sides. Drain off grease. Season chops with salt and pepper. Combine sauerkraut, apples, onion, brown sugar, and caraway seeds. Mix well. Place mixture in 9 x 13-inch pan. Arrange chops on top of sauerkraut mixture. Bake, tightly covered, in oven preheated to 350° for about 45 minutes. Uncover and continue baking about 15 minutes longer or until chops are done. 6 to 8 servings.

COLORADO CABBAGE BURGERS

Hearty yeast buns stuffed with seasoned pork and cabbage are a specialty in the farming areas of northeastern Colorado, where they can be found in a number of variations. Ground beef may be substituted for the pork, if desired.

Filling

1 pound lean, uncooked ground pork
1 medium onion, chopped
3 cups uncooked, coarsely-chopped cabbage
1½ teaspoons salt or to taste
Pepper to taste
½ cup water
1 teaspoon caraway seeds

Crumble pork into a 9- or 10-inch skillet which has been heated over moderate heat. Cook over moderate heat, breaking pork up in fine pieces with edge of spoon, until done. Add onion during the last 5 minutes of cooking time. Drain off all grease. Add cabbage, salt, pepper, water, and caraway seeds. Bring mixture to boil. Cook at rolling boil, uncovered, until all liquid has evaporated. Cool mixture to room temperature.

Dough

1 package dry yeast	2½ cups (about)
2 teaspoons sugar	unsifted all-
¼ cup warm water	purpose flour,
¾ cup milk, which has	spooned into cup
been scalded and	to measure
cooled to lukewarm	Melted butter or
½ teaspoon salt	margarine
2 tablespoons cooking	
oil	

Add yeast and sugar to warm water. Let stand a few minutes until yeast dissolves. In a large bowl, mix yeast mixture with milk, salt, cooking oil, and about 2 cups of the flour. Add more flour, if necessary, to make a moderately soft dough. Turn dough out on floured surface; knead several times until dough is smooth and elastic. Place dough in a greased bowl. Turn dough in bowl to grease all sides. Cover with a damp cloth, and let stand in warm place until indentation remains when two fingertips are pressed into dough, indicating it has doubled in bulk. (One of the best places for dough to rise is in the oven. Turn on oven to its lowest, warm setting while preparing dough. Turn off heat a few minutes before dough is ready, then place dough in its bowl with damp cloth in oven.) At altitudes above 5,000 feet, dough will rise in about 40 minutes. At altitudes below 5,000 feet, it will take dough about 10 minutes longer.

Punch dough down. Roll it out on lightly-floured surface to a rectangle about 12 x 18 inches. Cut dough into 8 squares of about 5 inches each.

TO ASSEMBLE:

Place about 2 heaping tablespoons of the cabbage filling in center of each dough square. Bring the 4 corners of each square together; pinch seams together to seal. Gently mold bundles into circular shapes. Place burgers, seam sides down, on greased baking sheet. Cover lightly with plastic wrap; let rise in warm place until puffy (about 20 minutes for altitudes above 5,000 feet, about 30 minutes for altitudes below 5,000 feet). Bake in oven preheated to 375° for about 30 minutes or until buns are golden brown. Brush tops and sides with melted butter while they are still hot. Makes 8.

Note: Cold Cabbage Burgers, wrapped airtight in foil, freeze nicely up to about 1 month. Thaw them in the refrigerator, wrap in foil, and reheat in a 400° oven for about 10 minutes. They are also good cold to be eaten out-of-hand.

SPICY CHINESE PORK WITH BROCCOLI

Prepared in the Szechuan manner, this dish is at its best when served with freshly cooked broccoli and rice. Speared with wooden picks, the spicy pork pieces also make delicious hors d'oeuvres.

½ pound uncooked pork, trimmed of fat and cut in bite-size pieces

2 tablespoons sherry

2½ tablespoons soy sauce

¼ teaspoon salt or to taste

1 tablespoon corn-starch

3 tablespoons vegetable oil

1 tablespoon finely-diced scallion

1 tablespoon finely-diced ginger root (it's easier to dice if ginger is partially frozen)

1 tablespoon minced garlic

1 tablespoon Szechuan bean sauce (a spicy, paste-like sauce available in Oriental groceries) *or* 1½ teaspoons red pepper sauce or to taste

2 teaspoons sugar

1 teaspoon sesame oil

1 teaspoon cornstarch dissolved in 1 teaspoon water

½ tablespoon vinegar

Pepper to taste

Broccoli, cooked until tender but still crisp

Cooked rice

Combine pork, 1 tablespoon of the sherry, 1½ tablespoons of the soy sauce, salt, and 1 tablespoon undissolved cornstarch. Mix well. Let mixture stand at room temperature 30 minutes. Heat vegetable oil over moderately hot heat in large skillet or wok. Add pork mixture. Cook over moderately hot heat, stirring constantly just until pork is done. Add scallions, ginger root, garlic, and bean sauce. If mixture seems too dry, add about 1 tablespoon additional vegetable oil. Mix well. Add remaining sherry, soy sauce, and sugar, sesame oil, dissolved cornstarch, vinegar, and pepper. Cook over moderate heat, stirring, until mixture is bubbly. Place pork in center of platter surrounded by hot broccoli. Serve with rice. 4 servings.

Note: 2 whole chicken breasts, boned, skinned, and cut in generous bite-size pieces may be substituted for pork.

JOHN MOSSETTI

Do you know a chap named John Mossetti? I don't. However, the elusive fellow's name has stuck with this recipe since it was printed in a 1959 issue of the *Denver Post*. The cook who submitted the recipe didn't know John Mossetti. The friend who gave her the recipe didn't know him either.

1½ pounds lean, uncooked ground pork	½ cup sliced ripe olives
1 large onion, chopped	1 can (about 4-ounce) sliced mushrooms, drained
1 package (8-ounce) noodles, cooked and drained	Salt and pepper to taste
2 cans (10¾-ounce each) undiluted tomato soup	¼ pound Cheddar cheese, finely diced

Heat a greased, 9- or 10-inch skillet over moderate heat. Crumble in pork. Cook over moderate heat, stirring frequently, until meat is very brown. Break up meat with edge of spoon as it cooks. Add onion during the last few minutes of cooking time. Drain off any grease. Arrange noodles on bottom of lightly-greased, 9 x 13-inch baking dish. Spoon pork on top of noodles. Spoon 1 can of the undiluted soup over pork; mix gently. Spread olives and mushrooms evenly over top. Sprinkle with salt and pepper. Spoon remaining can of undiluted soup evenly on top. (This time, there's no need to stir it.) Sprinkle cheese evenly over all. Bake, uncovered, in oven preheated to 325° for about 45 minutes or until bubbly. 6 to 8 servings.

HAM ROLLS

Buns with baked-in strips of ham go to luncheon or dinner as an entrée, or to parties as finger food. Simply change their size to suit the occasion. If there are leftovers, send them to school or work in the lunch box.

¾ cup tomato juice	1 tablespoon (or more to taste) minced onion
2 tablespoons packed brown sugar	
2 packages dry yeast	1 tablespoon salt
3 tablespoons melted bacon drippings at room temperature *or* cooking oil	1 egg, beaten
	2¾ cups (about) all-purpose flour, sifted before measuring and spooned into cup to measure
1½ teaspoons celery salt	

Heat tomato juice to lukewarm. Add tomato juice and sugar to yeast which has been placed in a large bowl. Let stand a few minutes, and stir to dissolve yeast. Blend in bacon drippings or oil, celery salt, onion, salt, and egg. Stir in half of the flour. Mix well. Using hands, work in remaining flour or enough to make a moderately stiff dough. Turn out dough on pastry cloth or lightly-floured surface; knead until it is smooth and elastic. Form dough into ball. Put dough in large, greased bowl. Turn dough to grease all sides. Cover bowl with damp cloth. Let rise in warm place until doubled in bulk. (This will take about 30 minutes at altitudes above 5,000 feet; about 45 minutes at altitudes below 5,000 feet.) The oven provides a good place to let dough rise. Turn oven to lowest setting (usually Warm) while preparing dough. Turn off oven a few minutes before dough is ready to rise. Place dough, in covered greased bowl, in oven to rise.

Strips of cooked ham at room temperature, cut in desired thickness and lengths	Cheese sauce, made from your favorite recipe or use All-Purpose Refrigerator White Sauce Mix (page 132)
Melted bacon drippings or cooking oil	

For medium-sized rolls, roll out ⅓ of dough at a time on lightly-floured surface into circles about ¼-inch thick. Cut each circle in 4 wedges. For larger rolls, divide dough in half, and roll it out into 2 circles. For hors d'oeuvre-sized rolls, make several small, thinner circles. Place a strip of ham at the wide end of each wedge of dough. (Incidentally, you can substitute frankfurters, sausages, etc., for the ham). Roll dough and ham toward pointed end. (Part of ham strips will be exposed as you work toward the point.) Place rolls, seam side down, about 2 inches apart on lightly-greased baking sheets. Brush rolls on tops and sides with melted bacon drippings or oil. Let rolls rise in warm place until double in bulk. Medium- to large-sized rolls will take about 20 minutes to rise at altitudes above 5,000 feet; about 30 minutes at altitudes below 5,000 feet. (Make certain ham is at room temperature. Cold ham will not allow the dough to rise as fast.) Bake rolls in oven preheated to 425° for about 20 minutes or until rolls are golden brown. Serve with sauce spooned over them. Makes 8 to 12 dinner- or luncheon-sized rolls.

Note: If you want to avoid last-minute preparation of the dough, it can be made in advance and refrigerated after the first rising period. When ready to use, remove from refrigerator, roll out, add ham, allow to rise until doubled in bulk, and bake.

SUPER BARBECUED RIBS

Baking starts with quite a bit of sauce but most of it is absorbed by the ribs, making the meat extra moist.

2 pounds meaty, country-style spareribs	½ cup vinegar
	1 cup pineapple juice
	⅓ cup brown sugar
1 small clove garlic, minced	1 teaspoon dry mustard
	2 tablespoons Worcestershire Sauce
1 can (8-ounce) tomato sauce	Thin slices onion
⅔ cup catsup	Thin slices lemon

Place ribs in a single layer on a rack in a shallow pan. Broil about 10 inches from source of heat until brown on all sides. Drain off grease. Remove rack from pan. Arrange ribs in a single layer in pan. Combine garlic, tomato sauce, catsup, vinegar, pineapple juice, brown sugar, mustard, and Worcestershire Sauce. Bring mixture to boiling point, stirring occasionally. Pour mixture over ribs. Arrange onion and lemon slices on top of ribs. Bake, uncovered, in oven preheated to 325° for about 1 hour or until sauce has thickened and most of it has been absorbed by ribs. Baste ribs frequently with sauce during baking period. (At altitudes above 5,000 feet, ribs will take up to 30 minutes longer to bake). 4 or 5 servings.

PORK CHOPS SUPREME

These chops need not be browned before baking them in their brandied sauce of heavy cream and fresh mushrooms.

8 strips bacon	2 cups whipping cream, unwhipped
8 center-cut, loin pork chops, trimmed of excess fat *or* 8 slices (about 2-inches thick) pork tenderloin	3 tablespoons flour
	¼ cup dry white wine
	3 tablespoons instant beef bouillon granules
¼ cup brandy	½ pound fresh mushrooms, sliced
Dry mustard	
Salt and pepper to taste	Parsley
	Cooked rice or noodles

Fry bacon until partially done but still pliable. (This is to remove excess grease.) Wrap a strip of bacon around outside edge of each pork chop. (Bacon strip probably won't extend all the way around chop.) Secure bacon to chop with wooden picks or skewers. Place chops in single layer in shallow, 9 x 13-inch baking dish. Drizzle brandy over chops. Sprinkle chops lightly with mustard (just shake mustard a couple of times over each chop). Sprinkle chops with salt and pepper. Bake, covered, in oven preheated to 350° for about 45 minutes or until chops are nearly done. Drain off drippings. Mix unwhipped cream with flour until smooth. Add wine and bouillon granules. Mix well, using wire whisk (but don't whip cream). Pour mixture over chops. Sprinkle mushrooms on top. Bake, covered, in oven preheated to 350° for about 15 minutes or until sauce is thickened and chops are done. (At altitudes below 5,000 feet, reduce first cooking period about 5 minutes.) Garnish with parsley. Serve with noodles or rice. 8 servings.

FRUIT STUFFED PORK CHOPS

Plumped pieces of dried fruit add zest to golden brown meat.

2 tablespoons butter or margarine

¼ cup finely-chopped onion

¼ cup finely-chopped celery

1 tablespoon minced parsley

Salt and pepper to taste

¼ teaspoon ground marjoram

1 cup soft, fairly-fine, whole-wheat bread crumbs (no crusts)

½ cup mixed dried fruit (apricots, prunes, etc.), cut in fine pieces

⅓ cup water

6 pork chops, cut about 1½-inches thick

Cooking oil

1 cup chicken broth

2 teaspoons cornstarch

Melt butter or margarine in medium-sized skillet over moderate heat. Add onion and celery. Sauté over moderately low heat until onion is transparent, stirring frequently. Add parsley, salt, pepper, marjoram, and bread. Mix well. Combine fruit and water and bring to full boil, stirring frequently. Add fruit and its liquid to bread mixture. Mix lightly but thoroughly. Using a sharp knife, make a lengthwise slit for a pocket on outside edge of each pork chop. Pack pockets with stuffing. Heat a small amount of cooking oil in a large skillet over moderate heat. Add chops, and cook over moderate heat until they are golden brown on both sides. Mix a small amount of broth with cornstarch until smooth. Heat remaining broth in a small pan over moderate heat. Add cornstarch mixture. Cook over moderate heat, stirring, until slightly thickened. Spoon broth mixture over pork chops. Simmer chops, covered, about 1 hour and 40 minutes or until done. (At altitudes below 5,000 feet, reduce cooking time about 15 minutes.) 6 servings.

ALL-PURPOSE REFRIGERATOR WHITE SAUCE MIX

This basic mix can be stored in the refrigerator for several weeks. It's always ready to thicken any type of liquid for sauces, casseroles, and soups of all kinds.

1 cup unsifted all-
purpose flour
4 teaspoons salt
3½ cups nonfat dry milk
granules

2 sticks (1 cup)
butter or margarine,
softened

In a medium bowl, mix together flour, salt, and dry milk granules. Using pastry blender, cut in butter or margarine until mixture resembles fine crumbs. Store in covered jar in refrigerator.

TO PREPARE SAUCE:

Using portions listed below, place mix in a heavy, medium-sized saucepan. Gradually add liquid (water, vegetable juice, broth, etc.). Cook over moderate heat, stirring constantly, until thickened. Season to taste with salt and pepper. Add mushrooms, shredded cheese, minced onions, seasonings, and other ingredients of your choice. Remember, shredded cheese will add additional thickening power so increase the amount of liquid for desired consistency.

Thin Sauce: Use ⅓ cup White Sauce Mix and 1 cup liquid, and follow preceding directions.

Medium Sauce: Use ⅔ cup White Sauce Mix and 1 cup liquid, and follow preceding directions.

Thick Sauce: Use 1 cup White Sauce Mix and 1 cup liquid, and follow preceding directions.

HAM-PINEAPPLE POMPONS

Leftover ham goes glamorous with pineapple slices. Serve the attractive mounds with a vegetable relish tray or cooked green vegetable.

2 cups cooked ground
ham
2 cups cooked rice
1 teaspoon prepared
horseradish
¼ cup finely-chopped
onion

½ cup finely-chopped
celery
1 egg, slightly beaten
¾ cup dairy sour cream
10 pineapple slices,
drained
Additional sour
cream (optional)

Combine ham and rice. Mix lightly but thoroughly. Add horseradish, onion, celery, egg, and sour cream. (If necessary, add more sour cream to hold ingredients together. Mixture should be fairly moist.) Mix lightly but thoroughly. Form ham mixture into 10 balls. Arrange pineapple slices in a single layer in a greased shallow pan. Place ham balls on top of pineapple slices. Bake, uncovered, in oven preheated to 450° for about 20 minutes or until hot. Serve with additional sour cream, if desired. 5 servings of 2 pompons each.

HAM-POULTRY LASAGNA MORNAY

Here's a way to use leftover ham and turkey for a special buffet-dinner casserole.

1 pound lasagna noodles	8 ounces (about) cooked turkey, sliced (or pieces enough to make a layer in a 9 x 13-inch baking dish)
½ stick (¼ cup) butter or margarine, melted	
⅓ cup chopped onion	
¼ cup flour	
1 teaspoon salt	8 ounces sliced Mozzarella cheese
¼ teaspoon pepper	
2 cups chicken broth	8 ounces (about) baked ham, thinly-sliced in about 3-inch squares (or pieces enough to make a layer in a 9 x 13-inch baking dish)
1 cup milk	
½ cup freshly-grated Romano cheese	
½ cup plus 2 tablespoons grated Parmesan cheese	
¼ cup dry sherry	½ pound fresh mushrooms, sliced
1 package (10-ounce) frozen asparagus pieces, thawed, uncooked, thoroughly drained	6 ounces sliced Provolone cheese
	Asparagus spears
	Paprika

Cook lasagna noodles according to package directions. Drain. Cover noodles with cold water. (This prevents noodles from sticking together while preparing remainder of recipe.) Melt butter or margarine in medium-sized saucepan over moderate heat. Add onion. Sauté over moderately low heat until onion is transparent. Add flour, salt, and pepper. Cook a few minutes over moderate heat, stirring. Gradually add broth and milk. Cook over moderate heat, stirring until thickened. Add Romano cheese, ½ cup of the Parmesan cheese, and sherry. Simmer, stirring occasionally, about 5 minutes or until thickened. Drain noodles. Grease bottom and sides of a 9 x 13-inch baking dish. Arrange a layer of noodles on bottom of pan. (Use the unbroken strips, and overlap them slightly. Repeat process when making remaining layers of noodles. The entire pound of noodles won't be used for this recipe.) Arrange asparagus pieces on top of noodles, then turkey slices, Mozzarella cheese, and ⅓ of the sauce. Add another layer of noodles, ham slices, mushrooms, Provolone cheese, and ⅓ of the sauce. Add another layer of noodles. Cover with remaining ⅓ of the sauce. Sprinkle with remaining 2 tablespoons Parmesan cheese. (Baking dish will be very full but don't worry; it won't run over.) Bake, uncovered, in oven preheated to 350° for about 45 minutes to 1 hour or until bubbly. Garnish with asparagus spears and sprinkle with paprika. Cut in squares with sharp knife to serve. (If assembled in advance, bring to room temperature before baking. Leftovers may be frozen and reheated, covered, in fairly hot oven.) 8 or more servings.

"CEC'S" HAM AND BEANS

A guy named Cecil, who also enjoys more Epicurean foods, has frequently requested this down-home dish since I first served it shortly after marrying him. A nutritious, main dish soup, it's delicious served with hot corn bread, slathered with butter, and drizzled with maple syrup. (There's a good corn bread recipe on page 106.)

2½ to 3 cups pinto beans, thoroughly washed	2½ to 3 cups diced ham or 6 to 8 meaty ham hock slices, trimmed of fat
5 cups water	Seasoned pepper to taste
1 medium onion, chopped	Salt to taste

(I have always cooked this in a pressure cooker, even before that appliance was touted as an energy-saver. The pressure cooker steam draws out a beautiful, thick broth from the beans and ham. It also eliminates the need for soaking the beans overnight.)

Put unsoaked beans, water, onion, and ham in a pressure cooker, at least 4-quart size. (If ham hocks are used, add the whole slices. At the end of pressure cooking period, remove and discard bones from hocks. Cut hocks in small pieces, and return to bean mixture.) At altitudes above 5,000 feet, cook mixture at 15 pounds pressure for 1 hour and 15 minutes. At altitudes below 5,000 feet cook mixture at 15 pounds pressure about 50 minutes. At any altitude, remove cooker from heat, and place it under a faucet of cold, running water to reduce pressure as fast as possible after cooking period. When cooker is completely cool, remove pressure control gauge and lid. The broth should be very thick and rich; in most cases, the beans will require further cooking. Add a generous amount of water so that mixture comes at least ¾ of the way up in the cooker. (During final cooking period, the liquid will thicken again.) Mix well. Add pepper and salt. Tightly cover cooker with its lid but do not add pressure control gauge. Cook over moderately low heat, stirring occasionally, until beans are done. Add more water, if desired, during final cooking period, and more pepper to taste. Serve in large soup bowls. (Leftovers will keep up to 3 days, if covered, in refrigerator. The mixture will thicken when refrigerated because the beans soak up the liquid. Thin with water to desired consistency when ready to reheat.) 8 to 10 servings.

GLAZES AND BASTING LIQUIDS FOR BAKED HAM

Whether you choose a cured ham, a "cook-before-eating" or "fully-cooked" ham, or any one of several other varieties available today, follow the wrapper directions for baking time and temperatures or consult a basic cookbook. The following mixtures will add glistening flavor to the rosy meat.

Carbonated Liquid Glaze

1½ cups packed brown sugar	2 cups pineapple juice
1 tablespoon dry mustard	2 cups diced, canned pineapple, drained
	Ginger ale
	Whole cloves

Mix together brown sugar and mustard. Gradually add pineapple juice. Mix until smooth. Add pineapple. Bake ham according to wrapper directions, placing ham on a rack even if not specified. Pour pineapple mixture over ham at the beginning of baking period. As pan drippings evaporate, add enough ginger ale to keep about ¼ inch of liquid in bottom of pan. Baste ham every 15 or 20 minutes with pan drippings. About 30 minutes before baking time is completed remove ham from oven, score ham fat in large crisscross pattern, making cuts about ⅛-inch deep; stud squares with cloves. Remove rack from pan. Place ham in direct contact with liquid. Bake about 30 minutes longer. This makes enough basting liquid for an 8 to 9 pound, boneless ham. Recipe may be cut in half for a 4 to 5 pound ham.

Brandied Ham

| Whole cloves | 1 cup lightly-packed |
| 1 cup brandy | brown sugar |

Bake ham according to wrapper directions. About 45 minutes before baking time is completed, remove pan from oven, score ham fat in large crisscross pattern, making cuts about ⅛-inch deep; stud squares with whole cloves. Pour off fat from roasting pan. Pour ½ cup of brandy over ham. Bake 30 minutes longer. Baste once with pan juices after 15 minutes. Remove ham from oven. Pour ¼ cup of the remaining brandy over it. Mix together remaining ¼ cup brandy and brown sugar; spread over top of ham. Bake about 15 minutes longer or until ham is glazed. Recipe makes enough basting liquid and glaze for a 5 to 6 pound ham.

Citrus Glaze

1 can (6-ounce) frozen orange juice, thawed and undiluted	1 tablespoon cornstarch
1 teaspoon dry mustard	
1 cup lightly-packed brown sugar	3 tablespoons butter

Heat orange juice in a medium-sized saucepan. Mix together sugar, cornstarch, and mustard; blend into orange juice. Cook mixture over moderate heat, stirring, until thickened. Remove from heat. Add butter. Mix until smooth. Bake ham according to wrapper directions. About 30 minutes before baking time is completed, remove ham from oven, score fat in large crisscross pattern, making cuts about ⅛-inch deep. Pour about ¼ cup of the glaze over ham. Bake about 30 minutes longer. Thin remaining glaze, if desired, with some of the pan drippings; serve as a sauce with slices of the ham. Recipe makes enough glaze and sauce for a 3 to 4 pound ham.

Quick, Glazed, Decorated Ham

Brown sugar	Canned pineapple rings,
Prepared Dijon-style	drained and cut in
mustard	halves
Whole cloves	Red or green
	maraschino cherries

Bake ham according to wrapper directions. Mix brown sugar with just enough mustard to make it of spreading consistency. The amount will vary, depending on size of ham. You'll want enough of the mixture to generously coat top of ham and to drizzle down sides. About 15 minutes before baking time is completed, remove ham from oven, score fat in large crisscross pattern, making cuts about ⅛-inch deep; spoon generous amount of brown sugar mixture over top of ham, and between cut portions. Stud squares with cloves. With wooden picks, secure pineapple semicircles in decorative pattern over top and sides of ham. Place a cherry in center of each semicircle. Spoon more of the brown sugar mixture over pineapple and cherries. Bake about 15 minutes longer.

GOURMET HAM SLICE

Cover a ham slice with a crown of delicious stuffing to make the meat go farther.

1 center slice ham, about 2-inches thick	2 tablespoons brown sugar
Whole cloves	1 tablespoon vinegar
1 can (1-pound, 4½-ounce) pineapple tidbits	½ of an 8-ounce package corn bread stuffing mix
1 tablespoon prepared mustard	¼ cup minced onion
	¼ cup minced celery

Stud sides of ham as desired with whole cloves. Place ham in shallow baking pan. Pour ¼ cup syrup from pineapple on ham. Drain remaining syrup from pineapple. Bake ham, covered, in oven preheated to 350° for about 30 minutes. Spread top with mustard. Arrange pineapple tidbits on top. Sprinkle with brown sugar. Drizzle with vinegar. Prepare stuffing mix according to package directions, adding onion and celery. Spoon stuffing on pineapple, pressing down lightly. Cover and bake 15 minutes. Uncover and bake 15 minutes longer or until lightly brown. About 8 servings.

HAM-HOMINY CASSEROLE

What a fast, appealing way to present leftover ham.

2 tablespoons butter or margarine	1¼ cups evaporated milk
2 tablespoons chopped green pepper	1 cup shredded, sharp Cheddar cheese
5 large, fresh mushrooms, sliced	2 cups hominy, drained
2 tablespoons minced, drained pimientos	Salt and pepper to taste
	2 to 3 cups cubed, cooked ham

Melt butter or margarine in a 9- or 10-inch skillet over moderate heat. Add green pepper and mushrooms. Cook over moderate heat, stirring, about 3 minutes. Add pimientos. In another pan, heat milk over moderate heat until steamy; remove from heat. Add cheese. Stir until cheese melts; add to mushroom mixture. Add hominy, salt, and pepper. Mix lightly but thoroughly. Spoon mixture into shallow, greased, 7 x 11-inch baking dish. Sprinkle ham on top. Bake, covered, in oven preheated to 350° for about 35 minutes or until bubbly. 4 to 6 servings.

HAM FURTERS

Too easy to be so good!

2 tablespoons cooking oil	1 slice precooked ham, about 1-inch thick
1 tablespoon lemon juice	6 frankfurter buns, toasted
1 teaspoon browning sauce for gravy	Horseradish (optional)
¼ teaspoon ginger	Pickle relish (optional)

Combine oil, lemon juice, browning sauce, and ginger. Score fat edge of ham to prevent curling during cooking. Brush both sides of ham generously with lemon mixture. Cook on grill over hot charcoal or under oven broiler 5 to 10 minutes on each side. Cut ham crosswise into strips, about 1¼-inches wide. Serve on frankfurter buns with horseradish and pickle relish, if desired. 6 servings.

SPICY PLUM SAUCE FOR BAKED HAM

Tired of the usual raisin sauce for ham? Then try this one.

1 can (1-pound, 14-ounce) purple plums	¼ teaspoon cinnamon
	⅛ teaspoon allspice
3 tablespoons corn-starch	2 tablespoons lemon juice
½ teaspoon salt	1 tablespoon butter

Drain plums, reserving syrup. Cut plums in halves, and remove pits. Combine cornstarch, salt, cinnamon, and allspice in medium-sized saucepan. Mix a small amount of plum syrup with cornstarch mixture until smooth. Add remaining plum syrup. Mix well. Cook over moderate heat, stirring, until thickened and clear. Add plum halves, lemon juice, and butter. Cook just until heated through. Serve over slices of baked ham. Makes about 3 cups sauce.

HAM-YAM SOUFFLÉS

A refreshing Honey-Lime Sauce adds a delicate finishing touch.

2 cups (about 1 pound) ground ham	2 tablespoons minced green pepper
1 cup mashed, cooked yams	2 egg yolks, beaten
½ cup evaporated milk	2 egg whites, stiffly beaten
¼ cup finely-chopped onion	Honey-Lime Sauce

Combine ham, yams, evaporated milk, onion, green pepper, and yolks. Fold in stiffly-beaten egg whites. Spoon into 6 greased custard cups (6-ounce size). Place in pan containing about ½ inch of hot water. Bake, uncovered, in oven preheated to 350° for about 30 minutes or until puffy and brown. Serve with Honey-Lime Sauce. 6 servings.

Honey-Lime Sauce

¼ cup lime juice	1 tablespoon butter
1 tablespoon corn- starch	1 tablespoon grated lime rind
¾ cup honey	

In a small pan, mix lime juice and cornstarch until smooth; add to honey; cook over moderate heat, stirring, until thickened. Stir in butter and lime rind. Serve with Ham-Yam Soufflés. Makes about 1 cup of sauce.

HAM-IT-UP CASSEROLE

A lot of good taste from a little recipe.

2 cups elbow macaroni, cooked according to package directions and drained	½ cup finely-chopped onion
1 cup (about ¼ pound) diced, cooked ham	¼ cup sliced, pimiento-stuffed olives
1 cup diced, cooked turkey or chicken	1 cup dairy sour cream 1 cup milk Salt and pepper to taste
1 cup (about 4 ounces) shredded Swiss cheese	¼ teaspoon dry mustard Additional olive slices for garnish

Combine macaroni, ham, turkey, cheese, onion, and olives. Mix lightly but thoroughly. In another bowl, thoroughly mix sour cream, milk, salt, pepper, and mustard. Combine macaroni and sour cream mixtures. Mix lightly but thoroughly. Spoon mixture into lightly greased 1½-quart round casserole. Bake, uncovered, in oven preheated to 375° for about 25 minutes or until bubbly. Garnish with additional olive slices. 4 servings.

BAKED CANADIAN BACON WITH ORANGE SAUCE

Enjoy your guests while this treat is baking for brunch.

1 pound Canadian bacon, cut in 12 slices
6 thin onion slices
6 orange slices, rind removed
2 teaspoons sugar
1 tablespoon cornstarch
1 cup orange juice
1 medium orange, peeled and cut in small pieces
2 teaspoons grated orange rind

Arrange 6 slices of the bacon in greased, shallow, 7 x 11-inch baking dish. Top each bacon slice with an onion and orange slice. Add another slice of bacon. Bake, covered, in oven preheated to 300° for about 30 minutes. Combine sugar and cornstarch in a small pan. Add orange juice. Mix until smooth. Bring to boil, reduce heat, and cook over moderate heat, stirring, until thickened. Add orange sections and orange rind. Serve sauce over baked Canadian bacon. 6 servings.

POULTRY

Poultry is probably just as welcome today as it was when our ancestors bagged wild turkeys in the woods, not as a sport but out of necessity, and farmers' wives depended on part of the barnyard chicken brood to feed their families. In fact, chicken and turkey are such popular American foods, it is difficult to suggest a brand new way to present them at the dinner table, but over the years there have been many cooking procedures developed to help "put a chicken in every pot."

While poultry prices might rise right along with those of other grocery items, chicken and turkey can still fit comfortably into most budgets. Whether it's family-style fried chicken or "Poulet Sauté au Vin Blanc" (better known as chicken sautéed with white wine), a cross section of prized poultry recipes are included in this section. Some use "from-scratch" cooking techniques, while others use convenience foods, such as canned or frozen fruits and vegetables, as short cuts. Turkey and chicken can be used interchangeably in some of the recipes, and many are well suited for economical entertaining.

ORANGE ROASTED CHICKEN

This chicken emerges from the oven succulent and fragrant with the flavors of orange juice, honey, and soy sauce used in its baste.

1	roasting chicken or capon (3½ to 5 pounds)		Cooking oil
1	teaspoon salt	1	medium onion, cut in thick slices
¼	teaspoon pepper	1	medium, unpeeled orange, cut in half
1	teaspoon garlic powder	1	cup orange juice
1	teaspoon paprika	¼	cup honey
		2	tablespoons soy sauce

Remove giblets from chicken. (Save giblets for gravy or use in casseroles, etc. Use Cooked Turkey Giblets recipe, page 165, as a guide for cooking them.) Wash and thoroughly dry chicken with paper toweling. Mix together salt, pepper, garlic powder, and paprika. Add just enough cooking oil to make the mixture into a paste consistency. Rub mixture on all outside surfaces of chicken. Tuck onion slices and orange into cavity of chicken. Place chicken, breast side up, on a rack in a shallow roasting pan and put, uncovered, in oven preheated to 325° for about 15 minutes. (This brief roasting period helps to "set" the seasoned oil on the bird.) Combine orange juice, honey, and soy sauce. Mix well. Remove chicken from oven. Pour orange juice mixture over chicken. Make a "tent" by creasing the center of a piece of foil large enough to cover chicken. Place tent loosely over chicken so that heat can circulate around it. Insert meat thermometer through foil into thickest part of thigh. Return chicken to 325° oven. Baste chicken several times during baking with orange juice drippings in pan. If necessary, remove foil tent during last 30 minutes of baking time so chicken will brown. Roast until drumstick moves easily and meat thermometer registers 190°, allowing about 25 minutes per pound baking time. Let chicken "rest" about 15 minutes. Remove and discard onion and orange from cavity before carving chicken. Yields about 6 servings, depending on size of chicken. (Allow from ¾ to 1 pound of uncooked chicken for each serving.)

MILLIONAIRE CHICKEN

Combine a Chinese recipe with a Mexican one for a mixture that's "worth a million" in attracting tastes.

3 tablespoons cooking oil
2 medium green onions and tops, sliced
½ teaspoon ginger
¼ teaspoon szechuan pepper (Chinese pepper available in Oriental sections of groceries) *or* cayenne pepper to taste
¼ teaspoon red pepper (not cayenne)
¼ cup soy sauce
2 tablespoons honey
1 medium clove garlic, crushed

½ teaspoon salt or to taste
2 cups (about) bite-size pieces of cooked chicken
1 package (6-ounce) frozen snow peas, cooked just until crisp-tender and drained or the equivalent in fresh, cooked snow peas
8 flour tortillas, wrapped in foil and heated in 200° oven until warm
1 small head lettuce, shredded

Heat oil over moderate heat in a 9- or 10-inch skillet. Add onion, ginger, szechuan or cayenne pepper, and red pepper. (For a less spicy flavor, reduce the amounts of szechuan or cayenne pepper, but, remember, the flavor of the finished dish will be toned down by the shredded lettuce, tortillas, and snow peas.) Sauté onion mixture over moderate heat, stirring frequently, until onion is transparent. Add soy sauce, honey, garlic, and salt. Mix well. Add chicken and snow peas. Mix well to glaze chicken and peas with honey mixture. Spoon chicken mixture into a serving dish. Arrange lettuce and tortillas on a platter. Let each person place portions of lettuce and chicken mixture on a tortilla. Roll tortilla, and eat with your hands. 4 servings.

GOUGÈRE WITH POULTRY

This version of a French Burgundian pastry crust filled with a vegetable mixture will fascinate guests and is easy to make, even though the directions may appear complicated.

1½ sticks (¾ cup) butter or margarine	broccoli, may be substituted)
2 medium onions, sliced, then sliced again in halves	5 medium tomatoes
	2 cups bite-size pieces of cooked chicken or turkey
½ pound fresh mushrooms, sliced	Salt and pepper to taste
2 medium zucchini squash, unpeeled, quartered, and sliced (other vegetables of your choice, such as	1 cup water
	1 cup unsifted flour
	4 extra-large eggs
	4 ounces shredded Gruyere or Swiss cheese

Melt ½ stick of the butter or margarine in a heavy, large pan over moderate heat. Add onions, mushrooms, and zucchini. Sauté over moderately low heat, stirring frequently, until onions are transparent. Cut 4 of the tomatoes in halves. Gently but firmly squeeze out as many seeds as possible from these tomatoes, holding each half in palm of hand. (The reason for seeding the tomatoes is to eliminate excess liquid in the filling.) Slice and reserve remaining tomato. Cut seeded tomatoes in fairly large chunks. Add tomato chunks, chicken or turkey, salt, and pepper to mushroom mixture. Mix gently but thoroughly. Cover mixture, and keep it warm over very low heat.

(This mixture may be made in advance and refrigerated, but do not add the tomatoes. When ready to use, add the tomatoes, and heat until warm before placing it in pastry-lined bowl.) For pastry, place remaining butter or margarine and water in heavy, medium-sized pan; bring to boil. Remove from heat. Add flour, all at once. Return to low heat and stir with wooden spoon until dough leaves sides of pan. Remove from heat. Add eggs, one at a time, mixing well after each addition with wire whisk. Dough will be very sticky, but keep stirring until it is smooth. Add about ¾ of the cheese. Mix well. Press pastry over bottom and part way up sides of ungreased, 2-quart, round casserole dish. Pastry should extend up the sides only about 1½ inches or less than half way. Mound chicken mixture in center of pastry. (There may appear to be too much filling, but the pastry will rise to the top of the casserole and the filling will shrink.) Bake, uncovered, in oven preheated to 400° for 30 minutes or until pastry is puffy and starts to get golden around edges. Arrange reserved tomato slices on top of casserole. Sprinkle with remaining cheese. Bake about 10 minutes longer or until pastry is brown around edges. At altitudes below 5,000 feet, reduce both cooking periods to about 25 minutes and 5 minutes, respectively. (Pastry will puff up into an interesting, irregular shape around filling.) 6 servings.

CHICKEN EN PAPILLOTE

You don't have to clean the oven or scour a sticky roasting pan when broiler halves are cooked in an oiled paper bag. They emerge from the oven a beautiful golden brown.

2 broiler chicken halves (about 1½ pounds each) Shortening	Cream-style French dressing Salt and pepper to taste Paprika

Wash chicken, remove extra-fatty portions, and pat thoroughly dry with paper toweling. Have ready a heavy, large, brown paper grocery bag. Using fingers, grease entire inside of bag with light layer of solid shortening. (This isn't as messy as it sounds.) Generously brush only the skin side of chicken with French dressing. Sprinkle chicken with salt and pepper, then generously sprinkle it with paprika. Lay bag on one of its largest sides on counter. Slip chicken halves into it, skin sides up. Do not allow chicken halves to touch each other or the top of bag. Close end of bag with double fold and secure with paper clips. Place bag, with chicken halves still skin sides up, on baking sheet. (This is necessary to catch any drippings that seep through bag.) Bake in oven preheated to 325° for about 3 hours for altitudes above 5,000 feet; about 2 hours for altitudes below 5,000 feet. In either case, test for doneness after 2 hour's baking time. Drumsticks should move easily when chicken is done. (Chicken browns fairly fast, so don't let this serve as a guide for doneness.) 2 to 4 servings.

POULTRY, MAC-CHEESE CASSEROLE

Don't turn up your nose at the canned macaroni and cheese here: It's the secret ingredient that makes this recipe a standout.

4 cups (about) coarsely-cut, cooked turkey or chicken	2 ounces (about) slivered almonds
2 cans (14-ounce each) macaroni and cheese	1½ cups shredded Cheddar cheese
1 cup sliced, fresh mushrooms	2 cans (10¾-ounce each) cream of chicken soup
1 can (8-ounce) water chestnuts, drained and sliced	1 cup packaged, herb-seasoned stuffing mix
	6 tablespoons butter or margarine, melted

Combine chicken, macaroni and cheese, mushrooms, water chestnuts, almonds, 1 cup of the cheese, and soup. (Reserve a few mushrooms for garnish.) Mix well. Spoon mixture into greased, shallow, 9 x 13-inch baking dish. Sprinkle remaining ½ cup cheese on top. Sauté stuffing over moderate heat in melted butter or margarine, stirring frequently, just until golden colored. Spoon stuffing on top of casserole. Garnish with reserved mushrooms. Bake, uncovered, in oven preheated to 350° for about 30 minutes or until bubbly. (At altitudes below 5,000 feet, slightly less baking time will be required.) This casserole can be made in advance, left uncooked, and refrigerated or frozen. When ready to use, bring to room temperature before baking. (It reheats nicely, too.) 10 to 12 servings.

ORIENTAL PEAR-POULTRY SAUTÉ

Oriental food has a big following in the Rocky Mountain West, really catching on "out here" during the past fifteen years. Time was, however, when our home cooks weren't all that familiar with the nutritious stir-fry technique. For example, in the late 1950's, the word *wok* had to be defined in the *Denver Post* food columns, or we would have been bombarded with "what's that?" letters.

3	tablespoons cooking oil	½	pound fresh snow peas
2	whole chicken breasts, skinned, boned, and cut in about ¾ -inch pieces	2	medium, fresh pears, unpeeled and cut in fairly thick slices
½	cup celery, sliced diagonally in pieces about ¼ -inch wide	1	tablespoon cornstarch
		1	teaspoon sugar
3	medium, green onions and a few of their tops, thinly sliced	3	tablespoons soy sauce or to taste
		1	cup rich chicken broth
1	can (8½ -ounce) bamboo shoots, drained and sliced		Salt to taste
		½	cup cashew nuts
			Cooked rice

Heat oil over moderate heat in wok or large skillet. Add chicken. Cook over moderate heat, stirring frequently, until chicken is almost done. Add celery, onion, bamboo shoots, and pea pods. Cook over moderate heat, stirring constantly, about 4 minutes. Add pears. Mix lightly but thoroughly. Have ready cornstarch which has been mixed with sugar, soy sauce, chicken broth, and salt until smooth. Add cornstarch mixture to chicken mixture. Cook over moderate heat, stirring constantly, until sauce is thickened and clear. Sprinkle mixture with cashews. Serve with rice. 4 to 6 servings.

SHERRIED, STEWED CHICKEN

This dish is a complete departure from the old-fashioned kind of stewed chicken that emerges from the kettle as pale as when it was uncooked. Here, the bird is browned before it goes into sherry-flavored liquid that thickens itself.

1 frying chicken (about 2½ pounds), cut in serving pieces, *or* the equivalent in chicken parts	3 medium carrots, sliced
	½ cup sliced celery
	2 green onions and tops, sliced
Biscuit mix	2 medium bay leaves
1 stick (½ cup) margarine	2 tablespoons Parmesan cheese
2 tablespoons solid shortening	1 teaspoon dry parsley flakes
2½ cups water	Rice or mashed potatoes
½ cup cream sherry	

Wash chicken. Drain off excess water but do not dry chicken. Roll chicken in biscuit mix, then with fingertips press more mix on both sides of chicken (as much as will stick to it.) The chicken should be well coated with mix since it thickens the cooking liquid that is used later for gravy. Melt margarine and shortening in Dutch oven. Add chicken, and brown on all sides. Remove chicken from pan. Add water, sherry, carrots, celery, onions, bay leaves, cheese, and parsley to drippings. Mix well, scraping brown bits that stick to bottom of pan into liquid. Return chicken to pan, placing larger pieces on bottom. Bring to boiling point, reduce heat, and simmer slowly, tightly covered, about 1 hour or until chicken is done. Remove chicken from gravy. Refrigerate gravy until fat rises to top. Skim off fat. Add chicken to gravy and reheat to serving temperature. Serve with rice or mashed potatoes. 4 servings.

ROAST TURKEY BREAST WITH BRANDIED CRANBERRIES

Of course, this juicy mound of meat can be served without the cranberries, but they do add a delectable, festive touch. The unusual baked berries can even be served for dessert.

1 uncooked turkey breast (4 to 6 pounds), thawed if frozen	Melted butter, margarine, or cooking oil
	Brandied Cranberries (optional)

Place turkey breast, skin side up, on rack in shallow pan. Generously brush breast with melted butter, margarine, or oil. Make a "tent" by creasing the center of a piece of foil large enough to cover breast. Cover breast loosely with the tent so that heat can circulate. Roast in oven preheated to 325° until done, allowing about 30 minutes to the pound. Test for doneness by inserting a meat thermometer into thickest part of breast so tip doesn't touch bone. Meat thermometer should register about 185°. Remove tent during last 40 minutes of roasting time if breast needs to brown. 10 to 12 servings.

Brandied Cranberries ·

4 cups fresh cranberries	2 cups sugar
	⅓ cup brandy

Combine cranberries, sugar, and brandy. Mix well. Place mixture in 9 x 13-inch baking dish. Cover with foil. Bake in oven preheated to 300° for about 1 hour. Refrigerate until cool or serve warm, if desired, for a different twist. Serve as an accompaniment to poultry, ham, or pork roast. The cranberries also make a delicious warm or cold topping for vanilla ice cream. Leftover reheats nicely. Makes about 4 cups.

CHICKEN OR TURKEY WITH BROCCOLI

Fresh broccoli or frozen, French-style green beans will vary the flavor and the preparation time of this recipe, which is bound to be repeated.

½ pound fresh broccoli *or* 1 package (10-ounce) frozen French-style green beans	1 can (10¾-ounce) cream of celery soup
	½ cup milk
	¼ cup hot water or chicken broth
Packaged corn bread stuffing crumbs (about 2¼ cups)	1 large rib celery, chopped
3 cups (about) coarsely-cut, cooked, chicken or turkey	¼ cup chopped onion
	Butter or margarine

Trim broccoli, discarding coarse stem ends and leaves. Cut stems of broccoli in small pieces. Separate flowerettes into small clumps. Pour about ¾ cup water into a medium-sized pan. Bring to boil, add broccoli stems, reduce heat, and simmer, covered, until stems are tender but still crisp. Add broccoli flowerettes during the last few minutes of cooking time. Thoroughly drain broccoli. If beans are used, thaw them just enough to separate them. (Frozen, thawed, chopped broccoli may also be used.) Sprinkle ⅔ cup of the dry corn bread stuffing crumbs over bottom of well-greased, 7 x 11-inch baking dish. Arrange chicken or turkey in an even layer over crumbs. Arrange broccoli or beans in an even layer over poultry. Mix together soup and milk until smooth, spoon evenly over vegetable. Thoroughly mix together hot water or broth and 1½ cups corn bread stuffing crumbs. Add celery and onion to stuffing mixture. Spoon stuffing mixture over soup mixture. Generously dot top of casserole with butter or margarine. Bake, uncovered, in oven preheated to 400° for about 30 minutes or until top is golden brown and mixture is bubbly. (At altitudes below 5,000 feet, casserole should be ready in about 20 minutes.) 4 to 6 servings.

PEEKABOO CHICKEN

Broth from cooked chicken is put to good use in this dining delight, which makes a hearty meal when served with a fruit salad and green vegetable. It's a budget-pleaser, too.

2 frying chickens (about 3 pounds each), cut in serving pieces *or* the equivalent in your favorite chicken parts	1 package (8-ounce) herb-seasoned stuffing mix
	½ cup chopped celery
	½ cup chopped onion
	1 stick (½ cup) butter or margarine
2 medium ribs celery with leaves	½ cup flour
	6 eggs, slightly beaten
1 medium onion, quartered	Mushroom Sauce (optional)
1 medium bay leaf	
Salt and pepper to taste	

Place chicken in large kettle. Add enough water to barely cover pieces. Add celery, onions, bay leaf, salt, and pepper. Bring to boil, reduce heat. Skim off residue that floats on top of water during first part of cooking period.

Simmer, covered, until chicken is tender. Remove chicken from broth. Strain broth, and discard vegetables and bay leaf. Refrigerate broth until fat rises to top. Remove and discard fat. Remove skin and bones from chicken. Cut chicken meat into bite-size pieces. (All of this can be done a day in advance of serving, if desired, but refrigerate broth and chicken pieces in separate containers.)

Prepare stuffing mix according to package directions, but add the ½ cup chopped celery and ½ cup chopped onion to hot liquid used for stuffing. If desired, some of the reserved broth may be used to substitute for water in preparing stuffing mix, but save at least 4 cups of the broth to use later in this recipe. Spread stuffing in greased, shallow, 9 x 13-inch baking dish. Place chicken pieces evenly on stuffing. Melt butter in fairly large pan over moderate heat. Add flour. Stir a few minutes over moderate heat, gradually adding 4 cups of the reserved chicken broth. (If there is not enough broth, add canned chicken broth to make 4 cups.) Cook over moderate heat, stirring, until thickened. Remove from heat. Stir a small amount of hot broth mixture into beaten eggs. Add egg mixture to remaining broth stirring constantly until smooth; season with salt and pepper. Pour sauce over chicken. Bake, uncovered, in oven preheated to 325° about 1 hour or until knife inserted in center comes out clean. (Mixture will puff up and may look like it is going to drip over edges of baking dish, but the eggs will hold it together and prevent this.) Let stand about 5 minutes. Cut in squares to serve. Serve with Mushroom Sauce, if desired. 8 to 10 servings.

Mushroom Sauce

1 cup dairy sour cream	Minced pimiento to
1 can (10¾-ounce)	taste
mushroom soup	Chopped parsley to
¼ cup milk	taste

Mix together sour cream, soup, and milk until smooth. Cook over moderate heat, stirring frequently, until hot but not boiling. Add pimiento and parsley. Makes about 3 cups sauce.

CHICKEN SALTIMBOCCA

The traditional Italian dish called Saltimbocca alla Romana is made with veal, prosciutto ham, fresh sage, and white wine. Here's the poor man's answer to it (and a delicious one).

3 whole chicken breasts, skinned, boned, and halved
6 wafer-thin slices boiled ham, 3½ x 3½ inches
6 slices Mozzarella cheese, about 3-inches long, 1½-inches wide, and ¼-inch thick
1 medium, unpeeled tomato, cut in very small pieces
½ teaspoon ground sage
⅓ cup fine, dry Italian-style bread crumbs
2 tablespoons grated Parmesan cheese
2 tablespoons dried parsley flakes
½ stick (¼ cup) butter or margarine, melted
Cream Sauce (optional)

Place chicken, boned sides up, on cutting surface. Place a piece of plastic wrap over each piece of chicken. Working from center out, pound chicken lightly with meat pounder to flatten each piece to a square shape, about 5 x 5 inches. (They won't be perfect squares but don't worry about that. Use your fingers to press chicken into shape and push together any tears.) The chicken pieces also can be flattened with a rolling pin: cover them with plastic wrap and roll from center out. Place a slice of ham on each piece of chicken. Place a slice of Mozzarella cheese in center of ham. Sprinkle cheese with some of the tomato pieces and sage. Bring sides of chicken up and over filling, jelly-roll style. Firmly tuck in all ends, pressing them together to seal well. (If filling starts to fall out, just tuck it back in. There is no need to use skewers to fasten seams if they are firmly pressed together.) Combine crumbs, Parmesan cheese, and parsley. Dip chicken rolls in melted butter or margarine, then roll in crumb mixture until thoroughly coated. (Hold them firmly while rolling in crumb mixture. If they come apart, just press back together.) Place rolls, seam sides down, in greased, shallow, close-fitting baking dish. (Their sides should touch.) Bake, uncovered, in oven preheated to 350° about 45 minutes or until golden brown. Serve plain or with Cream Sauce, if desired. Rolls may also be sliced and served cold as hors d'oeuvres, speared with wooden picks. 6 servings as a main dish.

Cream Sauce

2 tablespoons butter or margarine
2 tablespoons flour
1 cup half-and-half cream
Salt to taste
¼ teaspoon nutmeg (optional)
2 teaspoons lemon juice

Melt butter or margarine. Add flour. Stir a few minutes over moderate heat. Gradually add cream. Cook over moderate heat, stirring constantly, until thickened. Add salt, nutmeg, and lemon juice. Mix well. Makes about 1 cup sauce.

HONEY-GLAZED CHICKEN

The mustard mixture makes a delicious glaze for a whole roasted chicken, too.

1 can (20-ounce) sliced pineapple	¼ cup Dijon-style mustard
1 frying chicken (about 3 pounds), cut in quarters	¼ cup honey
	1 tablespoon sesame seeds

Add just enough pineapple liquid to barely cover bottom of shallow, 9 x 13-inch baking dish. Arrange pineapple slices in dish. Top with chicken, skin sides down. Combine mustard, honey, and sesame seeds; drizzle over chicken. Bake, uncovered, in oven preheated to 375° for 30 minutes. Turn chicken. Brush with pan drippings. Continue to bake until chicken is done. 2 to 4 servings.

DEEP DISH YAM-TURKEY CASSEROLE

Leftover turkey pieces are nested in a velvety yam "crust."

2 cans (16-ounce each) yams, drained, or 4 medium-sized, fresh yams, cooked and peeled	1 egg, slightly beaten
	1 cup sliced celery
	1 medium onion, chopped
5 tablespoons butter or margarine	3 cups bite-size pieces of cooked turkey
¼ teaspoon salt	1 can (10¾-ounce) cream of celery soup
¼ teaspoon poultry seasoning	

Beat yams with three tablespoons of the butter or margarine until smooth. Add salt, poultry seasoning, and egg. Mix well. Spread mixture evenly on bottom and about 2 inches up sides of greased, round, 1½-quart casserole dish. Melt remaining butter or margarine over moderate heat. Add celery and onion. Sauté over moderate heat, stirring frequently, until onion is transparent. Add turkey and soup. Mix well. Heat until very warm, stirring occasionally. Spoon turkey mixture into yam shell. Bake, uncovered, in oven preheated to 350° for about 45 minutes, or until bubbly. 4 servings.

MAKE-AHEAD SPINACH POULTRY BAKE

Have this casserole ready to pop in the oven for brunch, luncheon, or dinner.

1 stick (½ cup) butter or margarine	1 package (10¾-ounce) frozen chopped spinach, thawed, thoroughly drained, then squeezed as dry as possible with hands
2 tablespoons minced onion or to taste	
2 chicken bouillon cubes, crushed	
1¾ cups buttermilk	
2 cups (about 8 ounces) shredded, mild Cheddar cheese	8 standard-size slices slightly-dry white bread, trimmed of crusts, cut into cubes
4 extra-large eggs	
⅛ teaspoon cayenne pepper	2 cups bite-size pieces of cooked turkey or chicken
¼ teaspoon garlic salt	
Salt and pepper to taste	

Melt butter. Add onion and bouillon. Stir a few minutes over moderate heat. Add ½ of the buttermilk, cheese, and continue stirring over moderately low heat until cheese melts. Beat together eggs and remaining buttermilk. Add cayenne pepper, garlic salt, salt, pepper, and spinach. Combine cheese mixture, buttermilk-egg mixture, bread cubes, and turkey or chicken. Mix well. Spoon mixture into greased, round, 1½-quart casserole. Cover and refrigerate overnight. Before baking, let casserole stand about 15 minutes at room temperature. Set casserole in a larger pan that has about 1 inch of hot water in it. Bake, uncovered, in oven preheated to 350° for about 1 hour and 20 minutes or until lightly tinged with brown on top. 6 or more servings.

HOT TURKEY SALAD IN PASTRY SHELLS

The bonus in this combination? An old-fashioned pastry recipe that makes flaky pie crust, too.

½ cup mayonnaise	3 medium ribs celery, thinly sliced
1 can (10¾-ounce) cream of chicken soup	3 hard-cooked eggs, coarsely chopped
1 small clove garlic, minced	6 baked Extra-Rich Pastry Shells (about 4-inches top diam-
½ cup sliced almonds	eter, 2-inches bottom
2 tablespoons lemon juice	diameter, 2-inches deep)
2 cups bite-size pieces of cooked turkey or chicken	Paprika Parsley

Thoroughly mix together mayonnaise, soup, garlic, almonds, and lemon juice in heavy, medium-sized pan. Add turkey or chicken and celery. Cook, covered, over moderate heat until hot. Add eggs. Mix lightly but thoroughly. Spoon mixture into baked pastry shells, which should be at room temperature. Garnish with paprika and parsley. 6 servings.

Note: Turkey mixture may also be baked as a casserole. In this case, omit pastry shells. Sprinkle about 1 cup crushed potato chips in greased, shallow, 7 x 11-inch casserole dish. Spoon turkey mixture over chips and sprinkle with about 1 more cup of crushed potato chips. Bake, uncovered, in oven preheated to 450° for about 20 minutes or until bubbly.

Extra-Rich Pastry Shells

2 cups unsifted all-purpose flour	¾ cup lard
¾ teaspoon salt	¼ to ½ cup cold water

Mix together flour and salt in a bowl. Using a pastry blender, cut in lard until mixture resembles coarse crumbs. Sprinkle water over mixture, 1 tablespoon at a time, mixing with fork after each addition. Add just enough water for pastry to hold together. (At altitudes above 5,000 feet, it may be necessary to add the entire amount of water since moisture evaporates quickly at high altitudes.) Gather pastry into a ball. Roll out pastry to about ⅛-inch thickness on lightly-floured surface or between sheets of foil or waxed paper. (The latter method avoids adding more flour, which toughens pastry.) Remove top foil or paper. Cut pastry in circles to fit tart tins, allowing about ½ inch of pastry to extend above tops of tins since pastry will shrink during baking. Prick pastry in several places on bottom of tins with fork tines. Bake in oven preheated to 400° until golden brown. (Extra tart shells may be frozen. Use fluted tart tins for a fancier showing. This pastry also makes enough for a double-crust, 9-inch pie.) Makes 8 to 12 muffin-pan-size tarts.

CHICKEN BREAST, CHICAGO STYLE

About ten years ago, a Chicago restaurateur shared this, one of his favorite recipes, with me. It assumes a "Veronique" air when seedless grapes are added.

4 whole chicken breasts, boned, skinned, and cut in half
Flour seasoned with salt and pepper
3 tablespoons butter
3 tablespoons cooking oil
½ pound fresh mushrooms, sliced
1 teaspoon minced, dried chives
1 tablespoon flour

½ cup dry white wine
1¼ cups half-and-half cream
Dried leaf tarragon to taste
Seasoned salt to taste
1 cup halved seedless grapes (optional)
8 thin slices of toast, trimmed of crusts
8 large mushroom caps, lightly sautéed in butter

Dredge chicken on all sides with seasoned flour. Heat butter and oil over moderate heat in a large skillet. Add chicken. Cook chicken over moderate heat until golden brown on all sides. Remove chicken from skillet. Drain off all but 2 tablespoons drippings from skillet. Heat remaining drippings over moderate heat. Add mushrooms and chives. Cook a few minutes over moderate heat, stirring to coat mushrooms with drippings. Sprinkle flour into skillet; combine with mushroom mixture until thoroughly mixed. Add wine, cream, tarragon, and seasoned salt. Mix well. Add chicken breasts. Bring mixture just to boiling point, reduce heat, and simmer, covered, just until chicken is tender, about 20 minutes. If desired, stir grapes into sauce just before serving. Serve breasts on toast slices with sauce poured over them. Garnish with mushroom caps. 4 very generous servings.

CHICKEN OR TURKEY FRICASSEE

During the past two decades, this dandy dish has been a potluck favorite in western Kansas, where pheasants are plentiful and housewives know some of the best ways to cook them. Originally using cooked pieces of pheasant, this recipe was easily converted using chunks of turkey or chicken.

3 tablespoons butter margarine	3 extra-large eggs, beaten
1 medium onion, chopped	1 can (10¾-ounce) mushroom soup
1½ cups chopped celery	1½ cups shredded American or Cheddar cheese
4 cups bite-size pieces of cooked turkey or chicken (amount of poultry can be varied to suit taste)	1 box (8-ounce) Ritz crackers, rolled into fine crumbs
4 cups rich chicken or turkey broth or 2 cans (14-ounce each) chicken broth	½ teaspoon salt
	½ teaspoon pepper

Melt butter or margarine in large, heavy pan over moderate heat. Add onion and celery; sauté over moderate heat, stirring frequently, until onion is transparent. Add poultry, broth, eggs, and soup. Mix well. Add cheese, cracker crumbs, salt, and pepper. Mix well. Spoon mixture into greased, shallow, 9 x 13-inch casserole. Bake, uncovered, in oven preheated to 350° for about 1 hour or until bubbly. 12 servings.

LEMON-GRILLED CHICKEN

Long a flavor-friend of chicken, lemon does wondrous things here.

¾ cup cooking oil	Dash powered thyme
½ cup lemon juice	Dash poultry
1 tablespoon grated	seasoning
onion	1 frying chicken (about
½ teaspoon salt	2½ pounds),
½ teaspoon paprika	quartered
¼ teaspoon pepper	Lemon slices

Blend together oil, lemon juice, onion, salt, paprika, pepper, thyme, and poultry seasoning. Place chicken in shallow, close-fitting dish. Pour lemon mixture over chicken. Cover and refrigerate 8 to 12 hours, turning chicken occasionally. Drain chicken, reserving marinade. Broil chicken in oven or on charcoal grill until done. Baste frequently with marinade. Top each chicken piece with a lemon slice during last few minutes of cooking time. 4 servings.

Note: The same marinade can be used for other baked or broiled chicken and turkey parts.

CHICKEN BREASTS IN ONION CREAM SAUCE

This recipe takes a short cut by using a packaged gravy mix.

½ stick (¼ cup) butter	2 tablespoons tomato
or margarine	paste
3 whole chicken	2 tablespoons sherry
breasts, skinned,	1 can (3-ounce) mush-
boned, and halved	room slices, drained
1 envelope (1-ounce)	½ cup half-and-half
onion gravy mix	cream
1 cup chicken broth	

Melt butter or margarine. Add chicken breasts and brown lightly on both sides. Remove chicken from skillet. Stir dry gravy mix into drippings. Blend in broth, tomato paste, and sherry. Stir until well blended. Heat until bubbly. Return chicken to skillet. Add mushrooms. Simmer, covered, about 30 minutes or until chicken is tender. Remove chicken to serving platter. Stir cream into sauce. Heat and pour over chicken. 6 servings.

STUFFED GROUND TURKEY

Uncooked, ground turkey (available at most meat counters) tends to be dry unless it's given special treatment, as in this recipe.

2 tablespoons butter or margarine	2 eggs, slightly beaten
2 medium ribs celery, minced	1 can (10¾-ounce) chicken broth
¼ cup chopped onion	1½ pounds uncooked ground turkey
10 slices dry bread with crusts, broken into small pieces	⅓ cup evaporated milk
½ cup raisins	1 can (10¾-ounce) cream of chicken soup diluted with
1 teaspoon salt	½ soup can of evaporated milk
¼ teaspoon pepper	
1½ teaspoons sage	
½ teaspoon cinnamon	

Melt butter or margarine in large, heavy pan. Add celery and onion. Sauté over moderate heat until onion is transparent. Add bread pieces, raisins, salt, pepper, sage, and cinnamon. Mix well. Add eggs and chicken broth. Mix well. Let stand until bread absorbs any liquid in bottom of bowl. Stir occasionally. Mix with hands until stuffing holds together in a ball. Combine turkey, ⅓ cup evaporated milk, and additional salt and pepper to taste. Divide turkey mixture into 6 equal portions. With hands, press out each portion on waxed paper into a thin patty. Place an equal amount of stuffing in center of each patty. Form turkey mixture around stuffing into firm balls so there are no seams. (Most of the stuffing should be covered with the turkey mixture, but don't worry if some of the stuffing peeks through.) Place soup diluted with evaporated milk in shallow baking dish. Place stuffed balls on top of soup. (Use a baking dish small enough so that balls touch each other.) Bake, uncovered, in oven preheated to 350° for about one hour or until done. Baste balls occasionally with liquid in bottom of dish. 6 servings.

CHICKEN CONFETTI

The flavor of tomato is introduced into this time-tested treat.

4 slices lean bacon, cut in 1-inch pieces
¼ cup chopped green pepper
½ cup chopped onion
2 cans (10¾-ounce each) tomato soup
3 cups bite-size pieces of cooked chicken
1 can (1-pound) whole kernel corn, drained (or kernels from cooked, fresh corn-on-the-cob)
¼ teaspoon garlic salt
Pepper to taste
1 teaspoon vinegar
1 tablespoon Worcestershire Sauce
1½ cups buttered, fairly-coarse, bread crumbs

Fry bacon in large skillet until almost crisp. Remove bacon, drain on paper towels, and reserve drippings. Heat drippings over moderate heat. Add green pepper and onion. Cook over moderate heat, stirring frequently, until onion is transparent. Drain off grease. Add bacon and undiluted soup. Stir a few minutes over moderate heat. Add chicken, corn, garlic salt, pepper, vinegar, and Worcestershire Sauce. Mix well. Spoon mixture into greased, shallow, 7 x 11-inch baking dish. Sprinkle crumbs on top. Bake, uncovered, in oven preheated to 350° for about 30 minutes or until bubbly. (Altitudes below 5,000 feet may require slightly less baking time.) 6 to 8 servings.

TATA CHIP OVEN-FRIED CHICKEN

The chicken gets crisp on the outside but its meat stays moist. Children really go for this one.

1 package (5-ounce) potato chips, finely crushed
½ teaspoon garlic salt
¼ teaspoon seasoned pepper
1 teaspoon dried parsley flakes
½ teaspoon celery seed (optional)
1 frying chicken (about 2½ pounds), cut in serving pieces
1 stick (½ cup) butter or margarine, melted
Grated Parmesan cheese

An easy way to crush potato chips is to put them in a plastic bag, and whack them several times with a rolling pin. Then add garlic salt, pepper, parsley, and celery seed, if desired, to crumbs in bag, and shake bag to mix. Wash chicken, and pat with paper toweling until very dry. Dip chicken pieces in melted butter or margarine, one at a time, then drop in the bag of seasoned crumbs, and shake to coat chicken with crumbs. Place chicken, skin sides up, in a single layer in shallow 9 x 13-inch pan which has been lined with foil. Press any remaining potato chip crumbs firmly on top of chicken. Bake, uncovered, in oven preheated to 375°. Chicken need not be turned during baking. About 15 minutes before baking period is completed, sprinkle chicken with Parmesan cheese. Bake about 1½ hours or until done. (Altitudes below 5,000 feet may require less baking time.) 4 servings.

TURKEY STUFFING, ITALIAN-STYLE

The cook who perfected this recipe prefers to bake it in a casserole dish instead of stuffing a turkey with it. That's because the stuffing that sticks to the bones in the turkey cavity is usually wasted unless broth for soup is made by simmering the turkey carcass in water.

½ pound bulk Italian sausage
1 pound ground beef
1 medium onion, chopped
1 medium, green pepper, chopped
1 medium clove garlic, crushed
1 loaf (1-pound) Italian bread (cut bread in slices; spread them on counter to dry; place slices in plastic bag and roll into crumbs; use crusts, too)

1 cup not-too-finely grated Romano cheese
3 tablespoons dry parsley flakes
2 tablespoons dried leaf oregano
½ teaspoon poultry seasoning
1 egg, beaten
Broth reserved from cooked turkey giblets or chicken broth (see Cooked Turkey Giblets, page 165)

Heat a large, heavy pan over moderate heat. Crumble sausage and beef into pan. Cook over moderate heat, stirring frequently, until meat loses red color. Add onion, green pepper, and garlic during last few minutes of cooking time. Drain off grease. Add bread crumbs, cheese, parsley, oregano, poultry seasoning, and egg. Add enough broth to hold mixture together. Makes enough stuffing for a 12 to 14 pound turkey. (Stuffing may also be baked separately in a large, greased, uncovered casserole at 325° for about 1 hour. During last 30 minutes of baking time, occasionally spoon some of the drippings from roast turkey over stuffing.)

PORK CHOP VARIATION:

Brown 6 to 8 pork chops on both sides. Spread stuffing evenly over bottom of greased, 9 x 13-inch casserole. Place pork chops on top. Bake, covered, in oven preheated to 350° for 1 hour or until chops are done. Uncover during last 20 minutes of baking time. 6 to 8 servings.

COOKED TURKEY GIBLETS

Turkey giblets and their cooking broth can be used to heighten the flavor of stuffings and/or gravies.

1 teaspoon salt	½ medium onion, cut in
3 peppercorns	large pieces
1 small bay leaf	Turkey giblets and
2 medium ribs celery	neck, washed
with leaves	thoroughly

Combine all ingredients in large pan. Cover mixture with plenty of cold water, about 2 quarts, in order to yield a lot of broth. (Some cooks prefer cooking giblets in a small amount of water, then increasing the broth with other liquids.) Bring to boil, reduce heat, and simmer, covered, about 15 minutes. Skim off residue that floats on top of water at the beginning of cooking period. After 15 minutes, start testing the liver and remove when it is done. (Cooking time depends on size of liver.) Cover and continue to simmer remaining giblets and neck 1 to 3 hours or until gizzard is fork-tender and neck meat can easily be pulled off bones. (Again, cooking time depends on size and age of giblets.) Drain giblets, and reserve broth. Chop giblets finely, pull meat from neck and chop finely. (A food processor speeds up the chopping chore.) Immediately refrigerate giblets, covered, until needed.

Strain broth, discarding seasonings and vegetables. Refrigerate broth until needed. Use giblets and broth in stuffings, casseroles, soups, etc., or in the following gravy.

Turkey Giblet Gravy

The method for making this gravy may differ, but the taste fondly reminds me of my late Grandmother Heuer's giblet gravy, which she always made for Thanksgiving and Christmas dinners.

While the turkey is "resting" before it is carved, drain off drippings from roasting pan and reserve. The same pan can be used for making the gravy, so leave those delicious brown particles that stick to it; they will dissolve, adding color and flavor to the gravy while it is being cooked. Allow 2 tablespoons drippings and 2 tablespoons flour for each 1 cup of broth. To complete the amount of fat needed for gravy, add cooking oil to reserved drippings if necessary. Heat drippings over moderate heat in turkey roasting pan. Add flour. Cook a few minutes over moderate heat, stirring. Gradually add broth. Cook over moderate heat, stirring, until smooth and thickened. (Stirring with a wire whisk will usually insure a smooth gravy.) Stir in cooked, chopped giblets, continue stirring, and heat to serving temperature. Season to taste with salt and pepper. (If you are roasting a large turkey and want lots of gravy, just multiply the fat or drippings, flour, and broth to obtain the desired amount of gravy. For example, ½ cup fat, ½ cup flour, and 4 cups broth will yield about 4 cups gravy; double that for 8 cups, and so on. Larger amounts of gravy are better suited to using all of the chopped giblets.)

And whoever heard of giblet gravy without creamy mashed potatoes? Here's a way to prepare those potatoes the day ahead of serving time, eliminating frenzied, last-minute mashing.

Advance, Creamy Mashed Potatoes

The day before serving, boil, peel, and mash about 5 pounds of potatoes. While mashed potatoes are still warm, beat in with mixer enough milk to make them easy to stir with a spoon. (They should be moister than mashed potatoes that are to be served immediately.) Spoon potatoes evenly in greased 9 x 13-inch, shallow baking dish. Dot top of potatoes with ½ stick (¼ cup) butter or margarine, which has been cut in small pieces. Cover and refrigerate, up to about 16 hours. Bring potatoes to room temperature before they are ready to be reheated. Bake, covered, in oven preheated to 350° for about 30 minutes or until hot. 12 or more servings.

TURKEY CRUNCH CASSEROLE

It takes only a few minutes to toss together this treat.

1 can (1-pound)
French-style green
beans, drained
2 cups chopped,
cooked turkey
1 can (10¾-ounce)
cream of chicken
soup *or* 1 cup leftover
turkey gravy

¼ cup half-and-half
cream
1 can (2-ounce) sliced
mushrooms
1 can (3-ounce) chow
mein noodles
1 can (3-ounce) fried
onion rings

Place beans evenly over bottom of greased, 11 x 7-inch baking dish. Combine turkey, soup, cream, mushrooms, and mushroom liquid. Mix well; spoon over beans. Combine noodles and onion rings; sprinkle on mixture. Bake, uncovered, in oven preheated to 350° for about 30 minutes or until bubbly. 4 to 6 servings.

JOHNNY APPLESEED TURKEY STUFFING

One of the most popular stuffings from the *Denver Post* food pages. Remember, stuff the turkey just before it goes into the oven; NOT the night before.

1 stick (½ cup) butter
or margarine
1 small onion, chopped
1 cup chopped celery
2 medium, tart apples,
peeled and chopped

1 can (10¾-ounce)
chicken broth
1 package (8-ounce)
herb-seasoned
stuffing mix
4 slices bacon, crisply
fried and crumbled

Melt butter or margarine. Add onions and celery. Sauté until onion is transparent. Add apples and broth. Heat to boiling point. Combine apple mixture with stuffing mix and bacon. Mix well. Just before turkey is ready to be roasted, spoon stuffing in body and neck cavities. Makes enough stuffing for an 8 to 10 pound turkey.

HILDA'S CHICKEN CHOW MEIN

From a dear friend—and one of Colorado's best cooks.

2 frying chickens (about 2½ pounds each), cut in serving pieces
1 small onion, quartered
2 medium bay leaves
2 medium ribs celery with leaves
Salt and pepper to taste
Cooking oil
2 large onions, chopped
2 cans (16-ounce each) chow mein vegetables
1 can (8½-ounce) bamboo shoots
1 can (8½-ounce) water chestnuts, drained and sliced
¼ cup sugar or to taste
(amount of sugar depends on type of soy sauce used)
½ cup cornstarch
Soy sauce to taste
¾ cup slivered almonds
1 cup thinly-sliced celery
¾ pound (or more to taste) fresh bean sprouts, washed and thoroughly drained
1 jar (2-ounce) chopped pimientos, drained
Canned chow mein noodles
Fresh, quartered tomatoes (optional)
Quartered hard-cooked eggs (optional

Place chicken in large kettle. Cover with water. Add the quartered onion, bay leaves, whole celery ribs, salt, and pepper. Bring to boil, reduce heat, and simmer, covered, until chicken is tender. Remove chicken from broth. Strain and reserve broth, discarding vegetables and bay leaves from it. If necessary, add enough water to broth to make 3 quarts. Remove skin and bones from chicken. Cut chicken in bite-size pieces. Heat a small amount of cooking oil over moderate heat, in large kettle (at least 6-quart size.) Add the chopped onions. Sauté over moderate heat a few minutes stirring, frequently, until onions are transparent. Drain off oil. Drain chow mein vegetables and bamboo shoots. Slice bamboo shoots. Rinse these vegetables with cold water and thoroughly drain again. Add chow mein vegetables, bamboo shoots, water chestnuts, and chicken to onions in kettle. Mix well. Add reserved 3 quarts broth and sugar. Mix well. Bring to boil. Mix cornstarch with about ½ cup water until smooth. Add cornstarch mixture to chicken mixture. Stir over moderate heat until sauce is thickened and clear. Add soy sauce, almonds, sliced celery, bean sprouts, pimientos, salt, and pepper. Mix lightly but thoroughly. Cook over moderate heat a few minutes or just until piping hot. Stir occasionally. Serve over chow mein noodles. Garnish with tomatoes and hard-cooked eggs, if desired. Serve with additional soy sauce on the side. Makes about 6 quarts.

TURKEY- OR CHICKEN-RICE BAKE

Pieces of cooked poultry are extended by pork sausage and rice in an herb-flavored sauce. Cook the rice in chicken broth, instead of water, for a richer taste.

1 pound bulk pork sausage	Dried leaf oregano, marjoram, and thyme to taste
2 cans (4-ounce each) mushroom stems and pieces, drained	1½ cups uncooked rice (use a mixture of wild rice and long-grain brown rice, if desired)
1 medium onion, chopped	
2 cans (5-ounce each) water chestnuts, drained and sliced	3 cups coarsely-cut, cooked turkey or chicken
¼ cup flour	
½ cup milk	½ cup slivered, toasted almonds
2½ cups chicken broth	
Salt and pepper to taste	

Crumble sausage into large skillet, heated over moderate heat. Cook until done, breaking sausage into fairly small pieces with edge of spoon. Remove sausage from skillet; drain on paper toweling. Sauté mushrooms and onion in sausage drippings until onion is transparent. Add water chestnuts during last few minutes of cooking time. Drain off all but about four tablespoons grease. Stir in flour. Gradually add milk and chicken broth. Cook over moderate heat, stirring, until thickened. Add salt, pepper, oregano, marjoram, and thyme. Cook rice according to package directions. Combine rice, turkey or chicken, and sausage in greased 9 x 13-inch casserole dish. Pour sauce over top. Bake, uncovered, in oven preheated to 350° for about 30 minutes or until bubbly. Sprinkle with almonds before serving. 6 to 8 servings.

APRICOT-CORN BREAD STUFFING

To prevent the stuffing from becoming soggy, pack it lightly into the chicken or turkey's neck and body cavities.

1 stick (½ cup) butter or margarine
1½ cups chopped onion
2 cups chopped celery
1 can (30-ounce) apricot halves, drained and cut in small pieces
6 ounces toasted pecans, chopped

2 packages (10-ounce each) corn bread mix, baked and crumbled *or* 8 cups crumbled corn bread baked from your favorite recipe
⅓ cup (about) water

Melt butter or margarine. Add onion and celery. Sauté until onion is transparent. Combine onion mixture with apricots and pecans in large bowl. Add corn bread. Mix lightly but thoroughly. Gradually add just enough water to moisten stuffing. (Any leftover stuffing may be frozen and used later, or it may be baked, covered, at 325° for about 45 minutes.) Makes enough stuffing for a 12 to 14 pound turkey.

FRIEND-OF-A-FRIEND'S CHICKEN

Chicken parts turn a deep brown while they bake atop a bed of rice that has its own sauce when the dish is done.

1 can (10½-ounce) cream of celery soup
1 can (10½-ounce) cream of mushroom soup
½ cup milk

1½ cups instant rice, uncooked
1 frying chicken, cut in serving pieces
1 package (1¾-ounce) onion soup mix

Combine celery soup, mushroom soup, and milk. Mix thoroughly and heat over moderate heat. Sprinkle rice in greased, shallow, 9 x 13-inch baking dish. Spoon mushroom soup mixture over rice. Arrange chicken pieces on top. (Remove any excess fat from chicken.) Shake onion soup in package to mix it. Sprinkle onion soup over and around chicken. Bake, covered, in oven preheated to 325° for about 2 hours or until chicken is deep brown. (At altitudes below 5,000 feet, less cooking time may be required.) 4 servings.

CURRIED CHICKEN

Assemble this in the morning, then pop it in the oven for the evening meal— whether it's for guests or family.

1 frying chicken (about 3 pounds), cut in serving pieces	2 tablespoons butter or margarine
1 cup water	½ pound fresh mushrooms, sliced
1 cup dry sherry	½ cup slivered almonds
1½ teaspoons salt or to taste	1 package (6-ounce) long-grain and wild rice with seasonings
1 to 2 teaspoons curry powder or to taste	
1 medium onion, sliced	1 cup dairy sour cream
½ cup finely sliced celery	1 can (10½-ounce) mushroom soup

Place chicken in deep pan with water, sherry, salt, curry powder, onion, and celery. Bring to boil, reduce heat, and simmer, covered, about 1½ hours or until done. (It will take less time for altitudes below 5,000 feet.) Remove chicken from broth. Strain broth and refrigerate for later use. Remove chicken from bones. Discard skin. Cut chicken in fairly small pieces. Melt butter or margarine. Add mushrooms. Sauté mushrooms a few minutes over moderate heat until golden, stirring frequently. Cook rice following package directions for making firm rice, using reserved chicken broth instead of water. Combine cooked rice, chicken, almonds, and mushrooms. Reserve a few mushrooms to decorate top of casserole. Combine sour cream and undiluted soup. Combine sour cream and chicken mixtures. Bake, uncovered, in 9 x 11-inch casserole in oven preheated to 350° for about 1 hour. Arrange reserved mushrooms on top before serving. 6 servings.

BEEFED-UP CHICKEN BREASTS

It's rich and looks fancy, yet contains only five ingredients. And the chicken breasts require no prebrowning.

4 strips bacon	1 cup dairy sour cream
4 whole, boned (not skinned) chicken breasts	1 can (10¾-ounce) mushroom or celery soup
1 package (3-ounce) dried beef	Cooked rice or noodles

Partially fry bacon until nearly done but still pliable. Drain bacon. Remove fat from chicken breasts. Fold breasts into neat bundles, tucking edges into palms of hands so that skin of chicken forms a smooth surface on top. If necessary, secure underside with skewers or wooden picks. Arrange dried beef on bottom of 11 x 7-inch greased baking dish. Put folded chicken breasts on top of beef. Place a strip of bacon on top of each breast. Combine sour cream and soup, and mix until smooth. Spoon soup mixture over and around breasts. Bake, covered, in oven preheated to 300° for about 2 hours or until done. (At altitudes below 5,000 feet, check breasts for doneness after 1½ hours' baking time.) Serve chicken breasts and sauce over rice or noodles. 4 servings.

ASPARAGUS-CHICKEN BAKE

The crowning touch is corn bread, made from a mix or your favorite recipe.

½ pound fresh asparagus	1 package (8-ounce) corn muffin mix
½ stick (¼ cup) butter or margarine	1 can (10¾-ounce) cream of chicken soup
2 cups coarsely-chopped, cooked chicken (more chicken may be used if desired)	1 tablespoon lemon juice
¼ pound shredded, sharp Cheddar cheese	Chopped pimientos or sliced stuffed olives

Cut asparagus in pieces and cook in small amount of water until barely tender. Drain, reserving liquid. Melt butter in 8-inch square pan. Arrange asparagus in melted butter. Sprinkle chicken evenly over top. Sprinkle with cheese. Prepare muffin mix according to package directions. Carefully spoon batter on top of cheese as evenly as possible. Bake in oven preheated to 400° for about 30 minutes or until muffin topping is brown. Combine ½ cup of reserved asparagus liquid with soup and lemon juice. Stir until smooth and hot. Garnish with chopped pimiento or olive slices. Serve separately as sauce for casserole. 4 to 6 servings.

DOUBLE-DUTY CHICKEN

Stew a chicken when it's on special at the grocery. Then, freeze the meat and broth for two completely different meals at a later time.

1 stewing chicken (4 to 5 pounds), cut in serving pieces	1 large onion, cut in half
1 teaspoon salt	2 large carrots, thickly sliced
¼ teaspoon pepper	6 whole peppercorns
2 large ribs celery with leaves, cut in coarse pieces	Water

Place chicken in large kettle. Add salt, pepper, celery, onion, carrots and, peppercorns. Add enough water to barely cover chicken. Bring to boil and reduce heat. Skim off residue that floats on top of water during first part of cooking period. Simmer, covered, about 3 hours or until chicken is fork-tender. Remove chicken from broth. If desired, boil broth, uncovered, to reduce it for more richness. Strain broth, discarding vegetables and pepper-corns, and refrigerate until fat rises to top. Remove and discard fat from broth. Chicken broth should be refrigerated, for a maximum of 3 days, or frozen (in separate containers according to amounts needed) for a longer storage period. Remove skin and bones from chicken meat. Cut chicken in bite-size pieces. Divide chicken in 2 equal portions; refrigerate, covered, for a maximum of 2 days, or freeze each portion separately for a longer storage period. Use each portion of the chicken and some of the broth in each of the following recipes.

Chicken and Milk Gravy

2 tablespoons butter or margarine
1 small onion, chopped
¼ cup flour
1 cup chicken broth
1 tall can (13-ounce) evaporated milk
Salt to taste

2 cups (about) bite-size pieces of cooked chicken
Biscuits split in halves, toast, noodles, rice, or corn bread squares

Melt butter or margarine in 9-inch skillet over moderate heat. Add onion. Sauté over moderate heat, stirring frequently, until onion is transparent. Add flour. Stir a few minutes over moderate heat. Add broth, evaporated milk, and salt. Mix well. Cook and stir over moderate heat until thickened. Add chicken. Heat to serving temperature. Serve over biscuits, toast, noodles, rice, or corn bread squares. 4 servings.

Chicken-Fresh Vegetable Meal

1 cup chicken broth
1 medium onion, chopped
5 medium carrots, fairly thinly sliced
½ pound fresh green beans, snapped in halves
⅓ cup flour

½ teaspoon salt or to taste
1 cup evaporated milk
2 cups (about) bite-size pieces of cooked chicken
Hot mashed potatoes
½ cup (or more to taste) shredded Cheddar cheese

Place broth in fairly large pan. Bring to boil. Add onion, carrots, and beans. Return to boil, reduce heat, and simmer just until carrots are done. (If you prefer the beans crisp-tender, add them toward end of cooking period.) In another small pan, mix together flour and salt. Gradually add evaporated milk, mixing with wire whisk until smooth. Using wire whisk, gradually stir milk mixture into hot vegetable mixture. Stir over moderate heat until thickened. Add chicken. Mix well. Spoon mixture into greased, round, 2-quart casserole dish. Spoon mashed potatoes in a ring around edge of casserole. Sprinkle cheese on top of potatoes. Bake, uncovered, in oven preheated to 375° for about 20 minutes or until mixture is bubbly. 6 servings.

LAZY COOK'S CASSEROLE

As this dish bakes, the cheese melts and drizzles through it for added flavor.

½ cup milk
1 can (10¾-ounce) mushroom soup
3 cups (about) bite-size pieces of cooked chicken
2 packages (10-ounce each) frozen French-style green beans, thawed but uncooked

1 can (1-pound) chop suey vegetables, drained
⅓ cup chopped onion
Salt to taste
1½ cups shredded Cheddar cheese
1 can (3½-ounce) French fried onions

Combine milk and soup. Mix until smooth. Fold in chicken, beans, chop suey vegetables, chopped onion, salt, and cheese. Spoon mixture into greased, shallow, 7 x 11-inch baking dish. Bake, uncovered, in oven preheated to 350° for about 30 minutes. Arrange French fried onions on top of mixture. Bake, uncovered, about 10 minutes longer or until mixture is bubbly. (At altitudes below 5,000 feet, reduce first cooking period to about 20 minutes.) 8 servings.

CHEESY TURKEY PIE

Uncooked ground turkey goes into a pie, which would be complemented by a tossed green salad and buttered lima beans.

1 pound uncooked ground turkey
½ cup chopped onion
1 medium, green pepper, chopped
1 can (8-ounce) tomato sauce
1 can (3-ounce) sliced mushrooms, drained
¼ teaspoon dried leaf oregano

¼ teaspoon dried leaf thyme
½ teaspoon salt
⅛ teaspoon pepper
2 packages (8 rolls in each) refrigerated crescent rolls
3 eggs
1 tablespoon water
6 slices American cheese

Crumble turkey into greased skillet, heated over moderate heat. Add onion and green pepper. Cook over moderate heat, stirring frequently, until turkey starts to brown. Drain off grease if necessary. Add tomato sauce, mushrooms, oregano, thyme, salt, and pepper. Mix well. Remove mixture from heat. Unroll one package of the rolls. Press the 4 sections of dough together, forming a rectangle, 12 x 6 inches. Press perforations together. Roll dough into a 12-inch square. Fit dough into a 9-inch pie plate. Trim edge of dough. Separate 1 of the eggs. Mix egg yolk with water, cover, and refrigerate until ready to use. Beat egg white with remaining 2 eggs. Spread half of this mixture over dough in pie plate. Spoon turkey mixture on dough. Arrange cheese slices over turkey mixture. Spread remaining half of egg mixture over cheese. Brush edge of pastry with some of the reserved egg yolk and water. Roll second package of rolls into 12-inch square, according to preceding directions. Place dough on top of filling. Trim, seal, and flute edge. Cut a few slits in top of dough to allow steam to escape during baking. Brush dough with remaining egg yolk mixture. Bake, uncovered, in oven preheated to 350° for about 50 minutes. (If pastry gets too brown toward end of cooking period, cover it lightly with foil.) Let stand about 10 minutes before cutting into wedges to serve. 6 servings.

TAVERN CHICKEN, BRUNSWICK STYLE

Brunswick stew, a hearty, slow-cooking dish once made with squirrel meat (and sometimes rabbit) is modernized here. This recipe substitutes chicken for the squirrel or rabbit, and speeds up preparation by using canned and frozen vegetables.

2 chickens (2 to 2½ pounds each), cut in serving pieces	frozen lima beans, thawed
1 bottle (8-ounce) Italian salad dressing	1 package (10-ounce) frozen okra, thawed
1 can (28-ounce) whole tomatoes, cut in small pieces	1 can (1-pound) green beans, drained
1 medium bay leaf	1 can (12-ounce) whole kernel corn, drained
1 teaspoon salt	2 tablespoons corn- starch
1 teaspoon sugar	½ cup water
1 package (10-ounce)	

Place chicken in a layer in shallow, 9 x 13-inch baking dish. Pour ⅔ cup of the Italian dressing over chicken. Marinate, covered, in refrigerator for 3 hours, turning chicken occasionally. With chicken pieces, skin side up, in marinade, bake, uncovered, in oven preheated to 375° about 1¼ hours or until tender. Baste occasionally with marinade during baking period. (Baking time depends on size of chicken as well as how cold chicken is when it goes into the oven.) Combine tomatoes and their liquid, bay leaf, salt, sugar, and remaining ⅓ cup Italian dressing. Bring to boil, reduce heat, and simmer, covered, 15 minutes. Add lima beans, okra, green beans, and corn. Bring to boil, reduce heat, and simmer, covered, until vegetables are done. Mix together cornstarch and water until smooth. Add cornstarch to vegetable mixture. Stir over moderate heat until sauce is thickened. Serve with chicken. 8 servings.

MAIN DISH MELON-CHICKEN SALAD

Serve this with hot rolls for luncheon or supper. The idea for the recipe comes from one of Denver's male cooking pros.

4 cups cooked, diced chicken	½ cup sliced, blanched, toasted almonds
3 tablespoons lemon juice	½ cup (about) mayonnaise
1 cup sliced celery	1 cup halved seedless grapes
⅓ cup finely-chopped onion	1 cup pineapple chunks, drained
1 teaspoon salt	2 medium cantaloupes or honeydew melons
½ teaspoon pepper	Salad greens
1 can (2-ounce) pimientos, sliced and drained	Clusters of green and dark grapes

Toss together chicken and lemon juice. Add celery, onion, salt, pepper, pimientos, almonds, and mayonnaise. Mix lightly but thoroughly. Add grape halves and pineapple. Refrigerate until chilled. Slice off ends of melons to expose seeds. Scoop out seeds with potato peeler or knife to form hole through center of melons. Cut each melon into 3 even slices. Cut rind off slices. Place melon rings on greens. Add more mayonnaise to chicken salad, if desired. Spoon salad into center of each ring. Arrange clusters of grapes around outside of rings. 6 servings.

FRESH FRUIT-CHICKEN SALAD ON
PASTRY ROSETTES

If you lack a rosette iron, serve this refreshing salad on crisp greens; however, a rosette iron is a good investment (and not too expensive). With it you can easily turn out delicately designed pastries that look like they came from a French patisserie. The pastries can be topped with all kinds of hot, creamed meat or vegetable mixtures, or covered with ice cream and/or fruit sauces for desserts.

3 cups (about) bite-size pieces of cooked chicken	½ cup dairy sour cream
	1 cup thinly-sliced, fresh, peeled peaches
¾ cup coarsely-chopped celery	Seasoning salt to taste
1 cup halved seedless grapes	Pastry rosettes
	Thinly-sliced almonds
½ cup mayonnaise	Paprika

Combine chicken, celery, and grapes. Mix lightly but thoroughly. Mix together mayonnaise and sour cream until smooth. Combine chicken and mayonnaise mixtures. Mix lightly but thoroughly. Refrigerate mixture until chilled. About 30 minutes before serving, add peaches and salt. Mix lightly but thoroughly. Add more mayonnaise and sour cream, in equal proportions, if a moister salad is desired. Arrange desired number of pastry rosettes in a circle on individual serving plates. Place a mound of salad in center of plate only partially covering rosettes so that you can show off their beauty. Sprinkle salad with almonds and paprika. 6 servings.

Pastry Rosettes

1 cup milk	1 teaspoon sugar (for dessert rosettes use 4 teaspoons sugar)
1 cup unsifted all-purpose flour	
½ teaspoon salt	1 egg, unbeaten
	Cooking oil

Gradually add milk to flour in a small bowl, stirring with wire whisk. Add salt, sugar, and egg. Mix with wire whisk until smooth. In a medium-sized saucepan, heat about 1½ inch of cooking oil over moderate heat until it is hot enough to brown a small piece of bread in about 1 minute. Dip the end of rosette iron in oil about 15 seconds or just long enough to heat it. Quickly blot mold on paper toweling, then dip into pastry batter deep enough for batter to come barely to top of mold. Plunge mold with batter into hot oil. Fry over moderate heat until rosette is golden brown. Gently push rosette off mold onto paper toweling with the edge of a knife. (If rosette comes off mold in the oil, remove it with tongs.) If making dessert rosettes, sprinkle with powered sugar. Repeat process for each rosette. (Though the rosettes have to be made one at a time—unless the iron is designed with a double set of molds—you'll be surprised how fast they can be fried.) Keep oil over moderate heat. Add more oil, if necessary, as rosettes are being fried. Cool rosettes and store them, covered, in refrigrator 3 to 4 days, or they may be frozen. Bring to room temperature before serving. (This recipe is suitable for both low and high altitudes). Makes about 50 rosettes.

CHICKEN BREASTS WITH LEILANI SAUCE

Baby food in an elegant sauce? Well, it's an optional, time-saving step.

4 chicken breasts (no need to bone or skin them), cut in half	1½ cups water
1½ cups lightly-packed brown sugar	2 teaspoons dried, sweet pepper flakes
¼ cup granulated sugar	⅛ teaspoon cayenne pepper or to taste
1 cup cider vinegar	⅛ teaspoon instant minced garlic or to taste
1 jar (4¾-ounce) plum baby food *or* ½ cup cooked, puréed plums	2 tablespoons cornstarch
1 jar (4¾-ounce) apricot baby food *or* ½ cup cooked, puréed apricots	Sesame seeds to taste
	Cooked rice

Grease chicken breasts on all sides with cooking oil. Put breasts in shallow, close-fitting pan, skin sides down. Place on lowest shelf under broiler. Broil until well-browned on both sides, turning once. Combine sugars, vinegar, fruits, 1¼ cups of the water, sweet pepper flakes, cayenne pepper, and garlic. Mix well. Bring to boil, reduce heat, and simmer, covered, 15 minutes. Dissolve cornstarch in remaining ¼ cup water. Add to vinegar mixture. Stir over moderate heat until glossy and thickened. Place browned chicken breasts in a shallow, close-fitting casserole dish. Pour sauce over them and sprinkle with sesame seeds. Bake, covered, in oven preheated to 300° for about 30 minutes or until sauce is bubbly and chicken is done. Serve with rice. 4 servings.

OFF THE
BEATEN PATH

This section is not merely a catchall. It offers cooks opportunities to diversify menus with interesting recipes and ideas for serving something other than routine cuts of beef, pork, lamb, and veal.

Suggestions for turning leftovers into entrées with new taste appeal, as well as ways to utilize some of the many kinds of sausages available today, are also included. Variety meats (the edible inner parts of animals, such as liver) are treated with such flavorful respect that any prejudices against them are likely to disappear.

Most of the recipes are economical, something to keep in mind during these times of inflation, and every recipe provides substantial nutrition.

Game meats, both wild and domestic, share the honors here, but I have not dealt with the complete treatment of venison or game birds from the time of shooting to their arrival at the dining table. I strongly recommend contacting government, county extention services, or other reliable sources for information on safety precautions to be taken during all stages of handling any wild game—by hunters as well as cooks.

CHOW DON, DENVER STYLE

Some of Denver's top-notch Chinese cooks refer to stir-fried eggs as "chow don." But the eggs in this recipe only serve as a binder for a nutritious mixture of crisp bean sprouts, other vegetables, and any leftover meat, fish, or poultry.

8 eggs, well beaten	¼ cup chopped, drained pimiento
½ teaspoon salt	
1 teaspoon sugar	½ cup thinly-sliced water chestnuts
Soy sauce to taste	
½ cup cooking oil	½ cup sliced, fresh mushrooms
1 cup diced, cooked chicken, pork, ham, shrimp, or other meat, or fish of your choice	
	¼ cup sliced green onions and some of the tops
½ cup green pepper, cut in julienne strips	¾ pound fresh bean sprouts

Thoroughly mix together eggs, salt, and sugar. (About 4 teaspoons soy sauce may be added to mixture but it will discolor eggs. If soy sauce is omitted here, it may be sprinkled over the finished dish.) Heat oil over moderate heat in Dutch oven or large wok. Add the chicken, meat, or fish, green pepper, pimiento, water chestnuts, mushrooms, onions, and bean sprouts. Cook over moderate heat, stirring constantly, about 4 minutes. Do not overcook. Bean sprouts should be crisp-tender. Pour egg mixture in thin stream over bean sprout mixture, stirring constantly. Cook over moderate heat, stirring constantly, just until eggs are set. Do not overcook. Eggs should be moist. Serve, with soy sauce on the side, for brunch, lunch or dinner. 4 servings.

MAIN DISH SAUSAGE CHOWDER

A tossed green salad and chunks of crusty bread would complement this easy-to-make chowder.

2 pounds hot-flavored, bulk pork sausage (substitute 1 pound regular, bulk pork sausage and 1 pound of the hot-flavored variety, if a less spicy flavor is desired)	1 can (1-pound) whole tomatoes
	1 quart water
	1 medium bay leaf
	1 teaspoon garlic salt or to taste
	1 teaspoon dried leaf thyme
2 medium onions, chopped	2 cups peeled, diced potatoes
1 can (1-pound) kidney beans	2 medium, green peppers, chopped
	Pepper to taste

Crumble sausage into heated, large pan or Dutch oven. Cook over moderate heat, stirring frequently, until sausage is done. Add onion during the last 5 minutes cooking time. Drain off grease. Add beans and their liquid and tomatoes and their liquid, breaking up tomatoes with edge of spoon. Add water, bay leaf, garlic salt, and thyme. Bring to boil, reduce heat and simmer, covered, 45 minutes to 1 hour. (Use the longer length of cooking time for altitudes above 5,000 feet.) Add potatoes. Bring to boil, reduce heat and simmer, covered, until potatoes are almost done. Add green pepper and pepper to taste. Simmer, covered, until potatoes are done and green pepper is tender but still slightly crisp. Remove bay leaf. Serve in soup bowls. 8 servings.

LATTICE-TOPPED PIZZA RUSTICA

Different types of salami may be used to vary the taste of this Italian-inspired version of deep-dish pizza, minus tomatoes but brimming with cheeses and spinach. Don't let the length of the recipe discourage you from making it. I promise it's worth it, and leftovers reheat beautifully in a microwave oven, without a soggy crust.

1½ sticks (¾ cup) margarine, softened	½ pound Mozzarella cheese, cut in about ¼-inch cubes
3 cups unsifted flour (spoon it into cup to measure, don't pack it)	¼ cup grated Parmesan cheese
1 teaspoon salt	½ pound smoked, hard salami, cut in about ¼-inch cubes
7 extra-large eggs	
1¼ cups ricotta cheese	1 package (12-ounce) frozen, uncooked chopped spinach, thawed and thoroughly drained
⅓ pound Provolone cheese, cut in about ¼-inch cubes	

Using pastry blender, cut margarine into flour until mixture resembles coarse crumbs. Add salt while cutting in margarine. Lightly beat 2 of the eggs. Add these eggs to flour mixture. Have ready 1 of the remaining eggs which has been lightly beaten in a small bowl. Mix flour-egg mixture with a fork, then use hands to mix until it holds together. (At first, this pastry is very crumbly but it softens and holds together as you work with it. If necessary, add enough of the beaten egg to make it easier to handle. This additional egg may definitely be necessary at altitudes above 5,000 feet since moisture evaporates faster at higher altitudes but the pastry should not be too soft or it will become soggy during baking. Reserve what is left of the beaten egg to be used later.) Gather dough into a ball. Place it in a bowl, cover with a damp cloth and let stand at room temperature for about 30 minutes.

Combine ricotta, Provolone, Mozzarella, Parmesan, and salami. Mix thoroughly. Squeeze spinach with hands to release even more moisture after draining. Add spinach and remaining 4 eggs, which have been lightly beaten, to cheese mixture. Mix well.

Divide pastry into 2 equal portions. Keep 1 portion in bowl, covered with damp cloth. With short, very firm strokes, roll out the other portion between pieces of waxed paper into a circle about 13 inches in diameter. Lift circle into an ungreased 10-inch pie plate with sides at least 2-inches high. With fingers, press pastry over bottom and up sides of plate. If pastry breaks, just press it together with fingers. (This pastry is thicker than conventional pie pastry which prevents it from becoming soggy during baking. Even with all this handling, it turns out surprisingly flaky.) Spoon cheese filling into pastry-lined plate. Filling will mound slightly because there is so much of it but the cheese holds it together and it does not bubble over during baking.

Roll out remaining portion of dough between pieces of waxed paper to a circle about 13 inches in diameter. Cut circle into strips, about 1½-inches wide. (This is not a dainty creation so the strips should be wider than for a conventional pie crust.) Place some of the strips about 1½ inches apart over filling. Press ends of strips to edge of pie plate but avoid stretching them. Arrange remaining strips on top, lattice fashion, about 1½ inches apart. Press ends of these strips to edge of pie plate and avoid stretching them. (Again, if strips break, just press them together with fingers.) If desired, any leftover pieces of pastry may be pressed around edge of pie plate, then fluted with fingers. (Moisten dough with water before adding these pieces.) Add about ½ to 1 tablespoon water to reserved, leftover beaten egg. Brush pastry strips with egg mixture. Bake, uncovered, in oven preheated to 375° for about 1 hour or until pastry is golden brown and filling between lattice squares is fairly firm to the touch. Let stand about 10 minutes in plate before cutting in wedges to serve. 8 or more servings.

ITALIAN SAUSAGE BREAD ROLL

Inspired by a hand-me-down Sicilian family recipe called "Quachi" (meaning "conglomeration" in the Sicilian dialect), this recipe is far removed from its Old World version. It has been perfected to keep the bread dough fluffy while it bakes with its pinwheel, Italian sausage filling.

Filling

2 pounds bulk Italian sausage	¾ cup roasted sunflower kernels or piñon nuts
½ cup finely-cut, fresh parsley	¾ pound finely-diced Scamorza cheese

Crumble sausage into heavy skillet which has been heated over moderate heat. Cook sausage until it starts to lose red color, is almost done and grease starts to collect. (Do not cook until well done since a small amount of grease is necessary to flavor bread roll while it bakes.) Stir sausage frequently, breaking it up into small pieces with edge of spoon. Turn sausage into colander. Let stand until it is thoroughly drained of all grease. (Precooking the sausage in this manner removes excess grease and prevents the bread dough from becoming soggy while it bakes.) Cool sausage to room temperature while preparing dough. Have parsley, sunflower kernels or piñon nuts, and Scamorza cheese ready to spread on dough along with sausage. (Scamorza cheese may be finely diced in a food processor using steel blade.)

Bread Dough

5 to 5½ cups (about) unsifted flour	1½ cups water
2 teaspoons salt	½ cup milk
3 tablespoons sugar	3 tablespoons butter
1 package dry yeast	or margarine

Stir together 2 cups of the flour, salt, sugar, and dry yeast in large bowl of mixer. Combine water, milk, and butter or margarine in a pan. Heat milk mixture just until it is warm but not steamy hot. With spoon, gradually stir milk mixture into yeast mixture, then beat about 2 minutes on medium speed of mixer. Add about 1 cup of the remaining flour. Beat about 2 minutes on high speed of mixer, frequently scraping down sides of bowl with rubber spatula. Gradually add about 2 more cups of the flour or enough to make a soft dough. (Use hands to mix in most of this flour.) Sprinkle part of the remaining ½ cup flour on a board. Turn out dough onto board. Knead until it is smooth and elastic, about 10 minutes. Add more flour if dough appears too sticky. Place dough in large, greased bowl. Turn dough to grease all sides. Cover with damp cloth. Let rise in warm place until double in bulk or until indentation remains when 2 fingertips are pressed into dough.

(Rising time takes about 1 hour at altitudes below 5,000 feet. At higher altitudes, dough should be ready in 45 minutes or less. The oven is a good, draft-free place to let dough rise. Turn oven to lowest setting (warm on most ovens) while preparing dough. Turn off oven during kneading time, then place towel-covered bowl of dough in it to rise according to preceding directions.)

TO ASSEMBLE:

Roll out dough or pat, pull and stretch dough with hands on a lightly floured surface into a rectangle about 11 x 17-inches. Spread sausage evenly over dough leaving about 1-inch border around all sides. With fingertips, lightly press sausage into dough. Sprinkle parsley, sunflower kernels or nuts, then Scamorza on top of sausage. Lightly press in each layer with fingers as you proceed. Roll dough from long side, jelly roll fashion. Dust hands with flour, if necessary, to keep dough from becoming sticky. It dough tears, just pinch it together with water-moistened fingertips. Moisten ends and seam of roll with water; pinch together to seal. Place roll on greased, jelly roll pan, 10 x 15-inches. (A jelly roll pan with edges is necessary to catch any drippings that might ooze out of roll. An additional rising period is not necessary.) If desired, brush tops and sides of roll with an egg which has been beaten with about 1 tablespoon water. This gives roll a beautiful, golden color.

Bake roll, uncovered, in oven preheated to 350° for 45 minutes to 1 hour or until bread is golden brown and wooden pick inserted in center comes out relatively clean. (There will be some grease on pick from sausage filling.) Drain off drippings. Let roll stand in pan about 10 minutes before cutting in slices to serve. Serve hot for lunch, as a dinner main dish, or cold as a snack. The roll freezes nicely, and when ready to use, should be thawed in the refrigerator, then reheated in foil for about 20 minutes in a 400° oven. To change the character of any left over, serve the pinwheel slices with a topping of your favorite mushroom and/or cheese sauce. Makes 18 to 20 slices.

Note: The dough in this recipe makes excellent quick-mix, white bread. Follow preceding directions through the rising period. After dough has doubled in bulk, punch it down, cover, and let rest 15 minutes. Divide dough in half and shape into loaves. Place each loaf in a greased pan, 9 x 5-inches. Cover with damp cloth. Let rise in warm place until double in bulk or until indentation remains when 2 fingertips are pressed into dough. Bake in oven preheated to 400° for 25 to 35 minutes or until dough is golden brown, and sounds hollow when tapped with fingertips. Remove from pans. Cool on racks. Makes 2 loaves.

APPLE SKILLET SUPPER

Fresh apples and cabbage find their way into this family dish which is ready to eat in less than thirty minutes—in even less time if you have a food processor to shred the cabbage.

1 pound bulk beef sausage or bulk pork sausage	¼ cup cider vinegar
	4 cups coarsely-shredded cabbage
1 teaspoon dried leaf thyme	2 medium, unpeeled apples, cut lengthwise
⅓ cup packed brown sugar	in about ½-inch wedges

Crumble sausage into Dutch oven or large pan which has been heated over moderate heat. Stir frequently over moderately low heat until sausage is done. Drain off grease. Add thyme, brown sugar, and vinegar. Mix well. Add cabbage. Mix well. Bring to boil, reduce heat and simmer, covered, 2 to 4 minutes or just until cabbage is wilted. Add apple slices. Mix gently but thoroughly. Cook over moderate heat, uncovered, about 2 minutes or just until apples start to get soft. 4 servings.

SAUSAGE, BEAN ONE-POT MEAL

Fresh green beans are given a delightful new personality in this mushroom-sausage medley.

½ pound German sausage links, cut in bite-size pieces	1 teaspoon dried leaf summer savory
½ pound Italian sausage links, cut in bite-size pieces	½ teaspoon seasoned salt or to taste
3 medium onions, sliced and separated into rings	½ teaspoon freshly-ground pepper or to taste
1 pound (about) fresh green beans, snapped in halves	1 cup beef stock or bouillon
1 teaspoon dried leaf sweet basil	¼ pound fresh mushrooms, sliced
	Small, new, peeled potatoes, boiled until partially done (optional)

Heat a heavy, 5-quart pan or Dutch oven over moderate heat. Take a piece of sausage, and rub the cut side of it over bottom and sides of pan to grease it. Add all of the sausage pieces. Cook over moderately high heat until sausage is brown on all sides. Stir frequently. Remove sausage from pan; drain on paper toweling. Drain off all but 3 tablespoons drippings from pan. If necessary, add cooking oil to make 3 tablespoons drippings and heat over moderate heat. Add onions and beans. Cook over moderate heat, stirring constantly, until onions are transparent. Add sausage, basil, savory, salt, pepper, stock or bouillon, mushrooms, and potatoes if desired. Mix well.

Bring to boil, reduce heat and simmer, covered, about 20 minutes or until beans have reached desired degree of doneness and potatoes are cooked. (Add 5 or 10 minutes cooking time for altitudes above 5,000 feet.) 6 servings.

GAME HENS WITH VERMOUTH-SPLASHED STUFFING

These plump hens have been a party favorite in the Rocky Mountain region for more than a decade. Add a fruit salad, hot rolls, and a green vegetable to complete a feast that avoids last minute preparation.

½ stick (¼ cup) butter
6 small green onions with about 1 inch of the tops, sliced
1 can (3-ounce) chopped mushrooms, drained
½ cup chopped pecans
1 small, red, unpeeled apple, chopped
6 slices white sandwich bread with crusts,
torn into small pieces
Salt and pepper to taste
Dry vermouth
4 Cornish game hens, thawed, washed, dried with paper towel, and brought to room temperature
Cooking oil
8 slices lean bacon, cut in halves

Melt butter. Add onions and mushrooms. Sauté over moderate heat, stirring frequently, until onions are transparent. Toss together onion mixture, pecans, apple, bread, salt, and pepper. Add enough vermouth to hold mixture together. (It should form a ball.) Stuff each hen with mixture. (Don't be afraid to pack stuffing into birds. It is not supposed to have a fluffy texture.) Close cavities with skewers. Brush hens on all sides with cooking oil. Place hens, breast sides up, on rack in shallow roasting pan. Bake, uncovered, in oven preheated to 350° for about 1¼ hours. Arrange bacon slices on top of hens and continue baking for 45 minutes or until thighs on hens move easily. For altitudes below 5,000 feet, reduce cooking time about 15 minutes. (These game hens take longer to roast than Game Hens Elegante elsewhere in this section because they are stuffed and the heat will not penetrate them as fast.) 4 servings.

SAUSAGE-NOODLE DUO

Even purists who like to make sauces from scratch should consider this combination (using canned cream of chicken soup) when the day has been very busy and the cook is very tired.

1 pound mildly-hot, bulk pork sausage	1 cup shredded Cheddar cheese
4 ounces (about 2 cups) fine egg noodles	2 tablespoons chopped, drained pimiento
1 can (5-ounce) evaporated milk	2 tablespoons chopped green pepper
1 can (10¾-ounce) cream of chicken soup	Buttered bread crumbs

Form sausage into balls about the size of quarters. Flatten balls slightly. Heat a large skillet or Dutch oven over moderate heat. Add sausage. Cook over moderate heat until sausage is brown on all sides. Drain off grease. Cook noodles according to package directions, omitting salt in water. Drain noodles and add to sausage. Mix well. Thoroughly mix together evaporated milk and soup. Add cheese, pimiento, and green pepper to soup mixture. Mix well. Combine soup and sausage mixtures. Mix thoroughly and spoon into greased, 2-quart casserole. Sprinkle top lightly with buttered bread crumbs. Bake, uncovered, in oven preheated to 350° for about 35 minutes or until bubbly. 4 servings.

SHORT AND SASSY BAKED OMELET

Here's a lazy way to prepare sausage and eggs as a main dish for brunch or a light supper.

6 extra-large egg whites at room temperature	¼ cup cool tap water
¼ teaspoon cream of tartar	6 extra-large egg yolks
½ teaspoon salt	1 package (8-ounce) "Brown and Serve" sausage links

Place egg whites in large bowl of mixer. Beat on high speed until foamy. Beat in cream of tartar and salt. Gradually add water. Beat on high speed until stiff peaks form. (The water is an unusual addition but it's necessary in this recipe.) With the same beaters (there's no need to wash them), beat egg yolks in a small bowl until thick and lemon colored. Gently fold yolks into beaten whites. Lightly brown sausage, according to package directions, in an ovenproof, 10-inch skillet. Remove sausage. There should be a thin film of grease on bottom of skillet. If necessary, add a very small amount of cooking oil to skillet and heat until moderately hot. Spoon egg mixture into skillet. Reduce heat to low. Cook egg mixture on low heat about 3 minutes. Place sausages on top in spoke fashion. Bake, uncovered, in oven preheated to 350° for 15 to 20 minutes or until eggs are golden brown, and center springs back when tapped with fingers. (Altitudes above 5,000 feet will probably require the 20-minute cooking time.) Cut in wedges to serve. 5 to 6 servings.

DOUBLE-DUTY FRIED RICE

What a scrumptious way to disguise leftover meat—or omit the meat, and serve the rice as a side dish with your favorite roast.

1 cup rice (not instant)	2 eggs, beaten
6 slices lean bacon	4 tablespoons soy sauce
4 medium, green onions	or to taste
and some of the tops,	Pieces of cooked meat
sliced	(pork, ham, chicken,
1 can (4-ounce) sliced	etc.) *or* cubes of your
mushrooms, drained,	favorite luncheon meat
or sliced, fresh mush-	to taste
rooms to taste	Salt and pepper to taste

Cook rice according to package directions. Set aside to cool, fluffing occasionally with fork. Fry bacon until crisp in 10-inch skillet. Remove bacon from skillet, drain, and crumble. Drain off bacon drippings and reserve. Return about 3 tablespoons drippings to skillet and heat over moderate heat. Add onions and mushrooms. Sauté over moderate heat, stirring frequently until onions are transparent and, if fresh mushrooms are used, they are golden colored. Remove onions and mushrooms from skillet with slotted spoon. Add enough of the reserved bacon drippings to cover bottom of skillet; heat until moderately hot. Add eggs. Reduce heat to low. Cook eggs by lifting edges with pancake turner and tilting skillet to permit uncooked egg to run to bottom of pan, omelet fashion. (This method keeps eggs in a large pancake shape.) Remove egg "pancake" and cut into strips.

Add more of the reserved bacon drippings to cover bottom of skillet. Add rice. Cook over moderately low heat, stirring frequently, until rice is golden colored. Add crumbled bacon, onions, mushrooms, egg strips, soy sauce, meat, salt, and pepper. Mix gently but thoroughly. Cook over moderately low heat, stirring, until heated to serving temperature. 6 to 8 servings.

SAUCY SPOONBURGERS

Reminiscent of "Sloppy Joes," this dish has more substance and extends the ground beef with the addition of chunks of wieners and pork and beans. Serve it to a gang of hungry teenagers, at an after-ski, fireside gathering, or for a summertime patio party.

1 pound lean ground beef	2 cans (1-pound each) pork and beans in tomato sauce
1 medium onion, chopped	
2¼ cups water	Salt and pepper to taste
1 can (6-ounce) tomato paste	
1 envelope (1½-ounce) spaghetti sauce mix	1 pound wieners, each cut in 6 crosswise chunks
1 tablespoon (about) prepared mustard	12 hamburger buns, split and toasted
¼ cup (about) well-drained, sweet pickle relish	American or Cheddar cheese slices (optional)

Crumble beef into heated, large pan or Dutch oven. Cook over moderate heat until meat loses red color. Stir frequently, and break up meat with edge of spoon. Add onion during about the last 5 minutes cooking time. Drain off excess grease. Add water, tomato paste, dry spaghetti sauce mix, mustard, pickle relish, pork and beans and their liquid, salt, pepper, and wieners. Mix lightly but thoroughly. Add more mustard and sweet pickle relish to taste, if desired. Bring to boil, reduce heat and simmer, covered, about 15 minutes. Place a slice of cheese on each bun half if desired. Spoon hot bean mixture over toasted bun halves, allowing about ¾ cup for each split bun. 12 servings.

GAME HENS ELEGANTE WITH MILE HIGH PEACHES

A shiny brown glaze seals in the juices of moist game hen. Proudly present the little birds on a bed of long-grain and wild rice along with a garnish of peach halves piled high with fluffy meringue.

4 Cornish game hens, thawed, washed, dried with paper towel, and brought to room temperature
4 tablespoons honey
Salt and pepper to taste
3 tablespoons butter or margarine
3 tablespoons bottled teriyaki sauce
⅓ cup orange juice
Cooked rice (a mixture of long grain and wild rice)
Mile High Peaches for garnish (optional)

Place hens, breast sides up, in greased, shallow roasting pan. (Pan should be small enough so sides of hens barely touch each other.) Drizzle honey over breast and thighs of each hen. Sprinkle with salt and pepper. (Go easy on the salt since some brands of teriyaki sauce are extra salty.) Combine butter or margarine, teriyaki sauce, and orange juice in a pan. Simmer until butter melts. Stir occasionally. Pour sauce around hens. (Sauce recipe is easily multiplied if you want to use it as a gravy for rice.) Roast hens, uncovered, in oven preheated to 350° for about 1 hour or until done. (Thighs should move easily when hens are done.) For altitudes above 5,000 feet, add about 15 minutes roasting time. Baste hens frequently with pan drippings during roasting period. To serve, place hens over rice with pan drippings poured over top. If desired, arrange Mile High Peaches also on rice. 4 servings.

Mile High Peaches

1 can (1-pound) cling peach halves, thoroughly drained
6 to 8 tablespoons prepared mincemeat, drained
1 extra-large egg white at room temperature
⅛ teaspoon cream of tartar
2 tablespoons sugar

Place peach halves in buttered pan, cut sides up and close together to keep them upright. (There should be 6 to 8 halves.) Fill each cavity with about 1 tablespoon mincemeat. Beat egg white until frothy. Add cream of tartar and beat until stiff but not dry. Add sugar, 1 teaspoon at a time, beating to form stiff peaks. Spoon meringue on top of mincemeat. Bake, uncovered, in oven preheated to 400° until meringue is lightly tinged with brown.

Note: This recipe is excellent with any type of poultry or fowl.

STUFFING-CROWNED VENISON ROAST

A venison roast is made more delicious and retains more juices with an apple-bread stuffing on the outside of the meat.

1 venison roast (about 5 pounds), trimmed of all fat	1 teaspoon sage
	½ teaspoon dried leaf thyme
1 stick (½ cup) butter, softened so it can be stirred with a fork (but do not melt it)	½ cup chopped celery
	1 teaspoon parsley flakes
2 cups slightly dry, ¼-inch bread cubes	1 cup coarsely-chopped, unpeeled, tart apple
1 teaspoon salt	1 beef bouillon cube, dissolved in 1 cup hot water
½ teaspoon pepper	
½ medium onion, chopped	4 strips lean bacon

Place roast on a large sheet of heavy-duty foil. Spread butter over top and sides of meat. Combine bread cubes, salt, pepper, onion, sage, thyme, celery, parsley, apples, and bouillon. Mix well. Pat stuffing on top of meat with fingers. Arrange bacon on top of stuffing. Fold foil around roast, leaving some air space between foil and meat but tightly seal all seams with a double fold. Insert meat thermometer in thickest part of roast (through the foil). Place roast in a shallow pan (to catch any drippings in case foil tears.) Roast in oven preheated to 350° for 2 to 3 hours. Remove foil from meat pushing it down around sides of meat to allow stuffing to get crusty. Continue roasting for 1 more hour or until meat thermometer registers 170° to 180°. (The dark surface of venison is misleading; it may look done before it actually is.) To serve, lift stuffing from roast, slice meat, and thicken drippings, with flour, for gravy if desired. 10 or more servings.

ROAST GOOSE WITH SWEET-SPICY STUFFING

Today's commercially grown geese are more meaty and have less fat than their counterparts of several years ago. A tart, savory stuffing does wonders for the roasted beauty.

1	goose (8 to 10 pounds), thawed, washed, and dried with paper toweling	1	cup raisins
6	cups slightly dry, ¼-inch bread cubes	½	cup sugar
		1	teaspoon salt
		1	teaspoon cinnamon
		½	teaspoon allspice
		½	cup water
3	cups coarsely-chopped, unpeeled, tart apples	¼	cup melted bacon drippings

Remove neck and giblets from body cavity of goose. Cook giblets promptly in about 2 cups salted water to which a stalk of celery and a small onion have been added. Bring giblets to boil, reduce heat and simmer, covered, about 2 hours or until tender. Strain broth. Refrigerate broth and giblets separately for use later in gravy.

Combine bread cubes, apples, and raisins. Mix well. Combine sugar, salt, cinnamon, and allspice. Mix well. Sprinkle sugar mixture over bread mixture. Toss together lightly but thoroughly. Add water and melted bacon grease. Toss again lightly but thoroughly.

Remove excess fat from body cavity of goose and from neck skin. Remove wings at second joint. (This eliminates having to tie them to body of goose.) Fill neck and body cavities loosely with stuffing. Fasten neck skin to back of goose with skewer. Tie legs together or tuck in band of skin at tail, if it is present. (There is no need to truss goose.) Place goose, breast side up, on rack in shallow pan. Insert meat thermometer deep inside thigh muscle. Roast, uncovered, in oven preheated to 400° for 45 minutes for a small bird, 1 hour for a larger one. (There is no need to baste goose.) During roasting, remove accumulated fat from pan, and reserve it for gravy. (Fat should be removed frequently so that it does not scorch.) After the 400° roasting period, reduce heat to 325° and roast until thermometer in thigh registers 190°. Transfer thermometer to stuffing. Stuffing temperature should register 170°. Another test for doneness: meaty part of thigh should feel very soft when pressed between protected fingers, and after pricking thigh with a fork, juices running out should be clear. Let stand 10 minutes before carving. 8 to 10 servings.

Gravy

Heat over moderate heat 2 tablespoons of the reserved goose drippings. Add 2 tablespoons flour. Cook a few minutes over moderate heat, stirring. Gradually add 1½ cups of the reserved giblet broth and ½ cup dry, red wine. Cook over moderate heat, stirring frequently, until smooth and thickened. Meanwhile, chop goose giblets. Add giblets, and salt and pepper to taste. Serve gravy with slices of the goose and stuffing.

WILD DUCK IN PORT WINE SAUCE

This sauce is certain to tame any "wild" taste in the duck. It is equally delicious as a sauce for domestic duckling and rice or noodles.

1 wild duck, cut in serving pieces	¼ teaspoon ground ginger
Cooking oil	Red pepper sauce to taste
½ cup port wine	1½ tablespoons cornstarch
1 cup orange juice	
1 cup red currant jelly	Cooked Rice or Noodles with Almonds
½ cup lemon juice	
½ cup chopped onion	
1 teaspoon dry mustard	

Thoroughly wash duck. Cut breast meat away from bone, if desired. (Some people prefer only the breasts of wild game meat since the legs tend to be tough.) Place a small amount of cooking oil in a large, heavy pan or Dutch oven. Heat oil over moderate heat. Add duck. Cook over moderate heat until it is brown on all sides. Drain off grease. To make sauce, combine wine, orange juice, jelly, lemon juice, onion, mustard, and ginger. Mix well. Cook, covered, over moderate heat until jelly melts. Stir occasionally. Add red pepper sauce. Pour sauce over duck. Bake, covered, in oven preheated to 350° for 1 to 1½ hours or until duck is tender. (Baking time depends on age and size of duck.) Baste duck frequently with sauce during baking period. Remove duck from sauce. Mix a small amount of the sauce with cornstarch until smooth. Add cornstarch mixture to sauce in pan. Mix until smooth. Cook over moderate heat, stirring constantly, until thickened. Return duck to sauce. Serve duck and sauce over Cooked Rice or Noodles with Almonds. Number of servings depends on the size of the wild duck.

Use 1 or 2 domestic ducklings, thawed, washed, dried with paper toweling and cut in halves, lengthwise. Sprinkle both sides of duckling halves with salt to taste. Place duckling halves, skin sides up, on a rack in 1 or 2 roasting pans. Roast in oven preheated to 350° until drumstick meat is very tender, allowing about 45 minutes per pound for altitudes below 5,000 feet and about 50 minutes per pound for altitudes above 5,000 feet. Prepare wine sauce according to preceding directions and baste duck occasionally with sauce during last 30 minutes of cooking time. Turn halves several times during roasting period, ending with skin sides up. Serve duckling with remaining sauce and Cooked Rice or Noodles with Almonds. 1 domestic duckling yields about 4 servings.

Cooked Rice or Noodles with Almonds

Add ½ to ⅔ cup toasted, slivered, blanched almonds to about 4 cups of cooked rice or noodles, seasoned with salt and pepper.

MARINATED ROAST VENISON

When in doubt about the tenderness of venison, whatever the cut, marinating usually solves the problem.

1½	cups burgundy wine	1	tablespoon instant, minced onion
1	teaspoon ground ginger or to taste	1	venison roast (any size or type, trimmed of all fat)
2	teaspoons salt or to taste		
½	teaspoon pepper	6	strips lean bacon
¼	teaspoon garlic powder	½	cup water
		½	cup currant jelly

Combine wine, ginger, salt, pepper, garlic powder, and onion. Mix well. Place venison in close-fitting, glass dish. Add wine marinade. Marinate, covered, in refrigerator 12 hours or longer, turning meat occasionally. Drain meat thoroughly, reserving marinade. Place meat in shallow roasting pan.

Arrange strips of bacon on top. Pour water around meat. Roast uncovered in oven preheated to 450° for about 30 minutes. Reduce heat to 325°. Pour about ½ of marinade over meat. Roast at 325°, uncovered, allowing about 30 minutes per pound or until meat thermometer reaches 170° to 180°. Baste with remaining marinade during this roasting period. Remove meat from pan to heated platter. Skim off and discard any fat from pan juices. Blend jelly into juices and cook over moderate heat, stirring, until jelly melts. Serve as a sauce with sliced meat. Number of servings depends on size of roast.

SMOKY ROAST DUCKLING WITH FRUIT SAUCE

Here is a beautifully easy way to make certain guests enjoy duckling.

1 domestic duckling (4½ to 5 pounds), thawed, washed, and dried with paper toweling	1 teaspoon liquid smoke
½ teaspoon salt	½ cup apricot or peach preserves
¼ teaspoon ground ginger	¼ cup light corn syrup
1 medium clove garlic, minced	¼ cup water
1 tablespoon cooking oil	2 tablespoons vinegar
	6 whole cloves
	2 cinnamon sticks, each about 2½-inches long

Rub duckling cavities and skin with salt, ginger, and garlic which have been mashed together until smooth. Loosely tie duckling legs together. Place duckling on a rack in a shallow pan. Roast, uncovered, in oven preheated to 350° until drumstick meat is very tender. Combine cooking oil and liquid smoke. Brush duckling several times with this mixture during last 40 minutes roasting time. Roasting will take from 2 to 2½ hours. The longer length of time is usually required for altitudes above 5,000 feet. Combine preserves, syrup, water, vinegar, cloves, and cinnamon. Bring to boil, stirring constantly. Reduce heat to moderate. Cook mixture, uncovered, until slightly thickened. Stir frequently. Spoon sauce over duckling to serve, after removing cloves and cinnamon sticks. 4 servings.

MOIST LIVER-SAUSAGE LOAF

Confession: Liver is something I can live without, thank you. But I find this mineral-rich meat so well disguised here, I always forget it's in the recipe—though I'm the one who prepared it.

1 pound hot or mild bulk pork sausage
1 pound calf or beef liver, dried with paper toweling
1 medium onion, chopped
1 tablespoon lemon juice
Pepper to taste
¼ teaspoon dried leaf thyme
1 small, finely-crushed bay leaf
1 can (10¾-ounce) cream of mushroom soup
2 eggs, slightly beaten
2 cups finely-rolled, bacon-flavored crackers (roll them as fine as coarse meal)
Tomato Sauce (optional)

Crumble sausage into large skillet, heated over moderate heat. Cook over moderate heat until done, stirring frequently. Remove sausage from skillet and drain on paper towel. Drain off all but about 3 tablespoons of drippings from skillet. Heat skillet drippings over moderately high heat. Add liver. Cook over moderately high heat, about 4 minutes on each side, or until traces of pink have disappeared. Drain liver and mince. Mince sausage. (A food processor can speed up preparation time of this recipe. Using the steel blade, the sausage and liver can be minced but do not process beyond the coarsely-ground stage; the bay leaf can be crushed with the crackers which are processed into crumbs in seconds.) Combine liver, sausage, onion, lemon juice, pepper, thyme, bay leaf, mushroom soup, eggs, and crumbs. Mix well. (Bacon-flavored crackers provide the salt in this recipe.) Pack mixture into well-greased, 9 x 5-inch loaf pan. Bake, uncovered, in oven preheated to 350° for about 50 minutes or until top is firm but still springs back when touched with fingertips, and loaf does not feel too solid. (At altitudes above 5,000 feet, add about 10 minutes baking time.) Let loaf stand in pan about 10 minutes. Invert loaf onto serving plate. (Since this loaf is very moist, it is not unusual for some of it to stick to bottom of pan. If this happens, just remove portion that sticks to pan, and pat it on top of loaf. It will adhere to loaf in a few minutes.) Cut loaf into slices with very sharp knife. Serve with Tomato Sauce, if desired. 8 to 10 servings.

Tomato Sauce

2 tablespoons butter or margarine	Pepper to taste
2 tablespoons flour	Dried leaf oregano to taste
1 cup tomato juice	

Melt butter or margarine. Add flour. Stir over moderate heat a few minutes. Gradually add tomato juice. Cook over moderate heat, stirring, until thickened. Season with pepper and oregano. Heat to serving temperature. Makes about 1 cup sauce.

GAME BIRD BAKE

The cook who is "stuck" with remnants of the hunt—quail, dove, and other game birds—will find they mix very nicely in this combination.

2 pheasants or a mixture of pheasant, dove, quail, or other game birds of your choice
1 large stalk celery with leaves, cut in thick slices
1 medium onion, quartered
Salt and pepper to taste
1 can (10¾-ounce) cream of chicken soup
¾ cup mayonnaise
1 teaspoon lemon juice
⅓ cup half-and-half cream
Curry powder to taste (optional)
2 packages (10-ounce each) frozen chopped broccoli, thawed and drained
¾ cup shredded Cheddar cheese
1 can (3-ounce) sliced mushrooms, drained, *or* lightly sautéed, fresh mushrooms to taste

Place game birds in a large kettle. Add celery, onion, salt, and pepper. Cover birds with water. Bring to boil, reduce heat and simmer, covered, until birds are tender. (Cooking time depends on age and size of birds.) Remove birds from cooking liquid. Discard cooking liquid as well as celery and onion. Remove skin and bones from birds. Cut meat into fairly large pieces. (The amount of meat can be varied to suit taste.) Place meat evenly over bottom of greased, shallow, 9 x 13-inch pan. Combine soup, mayonnaise, lemon juice, cream, and curry powder if desired. Mix well. Add uncooked broccoli, cheese, and mushrooms. Mix lightly but thoroughly. Spoon broccoli mixture over meat. Bake, uncovered, in oven preheated to 350° for about 30 minutes or until mixture is bubbly. 6 servings.

Note: Pieces of cooked chicken or turkey may be substituted for the game meat, resulting in a very tasty dish with a slightly different flavor.

SPICY JERKY

Venison, beef, and buffalo have all been dried to make jerky—strips of seasoned meat. In one form or another, jerky has been chewed by everyone from yesteryear's American Indians to the '49ers and '59ers who rushed to California, then Colorado, in search of gold, to the cross-country skiers and summertime back-packers of today who keep the popularity of jerky alive.

3½ pounds venison,
cut from the round,
brisket, or flank,
trimmed of all fat
and partially frozen
(beef flank steak or
the lean end of fresh
beef brisket may be
substituted)
1 teaspoon seasoned
salt

½ teaspoon garlic
powder
¼ teaspoon pepper
1 teaspoon onion
powder
½ cup Worcestershire
Sauce
½ cup soy sauce or to
taste (soy sauce
intensifies salty
flavor)

Cut meat in ¼-inch-thick slices with the grain. (Length of the slices is a matter of personal preference, but remember they will shrink during the drying process. Meat must be partially frozen in order to slice it this thin. However, if frozen too hard, it cannot be sliced.) Combine salt, garlic powder, pepper, onion powder, Worcestershire Sauce, and soy sauce. Mix well. Place strips of meat in a shallow, glass dish. Add marinade. Mix to coat all of meat with marinade. Refrigerate, covered with plastic wrap, for 10 to 12 hours. Stir meat occasionally. Drain meat. Lay strips, sides barely touching, in a single layer on oven's center rack. (Do not let strips overlap or they will stick together.) Place a jelly roll pan or a piece of foil with sides built up on bottom oven rack to catch any drippings. Set oven temperature to 150°, leaving oven door ajar. Let meat dry 8 to 10 hours. During the last 2 hours, test meat for desired degree of chewiness. If more crispness is desired, let it remain in oven until desired texture is reached. Refrigerate jerky in jars, tightly covered, or freeze. It may be stored in freezer up to 6 months; in refrigerator up to 6 weeks. Bring to room temperature before serving. Makes about 1½ pounds.

GOURMET CHICKEN LIVER SCRAMBLE

It's rich and economical with a gourmet flair. Could you ask more of a brunch or supper entrée?

3 tablespoons butter or margarine	6 extra-large eggs, beaten
½ pound chicken livers, cut in halves and dried with paper toweling	1 package (3-ounce) cream cheese, softened to room temperature and cut in small cubes
½ medium onion, chopped	Salt and pepper to taste
½ cup coarsely-chopped celery	Paprika Parsley flakes

Melt butter or margarine in large skillet or Dutch oven over moderately high heat. Add chicken livers, onion, and celery. Cook over moderately high heat about 3 minutes or until livers are fairly firm when pressed with fingertip. Stir livers occasionally during cooking period but do it lightly so they do not break into small pieces. Do not overcook or livers will become mushy. Pour eggs over mixture, then sprinkle with cream cheese cubes. Cook over moderate heat, stirring very gently but thoroughly to keep eggs from scorching and sticking to bottom of skillet. Cook until eggs are thickened but still moist. (The cubes of cheese will not entirely melt and add an interesting, guess-what texture to the finished product.) Add salt and pepper during last few minutes of cooking time. Turn mixture into serving dish and sprinkle generously with paprika and parsley. (These final additions hide the fact that the livers have robbed the eggs of their golden color.) 4 to 6 servings.

PHEASANT A LA ORANGE

Young pheasants can be broiled or baked; older ones usually require braising or other forms of moist-heat cookery. This recipe combines the best of both techniques, making it unnecessary to try to guess the age of the bird.

2 pheasants	very thin, orange-colored top of rind, then cut in fine pieces with kitchen scissors)
Salt and pepper to taste	
Bacon strips or thin salt pork slices	
3 tablespoons butter	6 tablespoons currant jelly
3 medium, green onions and some of the tops, sliced	¼ teaspoon dry mustard
¾ teaspoon dried leaf tarragon	1 tablespoon (about) cornstarch
1¼ cups orange juice	1½ cups orange sections, well drained
3 tablespoons finely-cut orange rind (with potato peeler, remove only the	Cooked rice

Sprinkle pheasants inside and out with salt and pepper. Place pheasants, breast sides up, in shallow roasting pan. Completely cover breasts with bacon or salt pork. Roast, uncovered, in oven preheated to 400° for about 30 minutes. Remove bacon or salt pork. If bacon is used, reserve it to be used later as a garnish. If salt pork is used, save it for flavoring soups and casseroles. Melt butter in large pan or Dutch oven over moderate heat. Add onions and tarragon. Cook over moderately low heat, stirring frequently, until onion is transparent. Add orange juice, rind, jelly, mustard, and salt to taste. Place pheasants in sauce. Bring to boil, reduce heat and simmer, covered, until pheasants are tender. Turn pheasants occasionally during cooking period. For young pheasants, cooking time will take up to 1 hour; older birds will take longer. Remove pheasants to serving platter. Mix cornstarch to a paste with a small amount of water. Bring sauce to boil and add cornstarch. Cook over moderate heat, stirring, until thickened. (More or less cornstarch may be used, depending on desired consistency.) Add orange sections to sauce. Heat to serving temperature. Garnish pheasants with reserved bacon. Serve with cooked rice. Serve sauce separately to be spooned over pheasant and rice. (Sauce recipe may be doubled—even tripled.) Number of servings depends on size of pheasants.

MARY LOU'S MEATBALL-SAUSAGE DINNER

What would we do without friends like Lou?

1 pound uncooked, ground meat (use a combination of lean beef, pork, and veal ground together in desired proportions)
1 teaspoon salt
1 teaspoon dry parsley flakes
1 teaspoon pepper
1 teaspoon dried leaf oregano
2 teaspoons dried, sweet leaf basil
¼ teaspoon garlic powder
2 eggs, beaten
1 large potato, peeled, boiled, and mashed
¼ cup grated Romano cheese
¼ cup (about) fine, dry, Italian-seasoned bread crumbs
Shortening
1 pound lean, link Italian sausage, cut at an angle in about 3-inch lengths
1 can (28-ounce) peeled, crushed tomatoes with added purée and basil (available in most stores)
1 can (28-ounce) standard tomato purée
1 can (12-ounce) tomato paste diluted with ½ can water
Rigatoni Casserole

Thoroughly mix together ground meat, salt, parsley, pepper, oregano, 1 teaspoon of the basil, garlic powder, eggs, potato, cheese, and crumbs. (Mixture should be fairly moist. If necessary, add a few more crumbs for rolling consistency. If too many crumbs are added, meatballs won't have a fluffy texture.) Divide mixture into 10 or 12 portions. On waxed paper, roll each portion over and over into a ball. (The rolling process is very important to eliminate air holes and prevent meatballs from breaking during frying.) Heat a small amount of shortening in a large skillet over moderate heat. Fry meat balls over moderate heat until brown on all sides but not crisp. Drain meatballs on paper toweling.

Heat a Dutch oven over moderate heat. Rub cut side of a piece of Italian sausage over bottom and sides of Dutch oven to grease it. Add all of Italian sausage. Cook over moderate heat until sausage is brown on all sides. Drain off all but about 4 tablespoons of the drippings. (A certain amount of drippings are necessary to season sauce; they will be absorbed during cooking.

However, since the amount of grease varies in sausage, you should rely on your own judgment.) Add crushed tomatoes, standard purée, diluted tomato paste, remaining 1 teaspoon basil (or to taste), and additional salt to taste. Bring to boil, reduce heat and simmer, covered, 2 hours. Add meatballs. Return to boil, reduce heat and simmer, covered, about 45 minutes. Serve sausage and meatballs in 1 bowl. Serve sauce in another bowl to be spooned over meat and also over the Rigatoni Casserole. (Some of the sauce is also used for baking the rigatoni.)

Rigatoni Casserole

1 pound rigatoni	1 cup grated Romano
Cooking oil	cheese
Tomato sauce from	Salt to taste
previous recipe	1 pound round,
	Scamorza cheese

Cook and drain rigatoni according to package directions, but add 1 or 2 tablespoons cooking oil to the water (to keep rigatoni from sticking together), and don't rinse rigatoni after it is drained. Add enough of the tomato sauce to thoroughly coat rigatoni. Add about ½ cup of the Romano cheese, and salt to taste. Cut 10 or 12 slices, ¼-inch thick, from Scamorza cheese. (Don't substitute Mozzarella cheese; it scorches too easily.) Cut remaining Scamorza cheese into small pieces, and mix them with rigatoni. Place mixture in a greased, 9 x 13-inch baking dish. Add more tomato sauce if mixture seems too dry. Sprinkle with remaining Romano cheese. Place Scamorza slices in a single layer on top of casserole. Bake, uncovered, in oven preheated to 350° for about 30 minutes or until cheese melts and mixture is bubbly.

The recipe for this dinner may appear complicated, but it goes together quite easily. Meatballs, sauce, and casserole also freeze nicely if you'd like to make any or all of this ahead. Entire dinner yields 10 to 12 servings.

LIVER WITH SOUR CREAM-DILL SAUCE

Whether you prefer the delicate flavor of calf liver or the more full-bodied taste of beef liver, either one is suitable with this Danish-inspired sauce. Remember, liver of all kinds (including turkey, chicken, lamb, and pork) becomes leathery when overcooked, so pop it in the skillet at the last minute. Serve the liver rare to medium rare or while there are still some pink traces in the meat.

6	slices bacon		shire Sauce or to
¼	cup chopped onion		taste
1	can (2½-ounce)		Salt and pepper to
	sliced mushrooms,		taste
	drained	½	teaspoon sugar or
½	cup dry white wine		to taste
1	cup dairy sour cream	2	pounds beef or calf
¼	teaspoon dried dill		liver, cut into serving
	weed		pieces
¼	teaspoon Worcester-		Flour

Fry bacon until crisp in large, heavy skillet. Reserve all bacon drippings. Drain bacon on paper toweling, then crumble it. Return 2 tablespoons of the drippings to skillet and heat over moderate heat. Add onions. Sauté over moderately low heat, stirring frequently, until onions are transparent. Add mushrooms and wine. Bring to boil, stirring constantly. Remove from heat. Add sour cream, dill, Worcestershire Sauce, salt, pepper, and sugar. Mix well. Heat mixture to serving temperature. Do not allow to boil. Heat about 4 tablespoons of the remaining bacon drippings in a large, heavy skillet over moderately high heat. (If necessary, add cooking oil to make 4 tablespoons drippings.) Lightly dredge liver in flour. Add liver to drippings. Cook over moderately high heat, turning once, just until it starts to get golden brown. Reduce heat to low and cook about 3 minutes on each side or until liver has reached desired degree of doneness. Place liver on heated platter. Sprinkle crumbled bacon on top. Serve with sauce on the side or spooned over pieces of liver. 8 servings.

HIGH COUNTRY COOKING TIPS

The "never fail" cake recipe has been a family favorite for years. But the last time you baked it—what a shock to behold the batter rising, then running over the sides of its pan, creating a smoky mess in the oven.

Could this culinary catastrophe have anything to do with the fact that you recently moved to a higher elevation, such as Denver, Colorado, Albuquerque, New Mexico, or any of the many other places in the nation (and the world) where the altitude is more than 3,000 feet above sea level? Indeed it could, and no doubt the altitude caused the failure.

I always receive many inquiries from newcomers to high country areas wanting to know what adjustments need to be made in cooking. I wish I could give a straightforward answer. But, the fact is, there are only guidelines to be followed, and they don't always insure perfect results. (Even food technologists at institutions such as Colorado State University, Fort Collins, Colorado, where a lot of scientific investigation of high-altitude cooking has been conducted, acknowledge the vagueness of the subject.)

However, those who have dealt extensively with high-altitude cookery usually agree that experimentation—along with the guidelines—results in the best solutions to problems of all kinds. Adjustments need not be drastic and often are not necessary at all. So, if you move to a higher altitude, hang on to your favorite recipes and just plan on the "adventure" of experimentation.

The culprits mainly responsible for high-altitude cooking failure are decreased atmospheric pressure and a lower boiling point. For example, water boils at about 202° F at 5,000 feet compared with 212° F at sea level. Therefore, potatoes cooked on top of the stove in boiling water in Denver won't get done as fast as they would in boiling water in San Francisco.

It doesn't help to increase the heat because once the boiling point is reached, water maintains that temperature and doesn't get any hotter. This principle doesn't apply to oven cookery, however. At high altitudes, it is often helpful to increase the oven temperature by about 25 degrees in order to speed up the cooking process, and to prevent the food from becoming dry.

The three main guidelines to remember when cooking at higher elevations are: many foods take longer to cook; they lose moisture faster; and they tend to expand too much if they contain leavening. Following are some general rules for cooking specific types of foods at altitudes above 3,000 feet.

CAKES MADE WITH SHORTENING AND SWEET QUICK BREADS: Use all-purpose or regular cake flour. Don't use self-rising flour because the amount of leavening it contains can't be measured. Liquid evaporates faster at high altitudes, sometimes resulting in a greater concentration of sugar in the batter or dough. This can weaken the cell structure, causing the cake to collapse. Cell structure also can be adversely affected by lower atmospheric pressure, which may cause a cake to rise too fast, then fall either during or immediately after the baking period. Thus, more liquid, less sugar, less baking powder and/or soda may be required. The chart included here is to be used as a guide for making adjustments on cakes and sweet quick breads. Use the smaller modification first, then use the larger one, if necessary, the next time the cake is baked.

Altitudes:	3,000 to 4,000 ft.	4,000 to 6,000 ft.	More than 6,000 ft.
Reduce baking powder:	⅛ teaspoon for each teaspoon	⅛ to ¼ teaspoon for each teaspoon	¼ teaspoon for each teaspoon
Reduce sugar:	up to 1 tablespoon for each cup	1 to 2 tablespoons for each cup	2 to 4 tablespoons for each cup
Increase liquid:	1 to 2 tablespoons for each cup	2 to 4 tablespoons for each cup	3 to 4 tablespoons for each cup

Oven temperature:	Sometimes it is helpful to increase the oven temperature 15° to 25° but do not increase it above 375° unless specified in the recipe.
Shortening:	For very rich cakes, it is sometimes helpful to reduce the shortening 1 to 2 tablespoons.

ANGEL FOOD AND SPONGE CAKES: Avoid beating too much air into the egg whites and egg yolks. It is also helpful to reduce the sugar slightly, to add a small amount of flour and to increase the baking temperature. Sponge cakes also may require more liquid and less baking powder when the recipe calls for it.

YEAST BREADS: Because flour absorbs more liquid at high altitudes, slightly less flour may be needed. Yeast bread dough rises more rapidly at high altitudes, resulting in a 10- to 20-minute shorter rising period. Let the dough rise just until it is double in bulk or until indentations of two fingertips remain when pressed into dough. For some recipes that call for fairly lengthy rising periods in order to develop flavor in the bread, maintain those rising periods by punching down the dough twice.

COOKIES: A slight reduction in sugar and/or baking powder may be helpful along with a slight increase in the oven temperature. Like pie crust, which absorbs moisture faster at high altitudes, a small amount of extra liquid may be added.

CAKE MIXES: Follow package directions for making high altitude adjustments.

MUFFINS AND BISCUITS: The structure of these foods withstands increased internal pressure fairly well, however, it may be helpful to decrease baking powder and sugar slightly.

CREAM PUFFS AND POPOVERS: Recipes for cream puffs usually do not need to be adjusted since the heavy batter holds in the steam as its main source of leavening. Sometimes it is helpful to increase the amount of egg and decrease the amount of shortening in popover batter to strengthen it long enough for a crust to form.

CANDY AND SYRUP MIXTURES: The old-fashioned, cold water test for determining the soft ball, hard ball, crack stage, etc. is still reliable for high-altitude candy-making since sugar solutions, like water, boil at a lower temperature at high altitudes. The sugar mixture gets too concentrated by the time the specified temperature is reached, if sea-level directions are used. When a candy thermometer is used, certain adjustments need to be made in reading it to correspond with the altitude in which the candy is being cooked. County extension services are usually a good source of detailed information on this.

CANNING: This type of food preparation also needs more detailed modifications than space permits here. Processing time and steam-pressure cookery time increase as the altitude increases. Major manufacturers of canning equipment as well as county extension services are among the sources that should be consulted.

DEEP-FAT FRYING: A lower temperature of fat is required at high altitudes to prevent food from browning too much on the outside and being under-cooked within. Lowering the frying temperature 10° to 15° (depending on the type of food being cooked) usually solves the problem.

PUDDINGS AND CREAM PIE FILLINGS: Cooking the cream mixture over direct heat, not in the double boiler over hot water, will result in its thickening to the desired consistency. Mixtures using cornstarch should always be cooked over direct heat at high altitudes.

METRIC TIPS

America's move to the metric system, and how we deal with it in the kitchen, need not be uncomfortable or difficult. Nevertheless, how should we handle it?

First, don't bother to convert all of your favorite recipes to metric measurements (unless you have a lot of time on your hands). Second, use your present measuring cups and spoons for conventional recipes; use new ones marked with metric units for new recipes.

If you do make metric conversions, many experts agree that exact measurements aren't necessary, providing the amounts are close. For example, 2 ml. (milliliters) are slightly less than ½ teaspoon; the 250 ml. cup is about 2 teaspoons more than the 240 ml. cup. That's all very well and good if you're dealing with casseroles and other non-critical foods. But for those delicate cakes and other exact-amount recipes (especially those affected by high altitudes) I offer this word of caution: stick to U.S. Customary System measurements, otherwise the result might be a disaster.

Following are tables for making some of the more common conversions to the metric system. In many cases, for easier interpretation, I have listed the units in "rounded" quantities, such as 30 grams (instead of 28.35 grams) in 1 ounce.

SOME APPROXIMATE METRIC CONVERSIONS
OF WEIGHTS AND MEASURES

Units of Volume: Milliliters (ml.) and Liters (l.)

U.S. Customary quantity:	*Metric equivalent:*
¼ teaspoon	1.25 ml.
½ teaspoon	2.5 ml.
¾ teaspoon	3.75 ml.
1 teaspoon	5 ml.
2 teaspoons	10 ml.
3 teaspoons or 1 tablespoon or ½ fluid ounce	15 ml.
4 fluid ounces or ½ cup	119 ml.
8 fluid ounces or 1 cup	240 ml.
2 pints or 1 quart	946 ml. or close to 1 l.
4 quarts or 1 gallon	3,785 ml. or close to 3¾ l.

Units of Weight: Grams (g.) and Kilograms (kg.)

U.S. Customary quantity:	*Metric equivalent:*
½ ounce	15 g.
1 ounce	30 g.
4 ounces or ¼ pound	113 g.
8 ounces or ½ pound	227 g.
12 ounces or ¾ pound	340 g.
16 ounces or 1 pound	454 g.
2.2 pounds	1 kg.

SOME TEMPERATURES WITH FAHRENHEIT
CONVERSION TO APPROXIMATE CELSIUS

Fahrenheit:	*Celsius (Centigrade):*
275	135
300	149
325	163
350	177
375	190
400	204
450	232

SOME APPROXIMATE BOILING TEMPERATURES OF WATER AT VARIOUS ALTITUDES WITH APPROXIMATE FAHRENHEIT CONVERSION TO CELSIUS

Altitude:	Fahrenheit:	Celsius:
Sea Level	212	100
2,000 feet	208	98
5,000 feet	203	95
7,500 feet	198	92
10,000 feet	194	90

SOME HELPFUL EQUIVALENTS

(Approximate)

Beans:
    1 pound dry, lima = 5 to 6 cups, cooked
    1 pound dry, navy = 5 to 6 cups, cooked

Cheese:
    2 ounces = ½ cup, shredded
    4 ounces = 1 cup, shredded
    6 ounces = 1½ cups, shredded
    8 ounces = 2 cups, shredded

Cream:
   1 cup heavy = 2 to 2½ cups, whipped

Crumbs:
   1 standard slice, fresh bread, trimmed of crusts = 1 cup soft crumbs
   30 soda crackers = 1 cup very fine crumbs
   22 vanilla wafers = 1 cup fine crumbs

Lemons:
   6 medium = 1 cup juice
   1 medium = 2 to 3 tablespoons juice
   1 medium = 3 teaspoons grated rind

Mushrooms:
   (drained and sliced): 6- to 8-ounce can = 1 cup= ½ pound, fresh
                         3- to 4-ounce can = ½ cup = ¼ pound, fresh
   (stems and pieces):   3- to 4-ounce can = ⅓ cup = ¼ pound, fresh
   (whole): 6- to 8-ounce can = 18 small whole = ½ pound, small fresh

Nuts:
   1 pound unshelled almonds = 1¼ to 1½ cup nut meats
   1 pound unshelled pecans = 2 cups nut meats
   1 pound unshelled walnuts = 1¾ to 2 cups nut meats

Oranges:
   2 to 4 medium = 1 cup juice
   2 medium = 1 cup bite-size pieces
   1 medium = 4 teaspoons grated rind

Pasta:
   1 pound raw noodles = 7 cups, cooked
   1 pound raw macaroni = 8 cups, cooked
   1 pound raw spaghetti = up to 8 cups, cooked

Rice:
   1 cup uncooked regular = 3 cups, cooked
   1 cup uncooked converted = 3 to 4 cups, cooked
   1 cup quick-cooking = 1 to 2 cups, cooked
   1 cup uncooked brown = 3 to 4 cups, cooked

INDEX

Potato puff ground beef casserole,
23–24
Potatoes, mashed, creamy, 166
Poultry, 145
bake with rice, 169
bake with spinach, 157–158
with broccoli, 152–153
casserole, with macaroni and
cheese, 149
fricassee, 160
and ham Lasagna Mornay,
134–135
Oriental pear-poultry sauté, 150
pastry (gougère), 147–148
with peaches, 194–195
(*See also* Chicken; Duckling;
Game birds; Goose;
Turkey)
Prune sauce Suzette, for lamb, 84–
85
Puff(s):
potato ground beef casserole,
23–24
shrimp-crab, 71
tuna mayonnaise, 53

Queen City steak au poivre
(pepper steak), 35
Quiches:
seafood with Madeira, 73
shrimp, 72–73

Red sauce, 75
Red snapper, baked, 76–77
Refrigerator white sauce mix, all-
purpose, 132–133
Relish, sauerkraut, 120
Riblets, lamb, 91–92
Ribs, beef (*see* Short)
Ribs, pork, barbecued, 130–131
Rice:
with almonds, 198
and baked chicken, 170–171
brown, stuffed peppers, 101–
102
casserole, meatless, 108–109
fried, 192–193
and poultry bake, 169
and salmon pie, 45–46
Ricotta cheese filling, 22

Rigatoni casserole, 206
Roast dishes:
beef, citrus-sauced, 5–6
chicken, orange, 145–146
duckling, smoky, with fruit
sauce, 199
goose with sweet-spicy stuffing,
196–197
pork, spicy glaze for, 122
turkey breast with brandied
cranberries, 151–152
venison, marinated, 198–199
venison, stuffing-crowned, 195
Roll, lamb, 89–90
Rolls, ham, 129–130
Roll-ups, fish, 57–58
Romaine-steamed fish fillets, 57
Rosettes, pastry, 178–179
Roundup roll lamb, 89–90

Salads:
fresh-fruit chicken on pastry
rosettes, 178–179
hot turkey in pastry shells, 158–
159
melon-chicken, 177–178
spinach, 105
tuna, 54
Salmon:
patties, juicy, 48
with puffed topping, 47–48
and rice pie, 45–46
Saltimbocca, chicken, 154–156
Sauces:
amandine, 53
apricot, 92–93
bearnaise, 30–31
cheese, for corn cake, 106–107
for lamb rolls, 90
cream, 155–156
dill, 48
dill butter, 53
fruit, 199
honey-lime, 141
leilani, 179–180
lemon-parsley, 12–13
mushroom:
for chicken, 154
for Cornish pasties, 5
for trout, 52–53
olive, 46